THE POLITICS OF FREEDOM

An Analysis of the Modern Democratic State

THE POLITICS OF FREEDOM

An Analysis of the Modern Democratic State

BY C. W. CASSINELLI

Seattle   University of Washington Press   1961

This book is published with assistance
from a grant by the Ford Foundation.

CONTENTS

THE POLITICS OF FREEDOM

An Analysis of the Modern Democratic State

INTRODUCTION

Everyone knows that democratic states have elaborate constitutions, genuinely competitive elections and campaigns, complex legislatures and executives, and numerous interest groups, and that the citizens of democratic states enjoy civil liberties, social welfare, and high standards of living. All these are recognized as existing within and also as somehow indispensable to the democratic state. Yet, despite an extensive literature on democracy, the precise nature of this apparent indispensability is not clearly understood, and the democratic state itself thus remains unexplained.

In order to show the relationship of each of these political phenomena to the democratic state, their relationships with each other must be demonstrated. Although there are excellent descriptions of many of these institutions and practices as single and separate entities, the problem of a general integration of the most important elements of the democratic state has, on the whole, been neglected.[1]

The purpose of this analysis is to show how the principal political features of the democratic state are interrelated and how each is both necessary and sufficient for all the others. I use the term "democratic state" to refer to certain states recognized by common sense as fundamentally similar to one another and fundamentally different from other states. They are the United Kingdom, the United States, France, Canada, Australia, New Zealand, Norway, Sweden, Denmark, Belgium, the Netherlands, and Switzerland.[2] * These twelve states will provide the "raw data" for the inquiry which follows. Specific references to them, however, will only rarely be necessary, since the discussion will be concerned with characteristics which they all clearly possess.[3] Nevertheless, everything that is said about parties, govern-

* The adjective "democratic," in my usage, has neither ethical nor factual implications. It will serve simply as a label for a special subclass of state, and it has been selected solely because it conforms to customary usage. I shall also use the term "democracy" to refer to the democratic state.

3

ment, policy, and so forth, and about their interrelations, is consciously designed to apply to each of the twelve. There are important differences among democratic states, but their fundamental similarities are the subject of the present analysis.

Common sense recognizes that democratic states are similar in their institutions, policies, social and economic characteristics, and political beliefs. Political science goes beyond common sense to recognize that these characteristics are unique to democratic states, but it has paid too little attention to the reasons for this uniqueness. By attempting to show why each characteristic is indispensable to all the others, I hope to do more than simply list those that appear both necessary and sufficient. This requires describing each characteristic and then explaining how it is related to the characteristics previously examined.

The first characteristic of the democratic state to be described is its government, which I shall call "representative government." Taking this characteristic first has two important advantages. Although we have much information on individual representative governments, very few attempts have been made since John Stuart Mill to deal with representative government as a type of government. This neglect has probably impeded our understanding, not only of the structure and operation of the government itself, but of many other elements of the democratic state that are intimately connected with representative government. Dealing first with representative government will remove some of these impediments at the outset of our investigation.

Examining representative government first also makes easier the explanation of such things as democratic policy, leadership, class structure, and "ideology." The purpose of analyzing the democratic state's essential characteristics is the logical ordering of these characteristics, and the institutions of representative government offer a starting point more convenient than that provided by any other single essential characteristic. There is no assumption here that governmental institutions are "primary" in any way; it is simply a question of logical convenience.

Giving logical priority to the institutions of government may appear ill designed to cope with the problem of change within the democratic state, since institutions have a tendency to "lag" behind social, economic, and political developments. However, anyone interested primarily in the "dynamics" of the democratic state—as I am here concerned primarily with its "statics"—can utilize any connections among its elements brought out by the present study. Because all are both necessary and sufficient, he need only direct his attention to one of the more "dynamic" elements, like the economy, in order to discover how a change in one brings about changes in the others.

Occasionally, I shall discuss certain opinions about the democratic state which, although widely held, are erroneous or at least strongly misleading. These will not be serious digressions, for each directly contributes to understanding an important facet of the democratic state. For example, an extended discussion of "consent" is required to show that it is not, by itself, a sufficient condition for democracy. This account will also make clear that "consent" is still a necessary condition, and it will prepare the ground for explaining the special kind of "consent" always associated with the democratic state.

The study is divided as follows: chapter 1 examines the institutions of representative government; chapter 2 discusses the nature and function of political parties and their relationship to representative government; chapter 3 describes the general policy followed by representative government; chapter 4 deals with the unusual degree of civil liberty found within the democratic state; chapter 5 is concerned with the participation of the general citizenry in the processes of government; chapter 6 investigates the notion of the "consent" of the governed and shows in what sense it can be attributed to governments in general and to representative government in particular; chapter 7 examines the political myths, the reasons for governmental legitimacy, of the democratic state; chapter 8 explains the social and economic bases of the democratic state; and in chapter 9 I shall estimate the strengths and weaknesses of democracy.

The entire analysis is to be considered only a first approximation. My hope is that it will provide a stimulus for attempts at greater accuracy.

1: THE INSTITUTIONS OF REPRESENTATIVE GOVERNMENT

The democratic state has a unique type of government. Although it also appears in those transitional states consciously attempting to establish democracy, it is firmly founded only in the democratic state. The distinguishing feature of this type of government is the election to office of those men who possess the real and ultimate governmental authority, and I shall call it "representative government." This expression will be used here simply to name the concept derived from an analysis of the governments of the twelve contemporary democratic states. The word "representative," however, has connotations that may cause some misunderstanding. It may suggest that someone acts as someone else desires him to act. In politics, this idea applies to governmental policy-making, but chapter 3 will show the inaccuracy of saying that a representative government does what someone else (usually "the people") wants it to do. "Representative" also means "typical," and it has occasionally been said that the personnel of a representative government are typical of the general population. This opinion is factually incorrect.[1]

Despite the word's misleading connotations, there are no preferable substitutes, and little advantage comes from inventing a new name.[2] Furthermore, it is common usage to call a member of the kind of government in question a "representative," when no more is implied than that he has been elected to office. In short, "representative government" will refer to the type of government to be described; while it will be relevant to criticize the description as an inaccurate account of the twelve governments which are our basic data, it is beside the point to say that such a government is not "really representative."

I

Government is an organization consisting of many suborganizations and possessing a near monopoly of the means of violence within

6

a society. It determines and executes formal public policy, and it maintains an implicit but constant threat to make use of the means of violence in case it is not obeyed.[3] Governments differ from one another according to their internal structure and procedure and according to the policies that they pursue. The present chapter is concerned with the structure and procedure of contemporary representative governments.

The structure of a government is the arrangement of its several policy-making positions. One of the peculiarities of representative government is that there are several different arrangements of these positions. Its three major variations—cabinet government in states in the British tradition, assembly government in western European states, and presidential government in the United States—differ significantly in the location of power and the manner in which binding decisions are made. The ultimate control of the body called "parliament" is common to cabinet and assembly government, but presidential government, with its separation of powers, does not share this characteristic. Therefore, it is necessary to take as the essential feature of representative government the possession of the final decision-making power by men who are elected to their governmental positions. The manner in which these men obtain their power is the feature that distinguishes representative governments from all other governments.

The manner in which activities of individual human beings become activities of an organization is an integral part of the organization's structure; in the case of governments, each type has its own method of selecting people to perform its various functions. Stressing the special way in which individuals are chosen to fill positions of primary authority within representative government is the most convenient way to make clear representative government's relationships to the other basic features of the democratic state.

The essence of representative government has two aspects which must be explained in some detail: the nature of the elections used to fill the most important positions within the governmental organization and the nature of the positions themselves. In general, the elections must be uncoerced and periodic—and there are normally at least two candidates for every position to be filled. The positions themselves must be so related to the rest of the governmental apparatus that they have, in fact, the final word on all matters of policy which the government is competent to determine.[4]

II

An election is a method of filling an office in an organization, whereby a specified group of people express their preferences for one of several "candidates." The expression of preference by each elector is consciously directed to filling the position, and the method of determining the group's preference is formally decided upon before the electoral contest begins. Among representative governments, there are variations regarding the formal qualifications required for the electorate (possessing these qualifications gives one the "franchise" or "suffrage"), and regarding the method by which the preference of the group is determined (which is called the "electoral system"). These variations raise some problems of conceptualization, but they need not be dealt with immediately.

A representative system of government absolutely requires the election of the representatives to be periodic; that is to say, their terms of office must have definite and understood temporal limits. Election to office for life or for an indefinite period has occurred in governments which are quite clearly not representative.[5] This element of periodicity is an integral part of the twelve governments under consideration. That it is essential to representative government can be established by two general considerations. First, the policy pursued by representative government simply would not be what it is if the elected incumbents never had to stand for re-election, since one of the most powerful influences on policy decisions is the anticipated reactions of the electorate in future elections.* Second, the "political climate" of criticism and liberty that characterizes the democratic state would not persist and flourish without frequent electoral campaigns, because (as will be seen in chapter 4) these campaigns provide the single greatest impetus to unrestricted discussion. In the larger representative governments, the maximum term of office is usually five years, although some "upper" houses in bicameral legislatures have six- and even eight-year terms. In these latter cases, however, the terms of the individual representatives are usually staggered; and elections for at least some of the members occur at shorter intervals. It seems reasonable, therefore, to conclude that the terms of office in representative government, while not subject to any minimum duration, cannot exceed the maximum of five years. This maximum is to be waived only under extraordinary circumstances and by extraordinary means.[6]

III

The second condition indispensable to the elections of representative government is that they be what I have called "uncoerced."

---

* This matter will be discussed in detail in chapter 3. It should be mentioned here that in those cases where the representative is ineligible for re-election, he is usually associated with a political party which intends to contest the election; the circumstances in which the incumbent finds himself are thus basically similar to those which would prevail if he himself were planning to stand again.

Democratic states are generally said to have "free elections," in contradistinction to the elections in various kinds of dictatorships; this means, roughly, that in a democracy "everyone can vote the way he wants." This common-sense notion obviously must be refined. It must apply accurately to the actual situation in democratic states, and it must be useful in showing the interconnections of all the basic political characteristics of the democratic state.

The central role played by elections in the politics of democracy results from the belief, held by both electorate and candidates, that the outcome, not necessarily of every electoral contest, but at least of a series of elections, is in doubt. The span of time covered by the series may vary according to local circumstances, but it depends in every case upon the belief that the ultimate defeat of the dominant individual or party is a definite possibility. The constituent must believe that the election is a genuine contest, that its results are determined by the proper combination of votes cast by individuals who could reasonably have been expected to vote otherwise. Popular confidence in democratic elections depends upon this belief. Without this confidence, there can be no confidence in representative government itself, and thus no popular belief in the legitimacy of the democratic state. If the electorate believes, either correctly or incorrectly, that the result of an election has been determined other than by the voters themselves, this individual election does not meet the standards necessary for representative government.

The candidate, on the other hand, must know that both he and his competitors have an opportunity to win, if not any one election in his constituency, at least a subsequent election. If he believes he can do very little consistent with the electoral rules to change his chances of either winning or losing, his behavior as a representative or candidate will not lead to two of the most important political phenomena always found in the democratic state, i.e., the government's policy of promoting the people's material and social welfare and the existence of a remarkable degree of civil liberty. Elections under representative government, in short, must be genuine contests.

There are three commonly used methods of preventing elections from being genuine contests. The first controls the election's results by falsifying the distribution of the ballots, by miscounting them, or by "stuffing" the ballot box. The second uses bribery to induce the electorate to support one candidate or party, while the third threatens the voters' material and physical well-being if they do not cast their ballots in the prescribed way. In any case where any of these techniques is known to have been used, one can almost always predict the outcome of the election without knowing anything about the intentions of the electorate in question. Under these circumstances, the behavior of the electorate and the candidates will not meet the necessary standards of the democratic state.

The secret ballot, while not indispensable to democratic elections, is extremely useful in preventing the control of votes by anyone other than the voters themselves. Although genuine elections can occur and have occurred without the secret ballot, those people who do not want an uncontrolled election can make very good use of the information provided by open balloting, which indeed is a standing temptation to improper interference. This has been recognized in contemporary democratic states, and they all now use the secret ballot.[7]

Common sense recognizes that the three types of controlled situation differ from those wherein the election is fair but the outcome is nevertheless predictable with a high degree of probability. The constituency may be traditionally a "one-party" constituency,[8] or one of the candidates may be highly superior to his rivals in all those personal characteristics that normally influence the electorate. This difference between the controlled election and the "safe" election is accounted for in our formal description of democratic elections, which provides for the latter by requiring only that the situation not be static. There is always the possibility that the dominant candidate or party will be defeated by his or its own mistakes or by changes in the conditions that motivate the electorate. Unexpected victories have occurred frequently enough to oblige both voter and candidate to take the possibility into consideration. If the voter believes that the ballots have been cast without any outside control, he will be satisfied with the results. The candidate and the representative, on the other hand, must believe that the voters could, in all likelihood, have come to another decision, or their behavior will not be properly democratic. When the three techniques for controlling elections are not present, the candidate must assume that the electorate could have acted otherwise, and the conditions for a democratic electoral system are thus met.

In order to simplify and thus clarify the conditions for an "uncontrolled" election, the three methods of control must be further analyzed. In any stable society, the government is almost complete master of the system which fills its offices. When elections are used, the government is going to ensure that the proper methods of determining the distribution of votes are followed, and that the voters are neither bribed nor threatened into voting in a particular way—unless the government itself approves of the use of these techniques. Where the government has full control over its society, no private group can tamper with the ballots, bribe, or threaten without at least the government's acquiescence. In actual political practice, where governors have been chosen by periodic but "unfree" elections, governmental inter-ference has been the factor preventing the elections from meeting the conditions necessary for the democratic state.[9] To generalize, then, a genuinely representative government must not in any way, either ac-tively or by default, use its powers of physical coercion to control the decisions of the electorate. The second necessary condition of the elections of representative government is, therefore, that they be un-controlled and ultimately uncoerced.

IV

As can be seen immediately, the absence of coercion is a matter of degree. Controlled votes, of a few or perhaps many electors, may oc-casionally occur in contemporary democratic elections without under-mining the representative government in question. The proper degree of freedom is determined by the scope and frequency of any existing control, on the level of the individual constituency as well as that of the state as a whole.

A single election in an individual constituency will be coerced when control is applied to enough of the electorate to determine the elec-tion's outcome. If the control simply shifts votes from one candidate to another without determining the outcome, the rules of democratic elections have been broken, but the election itself is uncoerced. This rule expresses the most probable reactions of the electorate and the candidates: the existence of control will be recognized as an infringe-ment of the rules, but the final results of the election will not be considered irregular unless it is generally believed that they were de-termined by the control. The only assumption underlying the rule is that the electorate will believe the election to be controlled only when control has in fact been decisive. This assumption is reasonable enough. In the case of the candidates, since they have better sources of information they can often discount the controlled votes and con-centrate upon those they know to be uncontrolled. If they face a great enough handicap, they can always request the government to eliminate it, and a genuinely representative government will usually comply.

The system of uncoerced elections in an individual constituency will not be destroyed by an occasional recognizably controlled election. However, repeated violation of the rules will no doubt undermine both the voters' and the candidates' confidence in the genuineness of the contests, and "representation" within that constituency will be de-stroyed. The frequency of control is, therefore, an important factor, but its effect depends upon the tolerance of the electors and the opti-mism of the candidates. The limits to these attitudes vary from case to case, and it would be impractical, in the present analysis, to try to frame any generalizations about them.

Whether the elected branches of a representative government, whose personnel come from many constituencies, are properly constituted depends upon the situations in the individual constituencies. A workable rule is that the presence of controlled constituencies does not prevent a government from being representative, as long as the men whom they send to the seat of government to share in the country's highest policy-making procedures are neither so numerous nor so strategically placed that they can determine national policy. Again, this influence is a matter of degree. Whether or not it determines national policy depends once more upon the attitudes of the representatives and the citizens. As long as they both feel that decisions by the representative bodies are not beyond the control of the properly elected members, the citizens will retain their confidence in the system, and the representatives will support the welfare policy which necessarily accompanies representative government.[10]

V

An election has been described as a contest for office between at least two candidates; in an uncoerced election, the voter makes his own choice among the several candidates, despite the pressures of his social and economic position which incline him to support one rather than the others. The existence of more than one candidate is usually simply a result of the absence of control. Although contemporary representative governments occasionally exhibit unopposed candidacies, the possibility of opposition is definitely necessary for this type of government. The special results of representative government follow from the interactions of at least two candidates for practically all the elective offices, no matter how difficult the entry of a third candidate may be. These results will be examined in some detail later. We should look now at an interpretation of the common-sense belief that what distinguishes elections in the democratic state from what are called "elections" in places like Fascist Italy or the Soviet Union is the existence of "a real choice." Political scientists and others have often taken this to mean that the electorate has a real choice among different policy programs.

Those who present this interpretation are usually speaking more about what they consider desirable than about what they have observed, although they are not always clear about the difference.[11] American parties, which are diverse, "undisciplined," and overlapping in their policies, are very often thought incapable of providing their electors with a "real choice" among policies.[12] British parties, on the other hand, are usually thought to provide the best example of genuine but "democratic" policy differences, for they are relatively homogeneous, have hierarchical structures, and periodically publish programs to which the whole party is expected to agree. But a good case can be made that they are at least as close in their policies as American parties.[13]

Recognizing that the electorate only rarely has a choice between significantly differing policy programs, other writers have concluded that the real issue in a democratic election is the relative abilities of the several candidates to carry out wisely and efficiently the policies upon which they all agree.[14] Again, it is often unclear whether this opinion is supposed to apply to the actual situation under representative government, or whether it is an ideal which should at least be approximated.

The opinions that the choice before the voter is between policies or that it is between administrators are both misleading. It is true that there are often important differences between the policy programs of the competing candidates and that these candidates often differ in their administrative abilities. For the purposes of generalization, however, the "lowest common denominator" of all elections in the democratic state remains the existence of more than one candidate, any one of whom the individual voter is free to support. Differences in policy and capability are functions not of the democratic electoral system but of the variable circumstances under which an individual election takes place. In addition, stressing the choice among differing policies or capabilities results in a distorted picture of the value of selecting governors by means of elections. A representative government pursues a unique course of public policy, and its officials possess special abilities, both of which are worthy of our approval. It does not follow that the value of electoral contests comes directly from the competition of two or more policy programs, or that elections are especially suitable for selecting skilled administrators. In short, if the alternatives presented to the electorate are said to be more than the candidates themselves, the statement will not apply to the actual situation in the twelve democratic states, and it will unduly emphasize the moral significance of the differences among the candidates. As will be seen throughout the present analysis, it is the results of electoral competition, not the grounds of the competition, which are both factually and ethically important.

VI

The determination of who can participate in the choice of representatives is a central feature of the democratic system of elections. An electorate consists of the people who meet the formal qualifications specified by all representative governments, and who are not prevented from exercising their legal right to vote. Since a formally qualified elector can be prevented from voting only with the tacit support of the government, determining who is and who is not an elector follows the same procedure as determining the existence of an uncoerced choice between at least two candidates. It is necessary to call attention to the electorate's composition, although the point may seem quite obvious, because it determines to a great extent the kind of policy pursued by a representative government; it is one of the major influences on both what the government does and what it cannot do. These matters will be discussed fully in chapters 3 and 4, but it should be mentioned now that, for an analysis of representative government, it is the ability or opportunity to vote, rather than the particular manner of voting, which constitutes the importance of the franchise and, therefore, of the electorate. There has been a strong tendency to assume that the electorate's specific preferences are basic to the operation of representative government.[15] This assumption, as will be seen in chapter 5, leads to the untenable position of "majority rule," with its factual inaccuracy and ethical distastefulness. To repeat, in order to understand clearly the most important implications of the democratic electorate, attention must be focused upon the opportunity to vote and not upon any specific pattern of voting.

The electorate in all contemporary democratic states consists of all adult citizens; Switzerland, with no female suffrage, is the only exception.[16] In either case, the electorate includes every class, stratum, and section of the population. But universal suffrage came about only gradually,[17] and it was preceded by the genuine election of representatives by restricted electorates. The question might be raised whether the states were genuinely democratic when they had restricted franchises. This issue would have to be determined for each state, at each period of its development, and the decision would depend upon the presence or absence of the other, nongovernmental features of democracy. The existence of a fairly high degree of civil liberty is probably the best evidence that the state in question was democratic, despite its limited franchise.

Another way to determine the democratic nature of states with restricted electorates is to examine the attitudes of both those who can vote and those who cannot. If the state is democratic, the latter are content with their politically inferior position and willing to leave the business of government to others. The enfranchised groups, for their part, have no irremovable biases against eventually expanding the suffrage. They must view the unfranchised as only temporarily incapable or irresponsible, for reasons of poverty or ignorance. The political parties often provide a major element in this attitude, since they tend to view the unfranchised as future supporters. Moreover, when the latter finally demand the vote, as has always happened, those in power cannot deny them without undermining the system of uncoerced elections itself.[18] With these attitudes of acquiescence and tolerance, a state is probably democratic despite a restricted suffrage. However, our primary purpose is still to analyze the twelve contemporary states, all of which have universal suffrage.

VII

Representative governments do not all use the same method to translate the preferences of the voters into the composition of the elected branches of government. There are many differences in detail among the twelve "electoral systems," but three major varieties can be distinguished. The first is so-called proportional representation; it gives to any party a proportion of seats in the representative body approximating the proportion of votes it received from the electorate. The second might be called the "single-office, simple-plurality" system, under which the voter expresses a single preference for a single office; the office is given to the candidate who has received more votes than any other candidate. The third has been called the "second-ballot" system; it proceeds in the same way as the second, except that when no candidate receives over 50 per cent of the votes on the first ballot, another election occurs—either between the two candidates who received the highest number of votes on the first ballot or among any candidates who wish to stand.[19]

Each of these systems produces elections possessing the characteristics essential to representative government: they are uncoerced and periodic, and they are contests between at least two candidates. Although different electoral systems are connected with different types of political parties, with variations in the loci of decision-making, and with different attitudes among the general population, all of them are accompanied by the same general type of governmental policy, by the same emphasis upon civil liberties, and by the same kind of social and economic conditions. An examination of electoral systems is necessary to explain varieties of representative government and individual representative governments, but not representative government as a type of government.

One feature of some electoral systems does, however, require comment. This is "indirect representation," which provides that some members of the elected bodies are chosen not by the electorate but by men previously chosen by the electorate. "Indirect representation" usually applies to one chamber of a bicameral parliament, which is selected by the members of elected local-government bodies, while the other chamber is chosen directly by the electorate.[20] This "indirect" relationship between the electorate and the governmental official is basically the same as that between the people and the Swiss Federal Council or indeed any coalition cabinet. In the latter cases, a centrally or nationally elected body has made the choice, rather than a locally elected one, so "indirect" election is not as "unrepresentative" as it might appear. In contemporary democratic states, the electorate's influence upon the indirectly selected chamber is not significantly diluted by the presence of a body between them. This means that the normal effects of that influence accompany representative governments that have indirectly elected elements.[21] Nevertheless, too high a degree of indirectness would certainly be incompatible with representative government. Deciding when this incompatibility begins can proceed in the same way as deciding when the suffrage is too restricted for democracy, that is, by referring to the degree of civil liberty present in the given state. Again, this decision is peripheral to our inquiry, which is concerned primarily with governments whose "indirect" features clearly have no undemocratic effects.

VIII

The second major aspect of the structure of representative government is the nature of the positions that are filled by means of the uncoerced periodic elections. These positions must clearly possess a great amount of control within the government itself, the personnel of which is only partly elected. John Stuart Mill attributed to the elected representatives a very extensive power: they must exercise "the ultimate controlling power, which, in every constitution, must reside somewhere. This ultimate power they must possess in all its completeness. They must be masters, whenever they please, of all the operations of government." [22] However, since nonelected organs of government have at times been able to make their opinions prevail, even over the explicit objections of the elected bodies, Mill's statement seems too strong. Two important examples are the behavior of the United States Supreme Court during the early 1930's, and the British House of Lords from 1890 until 1910. In both of these cases, the Cabinet and the House of Commons in Britain and the President and Congress in the United States were able to overcome the resistance of the nonelected organs of government after a period of time. This suggests that the most reasonable restatement of Mill's principle is that the elected organs of government can always prevail over the nonelected organs, within a certain period of time and upon issues of a certain importance.[23] The proper length of time and the proper degree of importance are once more to be determined in each case where such questions might arise. Except for the possibility of another conflict between the Supreme Court and the elected branches in the United States, the future decisions of the elected bodies in any of the twelve democratic states will probably not be even temporarily frustrated by the nonelected bodies.[24] Any of these several problems of identification will no doubt occur only with regard to states like Mexico and India, which are trying to establish representative governments.

The elected bodies of a representative government must have ultimate control, whenever they so desire, over all policies pursued by that government. While nonelected bodies have occasionally prevailed over elected bodies, when an important issue was involved the latter were able, before too long, to assert their ascendancy. Such ascendancy is an indispensable condition of a representative government, which in turn is indispensable to the democratic state.[25]

IX

The essential features of the structure of representative government—elections and the position of the elected officials—have now been described. Representative government also differs from other governments in the procedure by which its binding policy is made. This is one aspect of what is called "constitutionalism," which has traditionally and correctly been considered an integral part of democracy.

Political scientists since Aristotle have recognized that the word "constitution" has several different meanings. It refers first to the "pattern of power" within any state. The special power structure of the democratic state will be examined in chapter 8. It also refers to the "arrangement of governmental offices," that is, the location of formal authority, which has been described in the present chapter. Finally, it means customary and effective restraints upon the actions of government.[26]

Although both the pattern of political power within the state and the arrangement of governmental offices are effective restraints upon a representative government, when one speaks of a constitutional government, or better yet of "constitutionalism," he is usually referring to the effectiveness of formal rules that describe in some detail the things which government must and must not do and the manner in which it must proceed. Representative government is constitutional government in this sense; although governments in western Europe were constitutional before they were representative,[27] the extent and formalization of the restraints upon representative government are significantly broader and more developed than they are upon any other type of government.

The ultimate foundation for constitutionalism is to be found in the dominant social class of the democratic state, which I call the "Middle Class." * The Middle Class favors a form of government with built-in "checks and balances," and it is anxious to limit the

* See chapter 8 for the definition of the "Middle Class."

government's sphere of competence. This attitude underlies the persistence of meaningful "bills of rights" and other guarantees of limited governmental activity. There is also a direct link between representative government and constitutionalism, which depends upon the special structure of the former. When they make authoritative policy, representative governments characteristically are required to follow procedures that are specified in unparalleled detail by provisions having constitutional force.* No other kind of government even approaches this degree of regularized restraint.

It is not difficult to discover why so many procedural matters are circumscribed in a rigid, constitutional manner. An electoral system is a very complex and delicate thing, and its position in representative government is absolutely crucial. Not only must there be many rules which define, clarify, and standardize the electoral process, but these rules must be protected as much as possible from intentional or accidental corruption. Hereditary monarchy, for example, was obliged to take pains to protect the procedure by which individuals became eligible for the highest authority. Such a simple procedure, however, required only relatively simple regulation. The method of selection in representative government, on the other hand, is undoubtedly the most complex yet devised.

The intricacy of representative government is not exhausted by its electoral system, for the structure of the governmental organization itself is highly complicated. The relationship between the controlling elected organs and the controlled appointed organs is necessarily very complex and, as we have seen, as crucial as the manner in which the former are selected. Because the elected bodies lack techniques of control possessed by other "sovereigns"—such as kinship ties, loyalty to the sovereign's person, and arbitrary control over the subordinate's person and property—the representatives must rely upon formalized rules and regulations.[28] In addition, formalized procedure is required by the extraordinarily large size of the elected bodies called "parliaments," to say nothing of the complications introduced by bicameralism and independently elected "executives." In these bodies, from two hundred to six hundred people share the formal authority for policy-making; even under cabinet government, where leadership in policy-making has been furthest concentrated and where the formal authority of the individual member of parliament has been most diluted, the opinions and preferences of no individual representative can be ignored.[29] Order must be brought to this remarkable division

* Although it would be misleading to draw a sharp line between method and content—between, in this context, "procedural" and "substantive" constitutionalism—a distinction can be made between what is basically procedural and what is not.

of authority and power; for this purpose, representative government has consistently utilized constitutional rules of procedure.*

X

The governments of the twelve democratic states are under the ultimate control of men selected for their offices by uncoerced and periodic elections. These two features are sufficient for representative government, although all twelve governments also have universal suffrage, at least two candidates in every electoral contest, and only a minimum of "indirect representation." These characteristics may appear at first sight obvious and unexciting, but developing their implications will bring out their enormous importance. A government constructed according to these few principles is necessarily associated with political phenomena of the highest significance. It is based upon certain social, communal, and economic circumstances; it pursues certain policies; and it is connected with certain beliefs, practices, and organizations. The organizations most closely connected with the processes of representative government are the political parties. It is logical to turn next to an examination of them.

* Because this complexity requires as much clarity as possible, it is practically indispensable that democratic constitutions be in writing.

2: POLITICAL PARTIES AND REPRESENTATIVE GOVERNMENT

Every democratic state has at least two political parties, and its party system—the organization, operation, and interrelationships of the parties—is an integral part of its institutional structure. Any analysis of democratic government and politics must include a description of the parties and the party system, and it must relate these features to the other major democratic political phenomena: the structure of representative government, the content of public policy, and the social and economic setting. The institutions of representative government provide the logically most convenient point of departure for this analysis; indeed, an explanation of parties could hardly otherwise be given.

The present inquiry, it will be recalled, is limited to an examination of those elements of the democratic state which are unique. A chapter dealing with political parties might thus appear out of order, for certain nondemocratic states also possess political parties. However, the democratic party differs so sharply in so many ways from the nondemocratic party that, far from being identical, they are only generally comparable. They belong to the same group of phenomena only in the way in which democratic and nondemocratic states belong to a single group. The current practice of including within one study, and ideally within one theoretical framework, the British Labour party, the French Radical Socialist party, the Italian Fascist party, and the Soviet Communist party is as misleading as including in a study of legislatures the House of Commons, the National Assembly, the Grand Council of Fascism, and the Supreme Soviet. Among these, only the British and French parties and parliaments are essentially similar. Regarding the parliaments, this point is generally conceded. However, despite the sharp differences between democratic and nondemocratic parties in membership, structure, purpose, function, and position, political scientists usually consider their

20

similarities more fundamental than their differences. The modern political party is an organization that arose to operate the institutions of government after the disappearance of the traditional principles of political legitimacy. Parties consequently differ from one another to the extent that their respective governments differ; and, since representative government is unique, so are the political parties of the democratic state.

To show that democratic political parties differ from nondemocratic parties, we must discover their essential properties and their relationships to representative government and to the rest of the democratic state. This is also required by our general analysis of the democratic state. Throughout the discussion I shall refer to democratic parties simply as "parties."

I

The essential characteristic of the more than two score parties in the twelve democratic states is that they "nominate" candidates for the elective offices of representative government. Only parties perform this function, a fact that has been generally recognized as distinguishing parties from other groups interested in the electoral process.[1] What has not been so commonly recognized is that the act of nominating itself is enough to bring a political party into being.

Defining the party as an organization which nominates requires some explanation, since making nominations is usually held to be only one of several primary characteristics of a party. A typical description of parties is that they are vehicles for capturing and maintaining control of important governmental positions, which they attempt to do by nominating candidates and conducting electoral campaigns.[2] This description is not satisfactory for several reasons. Not all parties are in charge of their nominees' campaigns; the act of nominating alone implies that the party is interested in winning the election; and only under special circumstances does the party "capture and maintain control" of important governmental positions.

The "national" parties of the United States provide the crucial evidence for eliminating the function of campaigning from the concept of party. The Democratic and Republican parties meet at four-year intervals to nominate candidates for the American presidency, an action which all students of American politics have interpreted as the parties' most important function. All agree, moreover, that in performing this function they are behaving as political parties. It has been realized that the parties "on the national level" do not persist in the periods between presidential election years, but there has been some reluctance to acknowledge that they simply do not persist beyond the duration of the national conventions themselves. The parties organize, with rules of procedure, specialization of function, and control over their membership; they appoint committees, draw up "platforms," and nominate candidates; then they disband. Campaigning for the two candidates is not undertaken by two nationwide organizations, but by a large number of smaller organizations (which may be parties in their own right), located in states, counties, cities, and so forth.[3] If conducting the campaign is a necessary condition of a party, there can be no "presidential" parties in the United States.

To nominate a candidate is to attach to his candidacy a label or symbol which is meaningful to the electorate and which ordinarily assures him of the votes of a number of electors. The whole purpose of nominating would be undermined if the candidate could not count, in the ensuing campaign, on support from the organization which gave him the label, or (if the organization had disbanded) from a number of organizations closely associated with it. In short, if the party remains in existence after nominating its candidate—as most but not all parties do—it will then attempt to get him elected. Although there are cases where the attempt is less than enthusiastic, campaigning can reasonably be considered a concomitant of nominating. For this reason, in addition to the intermittent nature of American parties, the function of nominating can be taken as the single essential characteristic of the political party.

II

One of the greatest difficulties for the theory of political parties is presented by the American "primary election." The primary is a device whereby a party nominee is chosen, usually from among competitors, not by a relatively compact organization, but by a large number of private citizens. Sometimes a single primary election serves as the real means by which a governmental office is filled. More often the device works as intended, and there is a meaningful general election among candidates each of whom has been previously selected by a primary. To be useful, a concept of the political party must help explain both of these situations. They should thus be examined from the point of view that nominating is both necessary and sufficient for the existence of a political party.

A primary that is the only significant election may or may not be accompanied by political parties.[4] Any nomination must occur before the primary, even though it will not be legally recognized as a nomination. The competitors may be standing simply because they feel inclined to do so, or because they have been asked by friends to stand; under these circumstances there is no nomination and hence no party. The candidate may, however, be associated with, and known to be competing under the auspices of, a particular group. Farmers' and businessmen's associations, "courthouse gangs," and "Organizations" (like that in Virginia [5]) are groups of this kind; when they have, either formally or informally, attached a meaningful label to a contestant they have made a nomination, and they are consequently rudimentary political parties. Experts on parties, it must be remembered, have pointed out that where such nominations are made, the political situation is similar to that where there are legally recognized parties.[6]

Parties also may or may not be present when the primary elections are followed by a meaningful general election in which there is real competition among the primaries' victors. In a primary, the candidate is chosen by a process ending in an expression of preference by all those citizens qualified to participate. There will be a real political party under these circumstances if, and only if, an organization which prior to the primary indicates its support of one of the contestants is usually successful in getting the voters to choose him. In the United States, there are many continuously functioning organizations which have almost unvarying success in obtaining the victory of their primary candidates.[7] Where this practice prevails, the party organization includes as real members those people who vote in the primary. They are members because they perform a specialized function that is an integral part of the system of functions making up the organization. There are, of course, varying degrees of cohesiveness in such political parties, and it must be determined in each case when the organization has disappeared because its directing agency has failed to retain the support of the primary's voters. There need not be special requirements which an individual must meet before he can participate in the primary, but it is highly probable that as the requirements are more strict, the organization will be more cohesive and more stable.[8]

In the absence of a directing group, a primary election cannot be interpreted as a majority decision made by a single organization, comparable, for example, to a decision of a party convention. The actions of the hundreds of thousands of participants in primary elections are not organized because they are never sufficiently defined and coordinated. Whenever a candidate is chosen by a primary in which the voting does not confirm the organization's preprimary choice, the conditions necessary for a political party are not present. Political scientists have recognized that when the results of primaries cannot be predicted, many features usually associated with parties, such as political leadership and governmental responsibility, are not in evidence.[9] Their judgment corresponds very well to our theoretical conclusion that the parties themselves are not in evidence.*

---

* There may, of course, be "parties within parties." That is, there may be competing groups which nominate candidates for the primary contest, in the same way in which this is done when the primary is the *de facto* election.

Considering the function of nomination as the distinguishing characteristic of a political party not only fits our experience of the amorphous American situation, with its "presidential parties" and "primary parties," but also corresponds closely to the facts of party cohesion. If the essential function is nominating, we would expect to find in highly organized parties a tightly controlled procedure of nomination. This is in fact the case in British parties, where the single most powerful formal bond holding a party together is the leaders' ultimate control of the party's label.[10]

Although a nomination is essentially an organization's attaching its label to a candidate, there is no reason why the candidate himself cannot be a member of the organization. Some candidates for nomination, usually but not always incumbent representatives, are very powerful in their parties and participate in their own nominations. This activity is not inconsistent with the essential function of the party, as long as the latter, as an organization, maintains control over the label in question. A British backbencher's modest participation in the activities of his constituency organization, and thereby in the activities of the nationwide party, differs only in degree from an American congressman's domination of the party machine he has constructed by himself and for himself in his own private constituency.[11]

III

It was said above that a party "maintains control of important governmental positions" only under special circumstances, and that, therefore, this "control" cannot be one of its essential characteristics. In order to explain this, a very simple distinction must first be made between two different kinds of organization, often called the "party in parliament" and the "party in the country" (and which I shall call the "parliamentary party" and the "party"). Thus far the discussion has dealt only with the latter. The parliamentary party is an organization of incumbent members of parliament, founded and maintained for the purpose of combining their voting strength. It is the result of the possession of decision-making power by a relatively numerous body, while the party is the result of choosing governors by means of elections. Not only are these two "parties" different types of organizations, but there need be no close connections between them. Parliamentary parties can exist without parties, and one of the most important ways in which the latter have come into existence is through the activity of parliamentary groups.[12] Often a party finds that its successful nominees do not form a parliamentary party, or that they form several.[13] Although this situation presupposes a weakly organized party, it nevertheless illustrates the independence of the party and the parliamentary party. When the two are connected, their relationships can take several important forms. Either may dominate the other, or they may be relatively independent of each other.[14]

The only time a party "controls" a representative government is when it controls its associated parliamentary party, which in turn controls the basic points of governmental decision-making. Whenever this relationship occurs, it is highly probable that the parliamentary party will eventually come to dominate the party; [15] but since the leadership of the two groups is in the same hands, it might be said that the party "controls the government." The British and some of the Commonwealth parties are the only ones which have found themselves consistently in this position, although occasionally cabinets have been formed elsewhere from single "disciplined" parties.[16] Since the special nominating group of representative government only rarely "controls the government," such a function obviously cannot be an essential feature of the democratic party.

IV

Because parties of the democratic state are unique, they cannot be treated solely as varieties of a single species that also includes autocratic and totalitarian organizations. Many studies of parties, however, begin with the statement that every party is an organization concerned with the control or exercise of governmental power, and thus with the means by which it can be obtained.[17] This is true only in the sense that both democratic and nondemocratic parties are engaged in politics, and it requires the most general interpretations of "control of power" and "means to power." The contemporary studies of parties clearly intend the comparison to be closer than this. The fact that the party is a recent development may underlie this assumption of similarity, but this fact implies only that the principle of organization has proven useful in almost every contemporary political context. How the principle is applied and what is done with the results are quite different under democracy, autocracy, and totalitarianism. The usual treatment of parties resembles a comparative study of the detection and prevention of crime by the Federal Bureau of Investigation and the Ministry of State Security, both of which use modern chemistry and modern communications.

In a comparison of democratic parties, autocratic juntas and action groups, and totalitarian movements, all operating under a representative government—the only place they can coexist and where their methods are comparable—the differences in their attitudes toward the constitution are most obvious, and the differences in the methods of subversion used by the autocrat and the totalitarian are only slightly less obvious. For example, the French Communist party seeks power in one way, and the French Socialist party seeks it in another; each also has its own organizational structure, propaganda, and basic aims. Dissimilar power-seeking methods signify fundamental differences in essence.*

All those groups called "parties" are no more comparable in their "exercise of power" than they are in their "search for power." A common way of expressing the belief that they all exercise governmental power or authority is to classify modern states into three categories, according to whether "one party monopolizes power, or two parties alternate in power, or several parties share power." [18] Rather than being variations of a single political type, however, these modern states are fundamentally different regarding their parties. The so-called one-party states are either autocratic, in which case the Party often monopolizes power, or totalitarian, in which case the Party has relatively very little power. In the two-party and multiparty states, on the other hand, the parliamentary parties may have a considerable amount of political power, although normally they do not, while the parties proper have power only under the exceptional circumstances of the British type of party system.

In the American two-party system, the parties have very little control over the parliamentary parties; and the latter, at best, agree only informally on legislative programs, which need not be supported by their individual members.[19] The parliamentary parties, even if the President is included, do not in any sense "possess" or "exercise" governmental authority, and least of all do they "monopolize" it. Even when a parliamentary party with a clear majority votes as a unit to pass a statute recommended by a President of the same party, the action is not that of an organization but, at most, only of a group of men with similar sentiments, opinions, and traditions.

In a multiparty system like the French the parliamentary parties do not share in controlling governmental power. The usual coalition cabinets almost invariably include members from weakly disciplined parliamentary groups. While some ministries may be headed by representatives responsible to, and perhaps even controlled by, their parlimentary parties, there will always be some ministers who are, for all practical purposes, independent of any organized parliamentary group. The French Radical Socialist parliamentary party no more controls a Radical Socialist minister than the Democratic party in the United States Senate controls a Democratic committee chairman.

Contrary to popular supposition, totalitarianism is not "one-party rule." Experts on the Soviet Union have recognized that under Stalin the Communist party was an impotent organization, and that the

---

* The Communist party, of course, can and does use nominations and campaigns as means to power, but these are not its sole or primary techniques. See section VI, below.

Party "apparatus," the hierarchical structure of Party functionaries, was simply one of several organizations used by the Leader as instruments of his power. The Party apparatus checked and was checked by the secret police and the economic ministries; in no sense whatever did it "monopolize power." [20] Everyone of any importance in the Soviet Union was a member of the Party, but this, rather than being an indication of the Party's power, is pretty conclusive evidence that Party membership in itself meant nothing. A man's authority came from his position in one of the bureaucratic hierarchies, including the Party apparatus; the mass Party was simply a club of the successful and would-be successful.

The Nazi party in Hitler's Germany was equally impotent. Although its membership was never as inflated as that of the Communist party, it soon became merely a "front" for various elite organizations drawn from its ranks. Power lay with these latter organizations, none of which can reasonably be called a "party." [21]

The final type of "party state" has a single autocratic but non-totalitarian organization. The Fascist party in Mussolini's Italy, which despite certain tendencies never became totalitarian, best exemplifies this kind of organization. Such an organization is the only party designed to monopolize governmental power. It has a genuinely hierarchical structure, and it places its members in all key governmental positions. The statement that the Fascist party ruled Italy is only a mild oversimplification.[22]

This brief survey of the various positions of power and authority occupied by the different types of "parties" has shown that only parties like those of the British and organizations like the Fascist party can be said to "have control over the government," but the differences between their controlling positions are much more striking than the similarities. British-type parties control the major departments of the administrative branch of the government and the majority of votes in the parliament. Fascist-type organizations control all the "legislative" policy-making positions, the civil service, the judiciary, the military services, and all organs of local government. A member of the majority party under cabinet government will probably have some special access to points of policy-making. A member of the ruling "party" in an autocratic state possesses political power.

In brief, democratic parties only rarely "control the government"; insofar as they do, they do not then create a particular variety of the "modern party state." This conclusion is consistent with, and gives force to, the other differences between democratic parties and non-democratic organizations usually called "parties"—differences in their methods of "gaining power," in their organization and membership, and in their general goals and purposes.[23] The empirical evidence strongly supports the proposition that the political party of the democratic state is a unique phenomenon.

V

The political party differs from other modern organizations for political action in its functioning, structure, and composition, because it was designed to accompany, and has developed along with, the institutions of representative government. The connection between them is the connection between electing governmental officials and giving nominations.

A democratic election involves the participation of a very large group of human beings. No matter which electoral system is used, the candidate's chances for success depend to a great extent upon the electorate's awareness of his candidacy and their understanding of its meaning. Communicating to great numbers of people is one of the candidate's major problems; in every democratic state it has been met by the technique of nomination. This method focuses the attention of the electorate upon the candidacy and informs them that the candidate already has the support of at least one group of political activists. A nomination also generalizes, so to speak, the qualities and attitudes of the candidate by associating him and his candidacy with a group whose interests and principles are reasonably well known. It is the most efficient method of communication available.

Without the technique of nomination, the electorate would face insuperable difficulties in attempting to get relevant information about the candidates. At best, the elector would be obliged to vote for candidates personally familiar to him, and, with a moderately large electorate, a very large number of candidates would be required. The elector's only alternative would be to inform himself of the background and views of each candidate, and this he would have neither the time nor the inclination to do.

The small minority actively concerned with the outcome of democratic elections are aware of this problem of communicating to the electorate, or they become aware of it after some experience with the operation of the electoral system.[24] Their problem is to make their favorite candidates known to the voters; but they are equally concerned with avoiding a wasteful fragmentation of potentially combinable votes among many candidates.[25]

The activists must consequently do two things: they must discover some principles which are likely to appeal to large numbers of voters, and they must devise a method which firmly associates these principles with their candidate. The most useful method is to adopt a shorthand expression or "label" symbolizing the principles, and then to apply it to the candidate in question. The label can be, and often is, informally applied, simply by "letting it be known" that so-and-so is the candidate of their group. As the electorate becomes larger and harder to communicate with, and as electoral contests become more complex and more in need of regularization because of an increase in relevant issues, the application becomes more and more formalized, until finally it is defined by law. Nomination is the normal method of associating a candidate with a set of principles; it varies from the great formality of presenting a "party list," under certain systems of proportional representation, to the informality of "letting it be known" that a candidate is standing under the auspices of, for example, a group of businessmen. The latter is a primitive method of publicizing the candidate and his principles which occurs only in primitive political circumstances, but it is, nonetheless, a nomination.

The principles which the nomination symbolizes must be designed to attract some relevant segment and proportion of the electorate. A new political party must normally rely very heavily on real principles which make significant statements about governmental policy, but this dependence usually decreases as the party ages. The label of an older party will attract voters because of loyalty, tradition, material interest, and remembrance of past principles, in addition to the political program the party currently espouses. The party label, in this case, possesses additional meaningfulness, and applying it to a candidate communicates to the electorate more than a statement of the candidate's views on past, present, and future public policy.

VI

The argument showing how democratic elections give rise to political parties has assumed throughout that the parties want to win elections. They may be interested in getting their men into important policy-making positions because they are genuinely concerned with realizing certain ideals, such as social welfare or governmental efficiency; or because they desire to control sources of patronage, like appointive offices or sources of governmental contracts; or simply because they want the prestige which results from their nominee's incumbency. They are not interested in "controlling the government," for even if they could exercise complete control over their nominees once the latter are elected (as most of them cannot), both they and the parliamentary parties accept certain limitations to their power, such as the short-term independence of the judiciary and the civil service. In addition, political parties always carefully avoid any suppression of rival parties, the action which would do most to assure their own control. The parties have no intention of abandoning the representative system of government and its periodic uncoerced elections; as it has been said, they accept the "rules of the democratic game." [26]

One of the peculiarities of representative government is that it permits nondemocratic groups to participate in its elections and in its policy-making process. Organizations like the Fascist, Nazi, and Communist parties can nominate candidates, conduct campaigns, vote on the budget, and participate in parliamentary committees. When they do these things, they are acting as parties and parliamentary parties, but it is manifestly clear that they are acting in other ways too. They are action groups and totalitarian movements using democratic devices for purposes inconsistent with the constitutional and ethical presuppositions of the democratic state. That is to say, they are not merely political parties, just as the political party which publishes a newspaper is not merely a publisher. These parties are anomalies; their electoral successes result from weaknesses in the social and economic foundations upon which representative government rests.

Groups of nondemocratic political activists not only have purposes and functions different from those of democratic groups, but they also differ in their organizational structure. They are more highly centralized, they have stronger articulation and a more formalized conception of membership, and they expect their members to participate much more extensively in the organization's affairs.[27] Members of nondemocratic "parties" have nondemocratic attitudes toward their organizations. They more fully identify themselves with their groups; in the case of Communism they practically lose their personalities to the organization.[28] The functions performed by the democratic party in the political process of representative government simply do not require a high degree of discipline and dedication; the nondemocratic group needs both for its tasks of subverting a constitutional order or ruling a "one-party" state.

VII

Although political parties do not "control governmental power" in the democratic state, they nevertheless perform vitally important functions. By means of their essential function of nomination, they simplify and thereby make meaningful the alternatives presented to the electorate. Without this simplification, the average voter would be unable to comprehend the great number of candidates and issues. There would be confusion in the election and in the resulting parliament, accompanied by the lowering of morale always associated with apparently directionless politics. Moreover, the original lack of comprehension, the simple psychological inability to grasp the alternatives being presented, would tend to undermine popular faith in the system of democratic elections.[29] A representative government depends to an unusual extent upon the confidence of its citizenry, and by their very existence the parties contribute to this confidence.

Providing political leadership for the democratic state is another very significant function of the party. The representatives make a great many basic governmental decisions, and they have the responsibility for all such decisions. The parliamentary parties often choose the most important leaders—the prime ministers, cabinets, and committee chairmen—from their own ranks, but the members of the parliamentary parties were themselves originally selected by the parties. Selecting qualified leadership is clearly central to the proper functioning of representative government and, therefore, to the maintenance of the democratic state.

The present discussion has emphasized the fundamental differences in structure, membership, and purpose between democratic parties and nondemocratic organizations. Similar differences occur in the kinds of men whom they select as leaders in making public policy. Although all politicians must be familiar with the arts of persuasion and compromise, and although they all must have some personal force and ability to handle men, the party politician must possess these techniques and characteristics to a very high degree, simply because he has little else to rely upon.[30] He cannot depend upon demagogic threats and promises because, even if his constituency is naïve or desperate enough to support such a program, he knows that he cannot put it into effect.[31] He cannot base his strength on his pocketbook, for election to office cannot be purchased.[32] Physical courage and ruthlessness may be vitally important to the leader of a military junta or action group, but they are at best incidental to a party politician. Organizational ability is desirable, but both the candidate and the representative can and usually do delegate direction of the organization to their lieutenants;[33] this delegation would be unthinkable in a bureaucratic or totalitarian state. The parties must, in short, nominate men skilled in attracting and maintaining the support of voluntary associations and uncoerced masses of voters. The political party supplies the democratic state with the special type of men who operate the special institutions of representative government.*

A third way in which the political party contributes to the operation of representative government is by creating a "collective responsibility" among the final arbiters of democratic public policy. When the candidate accepts a nomination, he becomes associated not only with his party and its supporters but also with all other

---

* The parties also provide leadership for most of the unorganized groups within the democratic state. This function will be discussed in the following chapter.

candidates identified by the same label. The strength of these links varies according to the degree to which the party and its allied parliamentary group are "disciplined"; but, even where the former is periodic and ephemeral and the latter fragmented, the label is considered by almost all elements in and out of parliament as their common possession. Outsiders naturally tend to identify the group's members with one another more strongly than do the members themselves. The general electorate will be unaware of or overlook divisions within a party which may be glaringly obvious to a politician or political analyst. But candidates and representatives often find it politically convenient to identify themselves formally and publicly with all who wear their label. They often find it even more convenient to refer to opposing parties as if they were monolithic in structure and sentiment.

The dynamics of the democratic party system strongly encourages the members of all parties to develop a sense of group identification. This sense leads both the parties "in power" and those "in opposition" to cooperate more closely within their respective ranks than they otherwise would, and to fear any attack, from one another or from a third source, upon their label or anyone associated with it. No matter how independent a representative happens to be, he must always allow for the possibility that an attack upon a fellow partisan, with completely different ideas and from a distant location, will adversely influence the attitudes of his own constituents. However, he also dislikes *ipso facto* any derogation of the political symbols with which he identifies himself.

The "opposition" party and its allied parliamentary party derive an immediate electoral advantage from criticizing the party "in power," and they are in a position to make informed and publicized criticisms. Their interest in enhancing the value of their party labels thus acts as a check upon the operations of government. The parties "in power," in their turn, must try to meet these criticisms and to expose the opposition's alternatives as undesirable or impractical. This kind of relationship is most highly developed in Great Britain, where there is a formally recognized Opposition; but mutual checks of party on party occur, to some extent, under all forms of representative government. Keeping the "Government" collectively responsible to the "Opposition" is one of the most important functions of the political party. This phenomenon occurs only in the democratic state.[34]

VIII

In discussing the organization, purposes, functions, and interrelationships of democratic parties, an account has been given of the democratic party system. Little more can be said about it as a type of system or institution. The number of parties, the degree of their "discipline," their relationships with the parliamentary parties, the geographical and social distribution of their electoral support— all these matters are determined by factors which vary from one democratic state to the next. Although we are not here concerned with these variations, it might be mentioned that each of the major sub-types of representative government—cabinet, presidential, and assembly government—is associated with a particular type of party system. Explaining the relationships between the formal structure of these governments and the party systems accompanying them is one of the more important tasks of political science.

Political parties perform many functions other than those just described. Throughout our examination of the democratic state, the political party will be conspicuously and significantly in evidence. It might be helpful here to list some of its tasks and to indicate where they will be discussed. The party participates in formulating the specific policy decisions of representative government, since its views and campaign statements cannot help influencing its parliamentary party. More important is the party's role in determining the general long-term policy of representative government, a role to be examined in chapter 3. The party is the most important champion of civil liberties in the democratic state, as will be seen in chapter 4. The expansion of the suffrage, which is closely related to both democratic welfare policy and democratic civil liberties, has been accomplished primarily through action by parties. This will also be dealt with in chapter 4. The operation of representative government depends upon certain popular attitudes, including a sense of political responsibility. How the parties aid in maintaining this sense of responsibility will be described in chapters 5 and 8.

The present chapter has been designed to explicate the concept of the political party and to show how parties are connected, as both necessary and sufficient conditions, to the institutions of representative government and, therefore, to the other principal political elements of the democratic state. Although in certain respects they resemble other organizations of political activists often called "parties," they differ from them precisely in the same way and precisely to the same extent as the democratic state differs from the autocratic or totalitarian state.

3: THE POLICY OF REPRESENTATIVE GOVERNMENT

The democratic state has unique governmental institutions and unique organizations of political activists; it is reasonable to suppose that the public policy of the democratic state is also unique. This supposition is supported by observation of the twelve contemporary democracies, wherein public policy is singularly concerned with both the material well-being of the broad masses and the special interests of the numerous organized groups. Only representative government goes beyond the provision of public sanitation, police protection, and communications, to institute workmen's compensation, old-age pensions, and unemployment and health insurance. Only representative government takes into very serious consideration the desires of small and economically unimportant groups of businessmen, laborers, and farmers. The present chapter will attempt to generalize this description as accurately as possible, and to explain why representative government makes this kind of public policy.

By "the policy of representative government," I mean all decisions made by government personnel acting in their official capacities. This "policy" obviously includes a great variety of decisions made by many different kinds of officials, from the parliament's passing the central budget to the policeman's issuing a traffic citation. In the analysis of the specific type of policy enacted by representative government, the decisions of the central government will be emphasized, rather than those of any of its subordinate units. Although primary attention will be paid to decisions made by the elected branches, the general conclusions will apply to all relevant governmental decisions, no matter what their source. The elected representatives, as its ultimate authorities, determine the spirit of the democratic state's public policy.

The problem is to describe and account for those policies that differentiate representative government from other forms of government. Thus not every governmental decision is relevant to the inquiry. Maintaining "law and order," providing military strength, and per-

forming services regarding the currency, post, measures, and so forth
are activities undertaken by all governments and need not be considered here.*

I

Generally speaking, a representative government acts so that every
segment of its citizenry—every stratum and locality and interest group
—enjoys a reasonably high standard of living and a reasonably high
degree of social deference. By "reasonable" I mean that the standard
of living is beyond mere subsistence and the social deference beyond
mere tolerance. Of course, this level of material and social welfare
is not the result of governmental action alone; the point is that a
representative government will guarantee it to each segment of the population. In maintaining this level of welfare each representative government faces special problems which require a greater or lesser degree
of social and economic regulation. One government may provide
family allowances and free dental care, while another may ignore
these but enforce "fair employment" practices. These differences in
the quantity and quality of governmental regulation are related to
the individual state's special socioeconomic circumstances. The basic
similarity, however, remains: every representative government provides a certain minimum standard of welfare and deference for its
entire population, when this does not result from unregulated social
and economic processes. No other type of modern government behaves
in this way.

The statement that welfare policy is empirically a necessary condition of the modern democratic state requires no proof. It is apparent
that the twelve representative governments pay close attention to the
welfare of their masses, as well as to the requests and demands of their
many "special interests." Evidence is required, however, for the statement that this policy is in fact sufficient for the democratic state. This
evidence can best be provided by a brief examination of certain
typical nondemocratic states.

States which can be classified as "old-fashioned" autocracies,
like Spain, Portugal, recent Central American dictatorships, Ethiopia,
and the states of the Arabian peninsula, are simply unconcerned with
the material welfare of their people; if they do not positively favor
social differentials, they at least are indifferent to discrimination.
Even Dr. Salazar, who is anxious to appear as "paternalistic" as
possible, does not concern himself with programs of "social welfare." [1]

---

* It has been said that any conscious abstention from action on the part
of government is as much policy-making as the passing of a statute. This is
well taken, but the present chapter will be concerned only with "positive"
policy. The special "negative" policy of the democratic state will be discussed
in chapter 4.

In "modern" autocracies, like the dictatorships of Perón in Argentina and Nasser in Egypt, the well-being of the general populace is generally ignored, despite protestations to the contrary.[2] Any pressure from organized or unorganized groups for governmental amelioration of economic and social conditions is resisted, or attempts are made to divert it, for example, toward military expansion or against alleged injustices from the outside. At best, the living standards of the people are raised only incidentally, as a result of governmental action to strengthen the state's economy.

Far from wishing to increase material welfare, totalitarianism has shown a studied indifference to anything but a subsistence standard of living, although subsistence in industrial states requires a higher standard than in agrarian states. Totalitarians have been interested almost exclusively in constructing an industrial foundation for military strength or in utilizing one for aggressive warfare. They maintain a standard of living only high enough not seriously to impair their workers' efficiency. The programs of "social welfare" which the totalitarian claims to have instituted are generally inoperative.[3]

The official attitude of both "modern" autocracies and totalitarian regimes toward social differentials is not always indifferent or approving as in the case of "old-fashioned" dictatorships. During the first years of their existence, both must destroy the status of their political opponents, and both may attempt to raise that of lower social groups whom they hope to use as allies.[4] Once these regimes have established themselves, however, new status differentials usually arise and are tolerated. The history of Communism, the movement most concerned with eliminating social stratification, illustrates this tendency.[5] In any event, the most that can be said about the two kinds of dictatorship is that they attack socially privileged groups. This policy is quite different from representative government's attempt to raise the status of the socially underprivileged, exemplified in such measures as "civil rights" legislation.

On the other hand, those states which, although they are not fully democratic, have adopted representative systems of government show concern for the welfare of their masses and make some attempt to translate this concern into positive policy. Their social-welfare programs are often restricted more by a lack of means than by a lack of will. Germany, Italy, and Japan exhibit this concern with welfare, but states like Mexico perhaps best exemplify this kind of political transition.[6] Of these, Germany alone approaches the well-established democracies in the comprehensiveness of its program.[7] The significant fact, however, is that only states which have representative governments seriously attempt to guarantee the material and social welfare of their entire citizenry.

II

Political science has recognized that representative governments follow a welfare policy and that this distinguishes them from other governments. But there have been too few attempts to give more than a superficial explanation of the relationship between welfare policy and the other principal political elements of the democratic state. The present analysis of democracy must explain this relationship; its conclusion will unsurprisingly be that, speaking roughly, the policy results from the parties' competition for votes.

One of the most persistent interpretations of the public policy of democracy is that it "carries out the will of the people." Although the proponents of this opinion rarely try to show why the people have this influence, it implies a particular relationship between the governors and the governed; thus it is a rudimentary explanation of welfare policy. Because it is a very common opinion, it warrants examination in some detail. During the course of this examination, the vital problems of evidence and meaning to be solved by the subsequent explanation of democratic policy will be clearly delineated.

There are several variations of this interpretation of democratic policy, but all of them include the notion that a representative government "reflects" the interests of its governed. The reliance upon one meaning of the word "representation"—"carrying out the will of someone else"—is evident here, but the notion is not merely concerned with the meaning of words. Its proponents believe that the governments of the twelve democratic states actually make this kind of public policy.[8]

Several questions immediately arise concerning the key phrases in the theory of interest reflection. Governmental action is supposed to correspond to certain beliefs, but what is the nature of these beliefs, who possesses them, and which governmental acts are in accord with them?

The beliefs are usually called the "interests," "desires," or "will" of the people. All these words must refer to what the people themselves possess; that is, the people have the interests and desires and they express the will. The notion of interest reflection does not mean that the government follows some transcendental General Will which it interprets itself; nor does it mean that the government does what is to the interest of the people, whether or not the latter are aware of this interest. Representation as the reflection of interests occurs in a situation where the people themselves define their own interests; representative government does what the people desire, not what it or any third party considers good for them.

"The people" are supposed to possess the interests that govern-

ment reflects. No matter what word is used, the implication is that
democratic policy is related to the desires of all the people, or at least
an overwhelming majority of them; no favoritism is shown to special
classes, strata, or sections. This conception of "the people" is meaningful; the group thus defined can possess interests, either in the sense
that they all have special interests or in the sense that they share a
common interest. It must only be remembered that, for the people to
have a common interest, each and every relevant individual must
himself consciously possess the interest.[9]

The last issue is to determine which of the government's actions
are in accord with which of the people's interests. Since the people
desire a multitude of things, the number of popular desires that governmental policy is supposed to reflect must somehow be restricted.
Similarly, the government makes a great number of policy decisions,
all of which are certainly not reflections of popular interest; another
restriction is thus in order. Finally, the theorists cannot claim that
only the government of the democratic state reflects popular interests,
since examples can be given of very popular actions by nondemocratic
governments.[10] The policy of representative government must be described as reflecting a certain quantity or a certain type of popular
interest.[11]

The quantitative restriction might be that a representative government reflects more interests, or acts more often in accord with
the desires or will of its people, than any other type of government.
The qualitative restriction might limit reflection to the most important
popular interests and perhaps to the government's most important
acts. The government might also be said to reflect only those interests
that the people desire to have promoted by governmental action; this
restriction seems fully consistent with the spirit of interest reflection.
If these qualifications are combined, the policy of representative government can be said to differ from that of all other governments in
that its more important elements are more often in accord with the
people's more important desires regarding governmental policy. Since
this version of the theory of interest reflection says the least, it should
best be able to resist criticism.[12]

III

The first impression given by this reasonably precise statement
of "a democratic government's acting in accord with the interests
of its governed" is of a remarkably involved and doubtfully accurate
attempt to say that representative governments enact policies of social
welfare. Since these policies distinguish democratic from nondemocratic governments, they must be the reflections of the important
popular desires to which democratic government pays more attention

than any other government. Nevertheless, the concept of interest reflection implies that these programs of welfare are desired by the people and for this reason put into operation. This is a suggested explanation of democratic public policy and, as such, requires evaluation.

The primary difficulty encountered by this theory is discovering what the people really want. The theory cannot be verified unless proof can be given that the people want social-welfare policy, or any other policy, before the government adopts it. It is easy to show, however, that what the people want the government to do is never clear, even after the government has taken the initiative.

To discover the people's attitude toward governmental policy, one might ask them directly what they wish the government to do. This questioning would have to be periodic, for the persistence of their preferences could not be assumed. Such polls of public opinion have not been taken, and there is no reason to believe that, if they were, their results would indicate that the representative government in question was doing a significant amount of what its people wanted it to do. This skepticism applies not only to one desire common to all the people, but also to many desires, each of which was being satisfied by governmental action. Most people's positive desires for action by government probably involve some detailed regulation of a minor annoyance or some prohibition of a common but disliked practice. If the surveys discovered any positive correlation between popular desires and public policy, this would have to be compared with the results of similar surveys of the people in nondemocratic states.

Representative government is notoriously sensitive to the demands of organized policy-aspiration or pressure groups. Their interests, which are expressed directly by the words and actions of their leaders, might be taken as those reflected by representative government. Since democratic policy is supposed to be in accord with the desires of the vast majority of the people, the membership of organized groups must include the "vast majority" of the people, and within each organization there must be no discrepancy between the interests of the rank and file and the words and actions of the leaders. Neither of these conditions is ever satisfied.

It might here be objected that the interests a representative government reflects are not specific and short-term, as has been unrealistically assumed, but much more general in nature. Representative government is in accord with the people's desires for peace and prosperity, which as human beings they naturally possess, or for the well-being of the national community with which they identify, or for the health of the governmental system which they believe to be legitimate. These interests are described in an extremely vague way, but if they were defined more precisely they could not be attributed to all the people. If this vagueness is ignored, there is no reason to believe that by reflecting them representative government differs from other governments. In short, the only interests which can possibly be attributed to the people as a whole are equally attributable to the masses of any state,[13] and nondemocratic as well as democratic governments promote peace and prosperity, the nation's well-being, and their own health.

In view of the difficulty of directly discovering what kind of public policy the people desire, it is sometimes said that, although one may not be able to determine *which* interests of the people are being reflected, he can know that these interests *are* being reflected. An examination of the people's general behavior under representative government will show that they are getting what they want, for they are submitting to governmental decisions without being forced to do so. When they refuse to obey the government, or when they obey it only under the threat of severe penalties, then their interests are not being reflected.[14] This argument changes the meaning of interest reflection from government's doing what the people want, to government's doing nothing to which the people are strongly opposed. The possibility that the people are completely indifferent to the acts of a representative government is not eliminated, and consequently no conclusions can be drawn regarding what the people want.

In summary, without reference to governmental activity, no proof can be given that the people desire any programs of public policy, either in the sense that all of them want a single policy, or in the sense that there is a group of special interests encompassing all the people. The population of the democratic state is simply too large for this information to be obtained. There is, however, a phenomenon of the democratic state thus far unmentioned which, it might be maintained, not only allows us to discover popular interests but shows us that they are reflected by governmental policy. This phenomenon is, of course, the electoral system.

IV

At the start of the present chapter, I said that the special policy of the democratic state resulted from the parties' competition for the people's votes. This statement might be interpreted to mean that, since the candidates are anxious to be elected, they will promise to do what their constituents want them to do, and that, once in office, their desire to be re-elected will cause them to keep their promises. This interpretation, although it sounds innocent enought, is incorrect. One cannot infer from the electoral process that the government is reflecting the interests of the governed, that it is doing what the people want it to do.

In the first place, under any electoral system which is not fully "proportional," the representative makes policy for people who did not vote for him. Democratic elections provide no evidence that the representative does what these electors want him to do.* In the second place, the theory of interest reflection assumes that the voters base their choice of candidates primarily on the latter's policies. It implies that the constituents ensure, through their control of the representatives' jobs, that the policy they want is put into effect. Our information indicates, however, that the voters neither are particularly aware of the policy issues of most campaigns nor cast their ballots primarily according to the issues familiar to them. They are motivated at least as much by factors such as their traditional party affiliations, their religious and ethnic preferences, and their taste regarding personalities, as well as by their pleasure or resentment at general developments such as changes in the level of economic activity and the course of international politics.[15]

Occasionally, an issue or set of issues, of overriding importance and simple enough to be understood by most of the voters, may be the crux of a campaign, and the competing candidates or parties may take stands on this issue which are sharply enough opposed to make their differences comprehensible to the voters. Given these conditions, it is not unreasonable to infer that the winners of the election have had their policy approved by a majority of the electorate. Even if the other objections to the idea of interest reflection through elections are omitted, these conditions occur in conjunction much too infrequently to support the statement that the policy of representative government is in accord with the will of its people.

The politician himself never knows what his constituents want him to do. He cannot take the continuous polls necessary to discover what they want government to do, nor can he rely upon the opinions of pressure group leaders. Even if he has been elected and re-elected, he cannot infer that he has been enacting the desires of his electorate. They may have voted for him for any of the reasons mentioned above, and his popularity may simply result from the unpopularity of his various opponents. The most that any representative can conclude from his electoral success is that the policy he has been pursuing is not greatly disliked by a majority (or plurality) of his electorate.

There is another view of representation closely connected with the concept of interest reflection, and some brief comments upon it

* This raises the familiar "problem of the majority," to be more fully examined in chapter 5.

might prove useful. The word "representative" is often synonymous with "typical," and it has been said that a person *politically* represents a group when he shares its values, customs, and beliefs.[16] From this, two inferences might be drawn: that the personnel of existing representative governments are typical of the general populations,[17] and that their policy reflects popular values, customs, and beliefs.

With respect to the first inference, the similarity between the representatives and the citizens in modern democratic states does not include those characteristics ordinarily considered relevant to political behavior. The representatives are atypical in their occupation, income, social status, education, religious affiliation, ethnic background, and age.[18] Nevertheless, the representatives need not resemble the citizens in all these respects in order to share the latter's values, customs, and beliefs; an absence of sharp differences of wealth, status, and so forth between governors and governed might suffice. This latter condition characterizes modern democratic states, but they are not, as a consequence, differentiated from many other types of modern state.[19] This general similarity of governors and governed is not a phenomenon of democracy, but of the disappearance of aristocracy as a viable social and political principle.

Even if the governors are assumed to be typical of the people, it cannot be inferred that the policy which they make reflects the interests of the people. There is no guarantee that people with typical interests will, when they are put into positions of authority, pursue these interests, thereby doing what the people "want" them to do. That is, it must be proved that a governor retains the ideas about governmental policy that he possessed before he himself became part of the government. A new environment and new responsibilities often give rise to new interests,[20] and even though the governor was typical in his origin, that he remains typical cannot be presumed.[21]

The concept of interest reflection does not provide a useful interpretation of democratic public policy. The most that can be said about the relationship between the government's policy and the people's interests is that they are generally compatible. The people "want" the policy in the same sense that they "want" law and order, a decent standard of living, and a representative system of government. This tells us very little indeed about the content of democratic policy, and it fails completely to connect the great welfare programs, which are its definitive element, with the periodic uncoerced elections similarly definitive of representative government.[22] The representatives do not simply discover that the people want "social security" and then legislate accordingly.

V

The distinctive welfare policy of representative government re-sults from the special relationship between the people and the govern-ors created by the system of periodic uncoerced elections. In order to show why it occurs, this relationship must first be described with some precision.

The basic element of the relationship is the normal desire of the candidates to win elections. Although there are often many competitors who have no serious expectations of success, who enter the contest to publicize a special viewpoint, to influence the distribution of votes, or to indulge personal or group whims, the problem concerns only those who have a real chance to win—and they invariably want to win. Their desire for success prompts them to take the initiative and pro-vide an electorally appealing campaign program. To understand what will appear to them as electorally appealing, it is necessary to deter-mine which part of their electorates they expect to provide them with the winning number of votes.

There are two relevant hypotheses about how candidates appeal to their electorates. The first is that they attempt to maximize their votes, to get as large a proportion as possible of the total vote; [23] the second says that they attempt to secure only enough votes for a com-fortable margin of victory.[24] If the first is correct, the candidate must take into account all the opinions that he suspects are prevalent in his constituency; this is, in effect, what the theory of interest reflection says that he does. Although our evidence is inadequate, the second hypothesis clearly has a higher degree of probability. Candidates and parties seem to focus their attention upon certain groups in prefer-ence to others. They seem to take as a normal principle their inability to defend a program pleasing to everyone. They no doubt usually realize that they receive disproportionate support from certain social strata or sections of the constituency, for reasons not entirely depend-ent upon their current policy programs. These people predisposed to support must not be alienated, and they must be fully "mobilized" during the campaign and election. If a winning number of votes can be had from these favorably inclined groups, courting voters pre-disposed toward other parties and candidates is a waste of time and energy. Regarding the appeals themselves, a platform that attempts to provide a plank for everyone must be constructed from lighter lumber; no candidate can afford to lose his friends by flirting with their enemies. He needs not only their votes but their money, their media of communication, and their volunteer labor.

If these arguments are correct, the candidate need take into account only the interests of that part of his electorate upon which he relies for success. At the least, every candidate realizes that his constituency contains groups which he simply cannot please, although he never knows precisely the size and location of these groups. Even if he attempts to get more than a "comfortable margin of victory," he has little reason to try for more than about 80 per cent of the votes in any individual election.[25] The candidate's problem is to present a set of campaign promises designed to appeal not to his entire electorate, but only to that proportion which he believes will give him a reasonably safe lead over his opponent or opponents. The problem of the incumbent representative is to support policy with the same kind of appeal.

Although the representative appeals only to a portion of his constituency, he still is unable to discover what this portion would like him to do. He must assume that the policy he pursues will influence the voting of these constituents, but he never can know exactly how and why. He can consult with the leaders of organized groups whose memberships he reckons among his supporters, and he can "sample" the opinions of the ordinary voters. But the information thus gained is not, as I have argued at some length, grounds for inferring what his special portion of the electorate wants him to do.

The candidate cannot even assume that the great masses of his unorganized constituents have any specific desires about the policy they would like him to pursue, and he cannot ascribe to the rank and file of organizations even an awareness of the policy aspirations of their officers. Given his very reasonable presupposition that issues of policy are nevertheless relevant, his problem is to present, in campaign promises and in official action, a program designed not to reflect the pre-existing interests of the governed, but to suggest, to a certain portion of them, governmental activities which they might well be wise to support.[26]

In the democratic state, proposals for both specific and general public policy are initiated by many different types of leaders. Officials of organizations, owners and editors of periodicals, teachers, and clergymen can effectively espouse policy because they possess the necessary means of publicity; this is also true with respect to occasional personages who, by virtue of past accomplishments, are normally assured of publicity for their individual views and opinions. Although all these "leaders of public opinion" influence the long-term trends of governmental policy, practical policy in the short run is most strongly affected by men who are held to speak for specific interests, whether of mass groups like the industrial workers, or of small groups like church congregations, or of individuals like a large manufacturer or landowner.[27] Since no constituency is fully organized, its great unorganized masses have no "spokesmen" among those leaders whose ideas carry weight in the day-to-day and even year-to-year making of governmental policy. But representative government, unlike any other kind of government, provides official leaders of mass opinion, because those men ultimately in charge of official policy and those who aspire to this power initiate policy programs designed to appeal to the great masses of the population.

My point here is not that only candidates and representatives attempt to please unorganized groups, or that only they have success in putting their programs into effect.[28] The point is that they are the only ones who have a vested interest in functioning as opinion leaders of unorganized groups. Since their power depends upon the electoral support of people whose interests are unarticulated, they must at least periodically attempt to devise "appeals to the people." No other system of government has anything resembling this.

In chapter 2 it was said that political parties often formulate governmental policy. The candidate can never know precisely how to capture and retain the support of the proper number of voters—a problem of communication which does not arise in connection with small organized groups and individuals. He therefore must devise a set of campaign promises; and once elected, he must fulfill them more or less faithfully. In most cases, the organization which originally nominated him is interested in the content of these promises, and, indeed, the act of nomination itself almost always associates the candidate with at least some items of a policy program. The extent to which the party participates in making the electoral appeals varies with the degree of its "discipline," which also determines its allied parliamentary party's participation in making them and faithfulness in adhering to them. Despite these differences in degree, all democratic parties have at least some part to play in the formulation of public policy, and the parliamentary parties are bound, in some measure, to respect the policy thus formulated.[29]

VI

The candidate who wishes to win an election must make some kind of appeal to certain sections of his constituency. He realizes that he should attempt to appear wise, intelligent, personally attractive, dedicated, trustworthy, and experienced. He also realizes that the voters on whom he is relying will very probably respond to what he promises to do regarding positive public policy once he is elected. He does not know which desires these voters have, so he must promise what he thinks they are likely to approve. He does not even know whether they have any desires with respect to governmental action, but he assumes they will support him if he informs them of possible action and then convinces them that they should be working for it. In effect, he expects electoral success from promising to satisfy desires which he himself has created. The result of this process in the modern democratic state has been the government's guaranteeing a minimum of material and social welfare to every electorally significant element of the population.

The first task for the candidate is to classify his electorate, as precisely as he can, according to certain indexes generally thought to have some correlation with its varieties or potentialities of political opinion. For example, in the United States he would consider occupation, membership in ethnic groups, standard of living, association with foreign countries or nations, traditional political affiliation, and religion. One of the most striking results of this rudimentary analysis will be the discovery, in almost every constituency, of a substantial number of people who are in a relatively inferior position regarding their material and social standing. They are always numerous enough to be a welcome addition to any candidate's electoral "coalition," and occasionally their votes would suffice to insure victory. The relatively less privileged in almost any constituency present a challenge and an opportunity which simply cannot be ignored. Indeed, excepting the United States and Canada, every contemporary democratic state has possessed, at one time or another, a powerful political party whose electoral appeal was directed almost exclusively to these "lower" strata of society.

Even if these groups are not especially large, they usually have enough votes to be a formidable factor in any candidate's calculations of success. At the very least, each underprivileged group in the modern democratic state will have one candidate and probably one political party purporting to "speak for its interests." The position of the American Negro in the period following World War II illustrates this principle very well. Although Negroes constitute only about 10 per cent of the American population—a percentage which is considerably smaller when the disfranchised Negroes of the South are subtracted—programs designed to appeal specifically to the Negro have been adopted by individual candidates of both major political parties; the national parties themselves have both gone on record as supporting such programs; and "civil rights" legislation has been passed by the federal Congress. This unorganized group, although it is not especially numerous, is seen by each party as occupying a critical position in its competition with its principal rival. The apparent eagerness of both national parties to compile a policy record which they believe will appeal to the as yet unfranchised Negroes of the South is another indication of the Negro's important place in American politics.

There will be no appeal to underprivileged groups which are

electorally negligible, and policy programs designed to solve their problems will not be initiated and defended by candidates and representatives. But the competition for office in most constituencies is normally intense enough to supply spokesmen for almost any group, no matter how small; and the construction of parliamentary majorities is usually difficult enough to give influence to the spokesmen who have been elected.

This electoral and parliamentary arithmetic motivates at least some candidates and parties to frame programs which will appeal to the people of lesser material and social standing. In the context of a democratic society, the broad outlines of the solution are obvious. From all relevant sources—the humanitarian tradition of the culture itself; individuals who have risen from the depressed groups; leaders of organizations with lower-strata membership; and the personal experience and conscience of candidates and party officials, no matter what their social origin—from all these sources comes the suggestion that electoral success is most likely to accompany promises to improve the position of the people in question. This appeal has been adopted by one or more parties—or large groups of candidates—in every democratic state. When they have been elected, these parties have enacted the policies which distinguish the democratic state: unemployment insurance, old-age pensions, bank-deposit guarantees, workmen's accident compensation, family allowances, wages and hours regulation, guarantees of "fair employment" practices, and insurance against illness. As these issues are more frequently discussed and as more and more of them are embodied in law, parties and candidates which originally opposed them become increasingly reconciled and often even adopt many of them as their own. The great majority of democratic leaders, both governmental and nongovernmental, cease to oppose at least the general principle of government's guaranteeing a minimum level of material and social welfare when it does not result from the unregulated course of economic and social processes.

All this does not imply that "the people desire" welfare policy. It does not even imply that the special minorities appealed to—the urban proletariat, the small farmer or peasant, the socially inferior ethnic or cultural group—want the government to enact welfare policy. What can be inferred is that the groups which profit from welfare legislation tend to approve of it, since campaigns based on promises of welfare have often been successful and since representatives and parties which have enacted the legislation have often been re-elected.[30]

VII

Welfare measures have become the distinguishing characteristic of democratic policy primarily because of the dynamics of the electoral system, but their conjunction naturally occurs in a special social, economic, and historical-traditional context. Representative government can be maintained only in what I call a "Middle-Class" society, a society, as Aristotle put it, dominated by those who possess the gifts of fortune in moderation. The Middle-Class society will be examined in detail in chapter 8, but the welfare policy of the democratic state cannot be fully understood without some references here to its basic properties.

All the people of the democratic state have a high standard of living, and this means that the underprivileged are by no means impoverished. They are "underprivileged" only in relation to other groups in the Middle-Class society; for this reason, the welfare appeals made to them only rarely come close to threatening expropriation of the more fortunate. The challenge of the lower classes is never so radical that it alienates more than a small minority of the upper classes. The rise of the British Labour party is the best known example of this, but similar developments have occurred in all democratic states.

Moderation also characterizes the classes and strata which do not stand to receive welfare benefits and which might even suffer a relative lowering of their material and social standing. They are obliged to accept, with reasonably good grace, the attempt by some politicians to win the favor of the underprivileged. Ultimately, they cannot resist the demand that the less favored be raised materially and socially, because they could do so only at the expense of the representative system of government itself. The logic of elections means that the franchise will eventually become universal, and that all underprivileged groups with any electoral strength will eventually be appealed to in the manner described above. To resist this tendency would require the suppression of any group, including political parties, which made welfare appeals or even recommended an extension of the suffrage. Suppression is incompatible with representative government; and the favored groups, because they are predominantly Middle Class, prefer the representative system above all others and are willing to accede to the moderate claims of the lower classes in order to preserve it.*

It should be noticed here that the element in the relationship between candidate and elector that gives rise to welfare policy is

---

* The reason why the Middle Class prefers representative government will be explained in chapter 8.

the latter's opportunity to vote,[31] or even, in the long run, the possibility that he will be enfranchised. Writers on representative government have often assumed that democratic policy results directly from the way the people cast their ballots. Naturally, no democratic policy at all would be made unless people voted, and no welfare policy would be made unless they supported candidates who favored it. However, as I have shown, welfare policy is designed to appeal to those who possess the franchise and who may be expected to vote; precisely how they vote and why they do so cannot be determined.[32]

VIII

The policy of representative government guarantees to every segment of the population a reasonably high standard of living and a reasonably high degree of social deference. This policy results from the competition for votes and the electorally strategic position of the relatively underprivileged groups. Such groups have this degree of political influence only in the democratic state. Given the system of uncoerced periodic elections, the situation could not be otherwise.

Contemporary nondemocratic states have no institutions providing official leadership for the underprivileged, and they are not obliged to take into immediate consideration the suggestions of nongovernmental leaders. In addition, nondemocratic government normally has a vested interest in resisting improvement of the masses' welfare. The power of nontotalitarian dictatorships depends upon small groups of the highly privileged who benefit from keeping the masses in a depressed position.[33] A rise in living standards would also serve to increase popular dissatisfaction with the autocratic government.[34] Totalitarian regimes, on the other hand, must resist any unnecessary increase in the living standards of their populations, for one result of material and social security is a relaxed independence quite incompatible with the regime's goal of total control of every individual.[35] Only a representative government can, does, and must persistently pursue a policy of welfare for all the people.

4: CIVIL LIBERTIES IN THE DEMOCRATIC STATE

The citizens of the democratic state enjoy a remarkable measure of civil liberty. This is probably the most striking of democracy's principal phenomena, and it is an integral part of the whole complex of democratic politics. It is intimately related both to the features previously examined—the institutions of representative government, political parties, and the policy of welfare—and to those yet to be discussed—the role of the general citizenry in government, the political myths of the democratic state, and the "Middle-Class" society. Following the usual procedure, the existence of civil liberty will be explained in terms of the operation of representative government and the behavior of the political parties. The relationships of civil liberty to the other political characteristics of the democratic state should thus become understandable.

Liberty has been generally recognized as a phenomenon of the highest factual and ethical importance, and a respectable amount of attention has been paid to its historical origins and traditional background.[1] There have also been attempts to explain its persistence, the best example being the theory of a political "equilibrium" among power-wielding groups, which prevents any dominance by one or a few over the others.[2] Although the conditions identified by these two approaches may well be necessary to liberty, together they are still not sufficient for liberty. I shall attempt to give a full account of the "liberal society" in chapter 8; I wish to emphasize here that the direct connection between civil liberties and the institutions of representative government has not been fully explored.

The failure of representative governments to restrict the civil liberties of their citizens can be considered the "negative" part of the special policy of the democratic state. Like the "positive" part of democratic policy, the guaranteeing of welfare, this tolerance of civil liberties is a direct result of the periodic uncoerced elections used to select the officials ultimately in charge of all public policy.[3]

50

I

The concept of liberty applies to the absence of governmental regulation of the citizens' behavior, and the condition of liberty exists, with respect to any category of human activity, when the government neither prohibits nor requires any variation of the activity in question. To take a simple example, men are at liberty (as we say) with regard to their diet when the government makes no regulations prohibiting or requiring the eating of any food. Liberty is defined solely in terms of the absence of governmental regulation, and it is thus the opposite of coercion.* Once again, I am using a familiar term to refer to a special kind of situation, without meaning to imply that the situation is one of "real liberty." Absence of governmental regulation is the important thing; it actually occurs in the democratic state; and naming it is simply a matter of approximating customary usage.

Liberty is a matter of degree in any aspect of a person's life and in his life as a whole; consequently, liberty in the state is also a matter of degree. States could be placed along a continuum according to the extensiveness and intensity of the governmental regulations imposed upon their citizens, but this continuum would exhibit clusters of states at several points in its spread. The cluster nearest the pole of complete liberty would consist of the democratic states; they would be in this position because, in addition to liberties exhibited by other states, they display what I have called "civil" liberties. Therefore, we may say that the democratic state is distinguished not merely by having more liberty but by having a different kind of liberty.

The term "civil liberty" usually designates two types of liberty: the absence of regulation regarding matters of conscience and expression, and the absence of arbitrariness in governmental procedure. The first type includes the great liberties of the First Amendment to the United States Constitution: liberty of religion, speech, the press, assembly, and petition. To this list should be added liberty of association. The second type includes the restrictions on governmental procedure found in Amendments II through IX, and others like the guarantee of habeas corpus and the prohibition of *ex post facto* laws and bills of attainder, stated in Article I, section 9.[4] In the present discussion of civil liberties in the democratic state, the emphasis will be upon the former type of liberty. The procedural liberties are more

* In chapter 1, section III, coercion was indirectly defined as the presence of directives specifying certain human behavior and backed by the threat to do physical violence to those who fail to abide by them. It is assumed throughout this study that the means of physical violence are practically monopolized by the government, that in any state relevant to the argument "law and order" are established.

closely connected with "constitutionalism" than with the factors which immediately promote the liberties of speech, press, assembly, and association. Representative government's need for formalized regularity of procedure has been described in chapter 1, and the affinity of the Middle Class for constitutionalism will be dealt with in chapter 8. Nevertheless, as the present chapter develops we must keep in mind that the extension of procedural guarantees, from the barons of the thirteenth century to the masses of today, is a function of the evolution of the democratic state and especially of the inevitable expansion of its suffrage.

One more qualification must be specified. It has been said, and for good reason, that religious liberty is the foundation of all other liberties. This statement implies that liberty of religion is not of the same order as the other liberties of the First Amendment, and it does in fact occur in nondemocratic states. In classifying the principal states according to the degree of religious liberty that they tolerated in 1938, M. Searle Bates placed nine of the twelve democratic states in the highest category, "a high degree of freedom from preferences and discriminations," but he also placed fifteen other states in this category. Not more than half of the latter at that time had governments with genuine representative features. The three Scandinavian democracies were placed in the second category, "preferences and discriminations minor or not generally acute," along with twelve other states, the great majority of which were clearly nondemocratic.[5] Although religious liberty is certainly a necessary condition of the civil liberties under consideration, it is not in itself sufficient for the democratic state and is thus beyond the scope of the present chapter.[6]

II

The civil liberties of speech, the press, assembly, and association are, as a matter of empirical fact, experienced by the vast majority of the citizens of the twelve democratic states which form the basic data for our study. In states which are not democratic, this condition does not occur. As in the case of welfare policy, civil liberties restricted in scope and subject to temporary suspension are present in several groups of states which have adopted representative forms of government but which are not yet fully democratic. Unlike welfare policy, however, civil liberties will not even be professed by those governments which are clearly nonrepresentative. The evidence for these statements must now be presented.

The best way to show that civil liberties are enjoyed by most of the citizens of the democratic state is to examine each of the arguments which might be used to disprove the assertion. In the first place, representative governments, like all governments, have the authority to restrict behavior deemed subversive of national defense, domestic tranquillity, and public morality. Such activity invariably includes instances of written and spoken ideas and opinions, of gatherings, and of organizations, and this means that civil liberties are at least qualified. Many of the most complex and delicate problems of public policy in a democracy involve the definition of concepts like treason, espionage, breach of the peace, inciting to riot, defamation, slander, vilification, indecency, and pornography. This extraordinary concern with specifying the exact limits of what can be said and printed and what associations and organizations are to be allowed is, in itself, very good evidence of the health of civil liberties outside the scope of these restrictions. The restrictions are, after all, simply manifestations of the "preservation of law and order," a function practically definitive of government. Democracy always shows a presumption in favor of liberty, even within this sphere of normal governmental regulation. This presumption is well exemplified by the British Parliament's sensitivity to charges of suppressing civil liberty and by the United States Supreme Court's custom of explaining in great detail its acquiescence in any executive or legislative act which restricts, or appears to restrict, the liberties of the Constitution.[7] In short, although civil liberties are restricted by prohibitions against inciting to riot, indecency, and so forth, the restriction is generally the minimum one consistent with the basic functioning of a political society.

Haranguing a crowd, advising resistance to military induction, forming a vigilance committee, castigating an opponent, and describing erotic activity do not, however, constitute the behavior most relevant to a discussion of civil liberty. They do not form "an essential part of any exposition of ideas," they have "a very slight social value as a step toward truth," and they offer "little opportunity for the usual process of counterargument."[8] The crucial issue concerns the liberties of speech, press, and assembly which are required for the "unmolested dissemination of unpopular economic, political, and social views" and in relation to which there may often be a conflict "between freedom and national security."[9] This distinction leads to the second argument that might be used to maintain that civil liberties do not prevail in the democratic state.

Representative government, it might be argued, has (like all governments) a political, economic, and social status quo to protect, and as a result it prohibits literature, speeches, and associations which it judges subversive of the prevailing order. Some, but certainly not all, representative governments do take rather stringent measures against what they consider subversive activity; at the present time, for example, both the beliefs and the organization of the Communist party are illegal in the United States. However, two facts must be noted in this connection. In the first place, subversion is defined in the United States solely in terms of the overthrow of the existing system of government by means of force or violence. This is, in comparison with the standards of nondemocratic states, a very mild conception indeed of the point at which the democratic status quo in threatened. In the second place, although the Smith Act of 1940 outlawed advocating the desirability of overthrowing the government by force, and the Communist party itself was forbidden legal existence by the Communist Control Act of 1954, the actual result has been to limit only slightly the traditional American liberties of press, speech, and association. One may believe that even advocacy of violent overthrow has a right to expression and that even the Communist party has a right to existence, and he may, with even better cause, deplore the atmosphere of fear created by these restrictions on speech and association. He nevertheless cannot deny that the liberty to criticize strongly and even bitterly this curtailing of liberty remains alike for congressmen, members of the Supreme Court, and private citizens. He must also remember that the government has been somewhat less than determined to give the Communist Control Act a rigorous enforcement.[10]

The inference to be drawn from these two facts is that in the United States, the democratic state which in recent years has been most subject to worries about subversion, the status quo is generally defined very broadly, and measures designed to protect it lack, to say the least, the full support of the American people. In other democratic states, the Communist party, at present the chief organized threat to democracy, is permitted to enjoy the normal civil liberties.

A third challenge to the contention that civil liberties characterize the democratic state might be that the restriction of liberty comes not from the government's prohibiting certain ideas and associations, but from its requiring certain others. Representative governments do require that oaths of allegiance be sworn and that groups like labor unions and professional associations be joined, but these requirements are always conditional upon the desire of the person affected to gain a particular end, such as citizenship, employment in the government service, or the right to pursue an occupation. The specific unconditional requirements of representative governments are very few in number and little more than ceremonial in content; and they may be waived in cases where they are judged in conflict with civil liberty.[11]

It might still be maintained that a representative government forces ideas and beliefs upon its citizens in a more subtle manner, through some kind of "indoctrination." It is true that ideas emphasizing the goodness of conditions in the democratic state are presented repeatedly: the government itself is proclaimed desirable, the "culture" or "civilization" or "way of life" of the people is highly praised, and social and economic circumstances are described in laudatory terms. This kind of "propaganda" is normal to any political society. In order to restrict liberty, it must possess a "captive" audience which has no legal access to ideas and interpretations different from the official ones. The democratic state may require that all school children be taught a certain version of history, and this is a mild form of "indoctrination," but other versions are available to these children and their parents, and compulsory education ends at a relatively early age. Representative governments attempt no other forms of indoctrination, so at most only a slight restriction of civil liberty comes from this source. Since the concept of civil liberty, as defined above, refers solely to the absence of governmental coercion, the statement that the "class structure" of democracy gives no opportunity for the expression of ideas "natural" to the suppressed classes is beside the point.

The final objection which might be raised to the proposition that there is a very high degree of civil liberty in the democratic state is that the legal right of employers to discharge their employees is a forcible restriction of the latter's civil liberties. There have been periods in the development of the democratic state when expression of unpopular ideas and association with unpopular groups were common grounds for dismissal from employment; this practice has not entirely disappeared even today. Nevertheless, it is not a very serious restriction upon civil liberties in the modern democratic state. Although employees have been discharged because of their unpopular opinions, they have always been able to find employment elsewhere. In other words, the employee's ability to earn a living has not been contingent upon the orthodoxy of his ideas and associations. The government could be indirectly responsible for lowering his standard of living, but he never was completely dependent upon the government through his dependence upon his employer.* [12]

The statement that civil liberties occur in every democratic state does not mean that each citizen can say and write anything he pleases and join any organization and attend any meeting which might strike his fancy without suffering some material deprivation supported by the law. It means that almost any idea can be made public and almost any group can congregate without being threatened with legal punishment. This condition is met by all contemporary democratic states. While perfect liberty is inconsistent with any ma-

---

* This argument also applies to the control over a worker's job which may be exercised by labor unions.

terial deprivation backed by the coercive power of government, my point is only that the democratic state exhibits a high degree of civil liberty enjoyed by a very large proportion of its citizens.

Civil liberty, as it has been described, is empirically both necessary and sufficient for democracy. Little proof is required to show that it is sufficient, and that the liberties of speech, press, assembly, and association are absent from modern nondemocratic states.

Civil liberties are obviously denied by both Communist and Fascist governments. Indeed, the Communists have succeeded in reducing all liberties to probably their lowest ebb in the history of political society. Certain nontotalitarian dictatorships are also notorious suppressors of civil liberties; even in the western European countries of Spain and Portugal the censorship of "undesirable" material is very strict. In general, censorship is practiced with varying degrees of intensity by all contemporary nonrepresentative governments.[13] Not only do they closely control material within their own borders, but they have recently been suggesting that international organizations be used to restrict the international circulation of material which they believe "presents them in an unfavorable light." [14] Professor Chafee's judgment that "the censor is the most dangerous of all the enemies of liberty of the press" should be remembered here.[15] In nondemocratic states, the liberties of assembly and association are generally strictly regulated. Liberty of speech is reduced at best to private conversation, but even there care must be taken not to express ideas which may appear critical of the prevailing pattern of power and privilege.

III

The presence of civil liberties in the democratic state is not a coincidence. They are the direct result of the uncoerced periodic elections used to select the highest governmental officials. Both *uncoerced* elections and civil *liberties* have been defined in terms of the absence of physical force applied or tolerated by the government, but this does not mean that the latter cannot be explained by reference to the former. Explanations of liberty usually concentrate upon the basic communal, social, and economic factors of the democratic state, without recognizing the influence of the institutions of representative government. Although these factors underlie both the liberties and the uncoerced elections, they are not sufficient to account for civil liberty's remarkable scope. It will be seen in chapter 8 how uncoerced elections result from the dynamics of the "Middle-Class" society; the present chapter will show how elections, in their turn, give rise to civil liberties.

Each of the two or more competitors in the uncoerced elections of representative government is obliged to communicate to the electorate certain information essential to securing the office at stake. He must tell them who he is, with whom he is associated, what opinions he holds on issues of political relevance, and what personal qualities he possesses. In addition to this minimum requirement, the candidate must somehow differentiate himself from his opponents. Unless he can do this by referring to his political philosophy or his personal capabilities, the contest itself will appear to have little purpose. Since he almost invariably wishes to win, he will attempt to establish his uniqueness by proving his superiority. Democratic elections cannot operate without at least enough liberty for the candidates and their immediate associates to disagree publicly regarding their respective qualifications for office. Furthermore, it has become universal practice to publicize candidacies through public meetings and to distribute printed material in order to reach even larger numbers of electors. These two techniques require at least some liberty of assembly and the press.

The electoral system has consequences wider than allowing the minimum of liberty required for the candidates to disagree among themselves. If the contest obliges the candidates to discuss their own merits in public, it is only natural that the electorate will begin to discuss these merits among themselves and that they will use the ordinary means—conversation, the press, the assembly hall, and the organization—to facilitate this discussion. Suppression of the electorate's civil liberties would simply be inconsistent with the fundamental principles of representative government.

Not only must the electorate be allowed to discuss, and therefore almost certainly to disagree upon, the assets and liabilities of the several candidates, but at least some of the candidates will stand to profit from this discussion. Popular discussion presupposes popular interest, and a candidate less well known than his competitors will find it advantageous to encourage any spontaneous discussion which might serve to increase the electorate's awareness of himself and his principles. The other candidates must then adopt the same devices of publicity in order to guard against the electorate's being not merely stimulated by the "campaigner" but attracted to him. Campaigning provokes popular participation in the disputes among the candidates, and they intend it to do so.

Thus far, the argument has referred only to the voter's discussions of issues which the candidates originally raised and disagreed upon. Once differences of opinion are allowed and even encouraged, no matter how innocuous they at first appear, the disagreement can easily broaden and become more intense. It may reach a thoroughness not contemplated by the candidates, and it may extend to matters upon which they themselves are in harmony. A small amount of liberty has a tendency to grow. Although the social and economic structure of the democratic state prevents disputes about the fundamentals of political life, disagreement takes place on almost every other issue. No factor exists to check the growth of liberty; or, to be more precise, the natural conservative tendencies toward restriction found in any human society are counteracted by equally powerful forces defending liberty. These forces are led by the political parties, the most important champions of civil liberty in the democratic state.

IV

The party's basic function is to nominate candidates, and it almost always attempts to secure the election of its nominee. The party has taken over the management of the campaign techniques described above, the techniques which require at least a minimum of civil liberty. A vested interest in civil liberties is thus possessed not only by an individual candidate and his immediate associates but also by a relatively permanent organization of many members and branches. Political parties, by virtue of their size, structure, and persistence, have more power than any individual candidate or informal group. They are the source of extensive material benefits and the object of powerful loyalties. Their influence in the politics of democracy can hardly be exaggerated.

The party relies upon large unorganized groups for votes and upon private organizations for aid in the form of money, labor, and the means of publicity. Consequently, it must be tolerant of the opinions held by the organizations and attributed to the unorganized groups. Moreover, it must defend these opinions, since an attack upon any of them is an indirect attack upon it. In the contemporary democratic state, there is no group of electoral importance that is not either claimed by a party or being wooed by a party. The competition for office, no matter which electoral system is used, provides a protector for each of these groups.

The parties can never be indifferent even to the organized and unorganized groups which seem to have committed themselves in the electoral competition. Although each party can depend upon electoral assistance from certain areas and social strata, these groups do not vote unanimously, and the proportion of their support is not fixed. The parties, therefore, can only rarely afford to neglect the (presumed) interests and opinions even of groups which normally give them overwhelming majorities. Even if defections to the opposition are unlikely, the possibility of abstention still remains. Regarding its organized support, the party experiences a similar kind of

insecurity. Sometimes a pressure group is the "captive" of a party—
or a party of a pressure group—but usually each can never be sure
that the other will not become at least indifferent to their partnership.
As a result, the parties must always be sensitive to the ideas, as well
as to the interests, of all the organized groups that concern themselves
with public policy.

The primary threat to an idea is the agreement to condemn it by
all the parties having influence on the conduct of government. A
substantial reduction of liberty in the democratic state thus depends
upon an unusual degree of consensus among its political activists.
Yet ideas have occasionally been suppressed in contemporary democracies. These ideas have been associated with electorally insignifi-
cant groups which were small, poor, and without prestige. As a
consequence, they were unfamiliar to the great majority of the citizenry and tended to appear threatening to established modes of behavior and thought. This suppression and the factors behind it have
been used as evidence by those who argue that civil liberties are
safer in the hands of an enlightened minority than at the mercy of
the "ignorant and narrow-minded masses."

Unpopular ideas can be suppressed in the short run under representative government, but the dynamics of democratic politics, and
especially the activity of the parties, make any permanent suppression
impossible. In order for ideas to be prohibited, each party must
believe that the prohibition will present neither an immediate nor a
long-term threat to its own electoral chances, and, even more important, it must anticipate some advantage from the attack. Parties are
not absolutely rational in their pursuit of votes, but the complexities
and uncertainties of electoral competition make them extremely sensitive to wasted effort and to committing themselves without fairly
good assurances of success. They must constantly ask themselves what
political activity their electorates would appreciate.

The democratic electorate as a whole can have no more than
a temporary interest in the suppression of any minority and even less
interest in the proscription of any idea or opinion. A serious and
imminent threat to the normal manner of life can create enough
popular insecurity to make a general attack upon an idea or association electorally profitable. However, even when the threat persists
and when the minority and its ideas are closely associated with it,
the electorate easily loses interest in the matter. The increasing indifference to the recent bipartisan attack upon the American Communist party has been a good example. If the Communist threat had
come primarily from within the United States rather than from a
foreign state—that is, if it had been closer to the electorate's experience—perhaps fear and antipathy would have persisted for a longer

time. As it was, the normal preoccupations of life soon became more important to the people than concern with subversion, and, in order to stimulate public interest, the parties were obliged to turn to other issues. A political party genuinely devoted to the methods of representative government can derive little advantage from the suppression of unpopular groups and the ideas associated with them.

In addition to this lack of advantage, it is probable that at least one powerful party will be put at a disadvantage by restrictions of civil liberties. The competition for votes requires the parties to differentiate themselves from one another. Each of them must take a stand along a segment of the "political spectrum," so that with either a two- or a multiparty system at least one important party appeals to, and expects electoral support from, every position from "left" to "right." The situation is similar regarding opinions associated with sectional, ethnic, cultural, or religious differences. As pointed out above, an offensive against an unpopular opinion can occur only when the opinion is held, or presumed to be held, by a relatively small group. In the case of a "left-right" political spectrum and a two-party system, these small groups are found at either extreme, where they are distinguished primarily by their refusal or inability to compromise their principles. A party receives only a very small percentage of its votes from its most extreme supporters, but it can never be sure that an attack on them will not be to its real disadvantage. The attack may alienate this group from the democratic process, and the party may anticipate a close contest in which these few votes will be needed; or the party may fear that the attack will spread to its supporters further toward the center, who are electorally very important to it; or it may suspect that an attack on its extremists is an attempt by the opposition to bring it into general discredit. An attempt to suppress a small group of Communists, for example, may not cause immediate damage to the left-wing party's voting strength; but the distinction between "communism" and "socialism" is easily forgotten or glossed over, and the attack may spread to ideas associated with the labor-union element and their spokesmen within the party. The party must naturally avoid any attempt by its opponents to label it "Communist." It must tactfully establish its independence of its extremists; although it may not be able actively to defend the Communists' civil liberties, from self-interest it should at least attempt to mitigate the attack and divert the public's attention from it.

The logic of the electoral system manifested in the behavior of the two parties applies, *mutatis mutandis,* to multiparty systems, where the party that must defend an unpopular opinion, while smaller and relatively less powerful than a party in a two-party system, is closer to the source of the opinion and electorally more dependent upon the group with which the opinion is associated. The electoral logic also determines the behavior of the parties in parliament. To the extent that a parliamentary party is allied with a party, its activity will reflect the electoral problems of the latter. Furthermore, as in the case of welfare policy, within the parliament itself the need for voting support obliges the parties to tolerate and often to defend the deviant opinions of representatives returned from atypical constituencies.

In brief, the dynamics of the democratic electoral system make it impossible for civil liberties to be denied to any group within the democratic state, and political parties, which originate to rationalize the electoral process, become the most powerful defenders of these liberties.

V

The principal concern of the party is electoral success, which may be defined differently by different types of parties, but which always involves votes from large numbers of electors and technical and financial aid from various organizations. Individuals and groups which can provide neither of these assets do not come under the party's immediate protection. As operating organizations, parties are not interested in civil liberty for its own sake; liberty for the scientist to pursue his research and for the teacher and clergyman to evaluate personal and social behavior means very little to the party official trying to win elections. Although the party leaders, and especially incumbent representatives, will publicly praise "freedom" and "liberty," it cannot be assumed that they possess any reasoned basis for this attitude, or that they even fully understand its implications. Yet the democratic state is always characterized by practically unrestricted inquiry into the very foundations of the personality, the society, and the universe.

Within the naturally permissive democratic society, electoral competition creates an atmosphere of liberty which allows the higher arts and sciences to flourish. Being almost always neutral in the politics of representative government, they are not specifically defended, but they cannot be attacked without an obvious appearance of inconsistency. A society in which the most powerful political figures defend the abstract right of every man to his own opinion, because this opinion might have some votes behind it, is a society which cannot help tolerating the speculations and criticisms of the professional intellectual whose electoral strength is invariably negligible.

In the case of civil liberties, as well as in that of welfare policy, the initiative is often taken by nongovernmental and even nonpolitical elites. Ministers, teachers, lawyers, and newspaper editors and commentators are probably more sensitive to infringements of civil liberties than are politicians, and they influence not only other leaders of public opinion but the politicians themselves.[16] Nevertheless, their power cannot be compared with that of the latter. They perform a vital service in the protection of liberty, but they do so only on the tolerance of the politicians and within the context created by the politicians. Without a system of government which requires the governors to defend diversity of opinion, the civil-liberty-oriented professors and editors and lawyers would be impotent indeed.

Since the parties are interested in the liberties of only those groups that can assist them, and since the liberty of electorally unimportant groups and individuals depends upon the parties' general defense of liberty, the health of civil liberties in a democratic state is influenced by the size of its electorate. If certain areas or certain social strata are not enfranchised, the parties have no reason to defend opinions and organizations connected with these people. The scope of their defense of liberty is narrower, and the political climate of the society is less favorable to those ideas which aim at abstract knowledge. Furthermore, whenever an electorate is more than temporarily restricted, potent forces of political repression are present. The unfranchised are intended to be kept in impotence; their gaining the ballot is something to be feared. Under these circumstances, any idea which can be interpreted as attacking the system of dominance and submission is very likely to be considered subversive. The Union of South Africa exemplifies this tendency to restrict gradually but steadily the scope of civil liberty, until only the minimum essential for conducting campaigns remains.[17]

The democratic states have moved more or less gradually from the restricted electorates with which most of them began to suffrage for at least all adult male citizens. The normal operation of representative government was responsible for this development. In order to maintain a restricted electorate, there must always be a very good reason for it, such as ignorance or poverty, which is accepted by the unfranchised themselves. Once the "lower classes" of all democratic states realized the importance of the vote, they demanded it; by that time the reasonable excuses for not giving it to them had disappeared. Literacy had spread remarkably, and the standard of living had increased significantly. These changes produced both the demand for the franchise and the disappearance of excuses for withholding it. Refusing the suffrage without reasons acceptable to those being denied would have required a policy of repression, and repression by its very nature is inconsistent with the representative system of government to which the already enfranchised classes were committed.

The political parties played a major role in the expansion of the suffrage. Their self-interested defense of civil liberties for some people creates an atmosphere favorable to civil liberty in general, thus making it easier to agitate for extending the right to vote. Their normal tendency to look about for additional sources of electoral support is even more important. When an electorate is restricted, some parties will usually work for, or at least encourage, the enfranchisement of groups expected to vote for their candidates. Similar pressure comes from organizations like labor unions and Socialist groups which derive their strength from the voteless strata, but parties can be credited with providing the main political impetus.[18] The parties' sensitiveness to the possibilities of increasing their mass support gives rise to a greater or lesser tolerance of the unfranchised segments of the population and the ideas and opinions commonly associated with them. This tolerance results from the same motives which prompt the parties to defend the enfranchised. The liberties of the unfranchised, however, are not secure until they receive the ballot and become actual rather than potential factors in the competition among the parties.

VI

We have seen that the civil liberties of speech, the press, assembly, and association are present in all contemporary democratic states, and their presence has been explained by reference to the democratic electoral system. We have also seen that these liberties are at times denied to people accused of advocating violent overthrow of representative government. Although these restrictions may well be criticized as "undemocratic," the surprising thing is that in these exceptional cases subversion is defined so narrowly.

The mutual challenge and criticism—among candidates, parties, and the general citizenry—required by the representative system make it very difficult to determine a point beyond which civil liberties are to be denied. Clearly, the state must protect itself against subversion, but the problem for the government is to determine when the exercise of liberty constitutes such a threat.

The prosperous citizen of the democratic state is particularly repelled by the thought of violent change; he wants very much to avoid it, and in times of stress he may come to believe that advocating it may increase its likelihood. The professional politician, who is fully committed to the electoral process, can easily share this belief, and the advocacy of violent revolution can be prohibited. However, there is little else upon which agreement regarding the suspension of civil liberties can be obtained.[19] Change in itself is not repugnant to most democratic citizens, and many different specific changes have their defenders. In addition, the political life of democracy is based on the conscious attempt to change at least the personnel of its leading governmental offices. Subversion can be only the attempt to bring about illegal change, which by definition means violent change. Even in the United States, where there has recently been the highest degree of sensitivity to the threat of subversion, one can advocate with full impunity the most fundamental changes in the government, the economy, and the society, as long as he intends them to be realized in a nonviolent way through the formal constitutional procedures. Any suggestion of this kind is perfectly respectable because, after all, one of the most basic beliefs of the democratic state is that "government derives its authority from the will of the people." Hence, the advocacy of any "revolution by a majority," while it may be considered odd or even threatening, is not to be suppressed.

VII

It has been shown that, as a matter of fact, civil liberties characterize the democratic state and are absent from the nondemocratic state, and that the constant conjunction of civil liberties and the institutions of representative government is no accident. It remains to be shown why civil liberties and nonrepresentative governments are incompatible, and that the democratic state is not only sufficient for these liberties but necessary as well.

In the first place, there is no reason why any nonrepresentative government should permit widespread liberty of speech, the press, assembly, and association. Totalitarianism and traditional and modern dictatorships do not require civil liberties for selecting officials, nor do they need them for making policy. Offices are filled by personal consultation, and decisions are made by small groups operating in private. Communication among politically important people, both in and out of government, is very simple, since they are so few in number.[20] Unlike their democratic counterparts, the officials of nonrepresentative governments need not keep in touch with the opinions of many groups in order to maintain themselves in office. Finally, political criticism has no function to perform in the nondemocratic state, where nothing resembles the critical interplay of electoral campaigns and parliamentary debates.

In the second place, and more important, there are very good reasons why nonrepresentative governments should not permit civil liberties. Unrestricted speech and an uncensored press will invariably give rise to at least some adverse criticism of any form of government, and adverse criticism is inconsistent with the fundamental principle by which nonrepresentative governments justify their rule. Autocracies, of whatever variety, justify themselves by reference to the superior wisdom, strength, and virtue of the autocrat and those associated with him—the "parties," aristocrats, plutocrats, or simply "the better elements" of the society.[21] Any criticism of individual officials or the policy they make is necessarily subversive of this claim to inherent superiority.

The nonrepresentative government is not equipped to deal with criticism, even if it decided that the inconsistency with its principles could be tolerated. It possesses no method to channel criticism along constructive or harmless courses, and it has no device to meet and try to refute criticism, assuming that such activity is not beneath its dignity. Normal complaints easily develop into real disaffection in the nondemocratic state because there is no way to make the complainants feel they are receiving proper attention. This problem is solved in democracy by the opposition parties, which take such complaints as their own, thus binding those who believe themselves aggrieved to the legitimate political processes of the democratic state. When it is remembered that the most typical characteristic of modern politics is the people's belief in their own importance, avoiding the growth of disaffection is seen to be even more difficult for the nonrepresentative government.[22]

Civil liberties not only encourage dissatisfaction with the nondemocratic regime; they also are incompatible with the structure of power and influence on which it is based. Any nonrepresentative government, whether or not it possesses the "acceptance" or "confidence" of its citizens, has as its base a small number of powerful and influential groups. Allowing power to spread in a nondemocratic state is as imprudent as allowing it to become concentrated in a democracy. If a nonrepresentative government permits its citizens to form any groupings they please, it is practically inviting new loci of power to arise, and, at the very least, it is increasing the difficulty of its political supervision. Since any civil liberty can be used by those who desire new groupings, a nonrepresentative government need only be aware of these basic principles of its existence in order to prohibit liberty. The principles themselves are so elementary that they have been recognized for millennia. In the modern era, improved techniques of communication have given the nonrepresentative government more control than ever before over what is said and printed, what meetings are held, and what associations are formed. In brief, any modern nonrepresentative government has no reason for allowing civil liberties, and it has very good reasons and very good means for not allowing them.

As in the case of welfare policy, civil liberties are found in states which have adopted institutions of representative government, but which cannot as yet be considered fully democratic. In these states there may be no popular myths of "liberty" and "freedom," and the leaders may often reveal their dislike or distrust of civil liberties, but the operation of representative institutions requires their presence. Since civil liberties are unique to the democratic state, their existence depends upon the transitional state's further evolution toward democracy.

VIII

It has been argued that autocracy is compatible with at least as much liberty as democracy because, unlike the democratic governor, the autocrat is not subject to the pressures of popular prejudice. Examples of the masses' desire to persecute minorities and the resistance of autocratic rulers to this pressure can certainly be cited,[23] but the argument fails to consider two facts. First, in the complex modern democratic state, the governors must deal with nothing as specific as the "passions of the masses." Even if there were an occasional genuine mass demand for the persecution of a minority, the processes of representative government (as shown above) would resist its fulfillment. It is a mistake to equate modern parliaments, cabinets, and presidents with the old-fashioned assembly of all the citizens, and it is equally erroneous to make the citizenry of the modern democratic state analogous to the mobs of the cities.

In the second place, contemporary autocracy only very rarely possesses the strong foundation of legitimacy and the resulting self-confidence necessary for tolerance and a sense of *noblesse oblige*. If the autocrat's power rests upon the "better elements," as does General Franco's in Spain, his position lacks the requisite stability, since the claims of aristocracy are no longer meaningful to the masses. If the autocrat has a modern power foundation, including an organization like Mussolini's Fascist party, his ability to protect minorities —assuming that he desires to do so—is seriously restricted by his dependence upon the members of this organization. The latter have no interest whatever in tolerance, and they will always be suspicious of any group not within their own ranks. Autocratic government in the contemporary period no more resembles traditional aristocracy than modern representative government resembles the direct democracy of the city state.

One reason for underestimating the bond between civil liberty and representative government may be the failure to appreciate the role of the professional politician in the processes of democracy. The politician's job, which is to maintain himself and his party in office, requires him to calculate as carefully as possible the opportunities for gaining and holding votes. He must, therefore, always think in terms of the next election; he must not be led by the advantages of the moment to disregard the welfare or the civil liberties of any segment of his electorate. This incentive to foresight does not exist for the nonprofessional, and it makes representative government superior to government in which the citizens themselves act as legislators. The professional politician, by virtue of his experience and personality, is also more tolerant of diverse attitudes and less likely to become intransigent in the face of opposition. His job is to compromise, to form and maintain coalitions, to keep the system operating as smoothly as possible. Here, too, government by the professional is superior to government by the citizen-legislator.

IX

At the beginning of this analysis of the democratic state, I stated that the results of electoral competition, rather than its grounds, form the most important aspect of the democratic electoral system; and I emphasized the opportunity to vote, the enfranchisement of the people, rather than the manner in which any individual voter or group of voters casts its ballots. The discussion of welfare policy in the preceding chapter and the present chapter's account of civil liberties have provided the basic evidence for these judgments. If the democratic state is studied as a type of state, specific disputes among the candidates and specific decisions by the electorate are not immediately relevant. Welfare policy and civil liberties, which occur in all democratic states, are necessary parts of the democratic political complex, and they are directly related to one another as companion results of the dynamics of representative government.[24]

It has been shown in this chapter why civil liberties are fundamental to the democratic state and how they are connected with its other basic political elements. Civil liberties are normally considered among the most desirable characteristics of democracy, but too little effort has been expended in explaining the reasons for their occurrence. Liberty depends upon a historical and traditional background, and it can thrive only in a "liberal society," but a major portion of the credit for its existence must go to the institutions of representative government.

5: THE PEOPLE'S FUNCTIONS IN REPRESENTATIVE GOVERNMENT

The significance of the functions performed by the people in the democratic political process has long been recognized, and these functions have generally provided the point of departure for treatises on the essentials of democracy. The unusual degree to which ordinary citizens participate in representative government requires description and explanation; but the most common attempts at this have been superficial and inaccurate, and those which have gone beyond the obvious have too often been incorrect. These opinions on popular participation should be examined here, although many of them may appear unworthy of serious consideration. Examining them will clear the way for an accurate account of the people's functions in government—the primary task of the present chapter—and it will also lay the foundation for relating them to the other principal political factors of democracy, to be undertaken in chapter 7. What philosophers, social scientists, politicians, journalists, and educators say about a political system, when it is intended to be descriptive as well as when it is a slogan or a rationalization, is an important fact of the system, and it must be accounted for by an analysis which aspires to a comprehensive explanation of the system.

Since representative government is found only in the democratic state, the democratic citizen obviously has unique political responsibilities. We have already seen how the operation of representative government depends primarily upon the parties and the professional politicians, and in the present chapter we will discover new aspects of this dependence. Despite this reliance upon specialists, the general citizenry still has functions that are essential to the democratic nature of the state. Attributing to the people functions performed by the politicians and parties is a very common error in the analysis of democracy, and it has tended to divert attention from the functions which the people really do perform.

The theory of democracy has traditionally been concerned with the people's capabilities to do what is required of them. Writers with antidemocratic biases have argued that the people are obviously incapable of meeting the responsibilities placed upon them by the democratic state. Democrats have retorted by stressing the rationality, good judgment, and sterling character of the "common man." Although the position of the antidemocrat has been recognized as weak, most defenders of the common man give the impression that they are not completely at ease with their own arguments. The strange thing about this discussion is that the people have been playing an important role in each of the twelve democratic states for a very long time. It seems clear enough that at least during this period they have possessed the needed capabilities. Just what these capabilities are can be determined only after the relevant popular political activity has been identified.

Throughout the discussion the term "the people" will refer to the electorate. Those who have the franchise are a very large proportion of the population, they have the special functions to perform, and it is about their "rationality" that doubts have been raised.

I

The democratic electorate selects, according to the electoral system in force, the men in ultimate control of authoritative governmental policy. Although differences in electoral systems cause some variations in this act of selection, its essence remains everywhere the same. The representative gains office through the support of a large proportion, at least one-fifth or one-sixth, of the voters within his constituency, and the more votes a party receives, the more parliamentary seats it obtains. According to these principles, the electorate as a whole chooses the men who govern it. The problem for the theory of democracy is to go beyond the obvious and discover the fundamental nature of this function and explain its implications.

There are several conceptions traditionally used to refer to this special relationship between governors and governed. Representative government has been called "self-government," "government by the people," and, less ambitiously, "government by the majority of the people." It has also been said that a representative government is "responsible" to the people, that the latter's function is not to conduct the actual business of government but to check or supervise those who do. Each of these conceptions goes beyond a mere description of the electoral process, and each is presumably intended to correspond to some basic aspect of the people's governmental functions.

The statement that democratic government is "self-government," despite its widespread occurrence in scholarly contexts, may intentionally be only a slogan.[1] If it is not just a slogan, and if it is supposed to have a meaning different from "government by the people," it could apply to areas independent of any government located outside their boundaries, the so-called self-governing areas. We also say that people are self-governing when their governors are drawn from their own ranks, but the democratic state has a monopoly of neither of these situations. Finally, "self-government" cannot mean that each person in the democratic state governs himself, since this implies the absence of government.

"Self-government" is probably most often an unconscious synonym of the more popular phrase, "government by the people," [2] which clearly implies that the people have a specific function to perform. What this function is supposed to be, however, is not easy to determine. If "governing" means making legislative, administrative, judicial, and diplomatic decisions, then the electorate does not govern and, because of its great size, could not govern. If "governing" means direct control over those who make the daily detailed decisions of government, then in this case, too, the electorate does not govern. In the type of government called "pure" or "direct" democracy, governing is carried on by the citizens, who correspond to the electorate under representative government. Their position is strictly analogous to that of representative government's elected bodies, and having ultimate control over all governmental actions can certainly be described as "governing." But the fundamental difference between representative government and pure democracy is precisely that the latter's citizens pass laws and control administrations, while the former's electorate does neither.

Contemporary political scientists have used this obvious difference between representative government and pure democracy to reject as irrelevant a common attack on the modern democratic state. Since the electorate does not govern, it is no criticism of representative government to argue the common man's inability to understand intricate matters of fiscal policy, international relations, military preparedness, and so forth.[3] The criticism, incidentally, is similarly irrelevant when applied to the representative. Although some democratic theorists say that the representative is "typical" of the citizens who select him, he is really not (as was seen in chapter 3) an average man. In intelligence, education, and access to relevant information, he is definitely atypical and superior.[4]

"Government by the people" cannot refer to what is done by the elected representatives and their appointees, but one might maintain that the people's "governing" occurs on another level, that they provide the broad outlines of governmental policy which their representatives then make specific and appropriate to the circumstances. This is probably the usual interpretation of "government by the people," and it leads directly to one of the most nagging problems of democratic theory, the problem of the majority.

II

Decisions are made by a majority at two very important points in the procedure of representative government. In the first place, representatives are selected by a majority or plurality of the electorate's votes; or, in the case of proportional representation, by a relatively large proportion of their votes, and the distribution of the parties' strength in parliament corresponds fairly closely to the nationwide distribution of votes they receive. Numbers prevail in all these cases, and this is the essence of "majority rule." In the second place, the decision of a parliamentary majority is binding with respect to ordinary policy issues, and, no matter how important the issue, unanimity is never required. As a characterization of representative government, the concept of majority rule must refer to the electorate, for majority decision in the government itself is a technique also used by nonrepresentative governments. It might be thought that the electorate provides the "broad outlines of governmental policy" directly in the electoral process, or indirectly in the parliamentary process. This belief seems to have been responsible for calling democracy "rule by the majority."

The idea that the electoral process implies that the majority of the people determines the general outlines of governmental policy has distressed the democratic theorist. He cannot ignore the apparent operation of majority rule, but he is reluctant to justify a system which may show complete indifference to the wishes of almost half the people. There is a real dilemma here, because the only practical alternative to majority rule (and the possibility of the "tyranny of the majority") is some kind of minority rule, which would be clearly "undemocratic." [5] However, the problem and the dilemma can be eliminated from democratic theory by analyzing the operation of majority decision in representative government.

When a majority "rules" over a minority, as in a small private association, the majority's opinion prevails over the minority's opinion on issues which are not agreed to unanimously and about which only two opinions are held. The majority opinion is put into effect by the officers of the association, and it binds the minority as long as the latter remains within the association. If the majority of the electorate "rules" the minority of the electorate in the democratic state, they both must have opinions which they express when they go to the polls.

That the majority has no such opinion was argued at length in chapter 3. It was shown there that examining an electoral majority will discover no items of public policy that determine the voters' decisions. Even when they cast their ballots for or against policies—rather than according to the candidates' personalities, traditional party affiliations, or religious and ethnic preferences—the policies they have in mind differ from one voter or group of voters to the next; the candidate or party whom they support may never have committed themselves to the policies; and voters both for and against a candidate may wish to support the same policy.[6]

It might be answered that the majority need not have a single opinion, that the several opinions of the majority prevail over the several opinions of the minority; but the majority still cannot be shown to hold one group of opinions and the minority another. In order to be relevant, these "opinions" must be about "policy"; they must concern actual or potential governmental activity. To say that the majority "rules" by expressing its opinion on candidates or parties is to say only that representative government uses elections to fill its most important offices. It is this device that the concept of majority rule is presumably intended to explain.

Even those individual elections whose results seem most clear—for example, the American election of 1936 and the British election of 1945—give no grounds for concluding that the majority wished a policy program to be put into effect. If any motive prevailed in the American election, it was probably a vague sense of gratitude for what the administration had done in its previous term of office. In the British election, the winning party's plurality was probably the result of an equally vague desire for a very generally conceived "new deal" for the less privileged classes. It must be remembered that these two elections were unusual in the definiteness of their results. Most are like the French election of 1951, where one might discover a majority against Communism, a majority against "Gaullism," and a majority against the "parties of the Third Republic."

"Majority rule" cannot mean that the opinions of the majority of the people are expressed indirectly by majority votes in parliament, for this is the previously rejected theory of interest reflection. No political scientist attempting to explain the policy-making process of contemporary representative government follows the hypothesis that each decision by parliament, or even each important decision, is an expression of a majority's opinion. The useful hypothesis is that special interests, usually organized but often unorganized, are compromised and adjusted by the policy-makers. Forcing an opinion of a majority of the electorate upon an opposed minority of the electorate occurs only rarely, and, far from being the essential feature, it is only a by-product of governmental action and thus of the representative system. If this argument is correct, any concern about representative government's resulting in a "tyranny of the majority" has no foundation in fact.[7]

III

In spite of the foregoing arguments, it still appears true that representative government requires that "the ultimate choice, the final act of decision, be that of the majority." [8] But this statement simply describes an aspect of representative government too obvious to be overlooked. "Rule" by the majority has been problematic only because too much has been read into the words, "the final act of decision." This phrase means only that a majority of the electorate has, for a great variety of reasons, preferred one candidate over another, and that a majority of the members of parliament has voted for a bill, again for many reasons. The device of majority decision is merely a technique of representative government, designed for the very practical purpose of permitting decisions to be made by large groups of electors and representatives. Unanimity is an impossible requirement, and giving a minority of formally equal electors and representatives the authority to make binding decisions would simply be nonsensical. The device of majority decision works very well. It permits decisions to be made in a manner accepted by all as legitimate, and no reference to any majority opinion on issues of public policy is necessary to explain it.

Saying that "majority rule" is solely a device of decision-making may appear to resolve the traditional problems only by refusing to admit their existence. However, the "dilemmas" associated with "majority rule" come from attempts to justify it rather than to understand it. When it is shown that the usual grounds for its justification are incorrectly chosen, there should be no reluctance to interpret decision-making by a majority as no more than a useful technique of representative government.

The traditional justification of "majority rule" has been puzzled by the fundamental question: why should an opinion, just because it is held by a majority, prevail over all other opinions? The difficulty results from the habitual assumption that the majority's opinions, and thus its decisions, are somehow always correct.[9] Since theorists have understandably been reluctant to say that the majority is by definition always right, its opinions must be justified on metaphysical or empirical grounds. The most important metaphysical justification identifies the will of the majority with a "general" will shared by both majority and minority. It is hopelessly confused and eminently unsatisfactory, as any such attempt must be.[10]

An empirical justification of the "opinion" or "will" of the majority refers to the results of majority decisions, both by the electorate and in the parliament. The men and the policies supported by the majority must be proved superior, in some definite way, to the men and policies favored by the minority. On the basis of objective indexes like administrative and organizational ability, diplomatic skill, and honesty, successful candidates cannot be proved superior to their unsuccessful rivals throughout the history of democratic elections. The conclusion is similarly indefinite when the choices of both electoral and parliamentary majorities are judged in terms of the long-run health of democratic states. The evidence indicates, and both common sense and social science strongly suggest, that majorities have been sometimes right and sometimes wrong. The decisions of the majority simply cannot be justified empirically.

Some difficulty also arises when the moral status of opinions held by one or more minorities comes into consideration. When the position of the majority is supposed to be correct, minorities are usually said to have a right to their own opinions so that they can work toward becoming themselves a majority. However, if the opinion of the majority is correct, it does not follow that a minority should be given the opportunity of becoming a new majority; in fact, it makes better sense to say that, since the minority is by hypothesis in error, it has no right at all to its opinions. Although a justification of minority rights could be provided by admitting that majority decisions are not always completely correct, "majoritarianism" tends to leave minorities in a position too precarious to be tolerated in democratic political ethics.

The impossibility of proving that majority decisions are always correct shows that the usual grounds for justifying them have been incorrectly chosen. We can return to the statement that majority decision is only a technique of representative government; we can praise or blame any specific decision by reference to its context; and we can defend the opinions of minorities in terms of each man's claim to civil liberties. The technique of decision-making itself is to be justified solely as an indispensable part of the institutional complex I have called "representative government." Its value depends upon the desirability of the latter.

IV

Another common interpretation of the people's function in representative government is that, rather than governing or ruling or making decisions, they "hold their governors responsible." [11] The notion of responsibility applies to action which, for various reasons, conforms to a norm. Governmental responsibility may mean that the official is responsible to the will of someone else, or that he is responsible to certain impersonal standards of professional, technical, or personal excellence.[12] Our problem is to determine whether representative government is responsible government, and, if it is, whether the people participate in making it responsible.

The statement that representative government is responsible government usually means that its policy conforms to the desires of the electorate, which are supposed to serve as the norms in the relationship of responsibility. However, the actions of government do not "reflect the interests of the governed"; the norms which the governed are supposed to provide are simply nonexistent.

Sometimes a distinction is made between two types of responsibility: accountability, where the responsible person is subject to a penalty in case he defaults in his duty or obligation, and responsiveness, where there is no external penalty available. It might be thought that even though the representatives cannot be responsible to the will of the people, they are still accountable to them at the polls. But accountability is relevant to "responsibility to the people" only if there is a method by which the governors can be held responsive to what the governed want. The electorate certainly possesses a penalty, but this "accountability" cannot be genuine responsibility, because responsibility implies that the agent has a duty or obligation to conform to a norm. Again, no norm can be discovered by examining the reasons why the electorate supports and opposes candidates and parties. In short, the representatives are in no sense responsible to the will of their electorates.

Nonrepresentative governments can be responsible to standards of professional, technical, and personal excellence. Monarchies, aristocracies, theocracies, bureaucracies, and dictatorships have been attached to and guided by norms of "public service." They have striven for efficiency, honesty, just application of the law, and service to their citizens in areas like health, morals, and national defense. These governments, however, because of their structure and power foundations, must obtain the norms which guide their conduct primarily on their own initiative and from within their own ranks. Their norms have been traditional, as in the cases of the British aristocracy and the German bureaucracy, or they have been self-devised, as in the cases of history's famous "reformers" and "lawgivers." The great advantage of representative government is that, while it utilizes both tradition and internal invention, it also must meet very powerful and effective standards which originate outside its own ranks and which do not depend upon its own initiative.

It has already been shown how the political parties come to espouse and implement policy that raises the living standard of the masses and eventually guarantees to each group a minimum of material and social welfare. As representative governments more or less regularly pursued welfare policy, there developed norms of governmental action considerably broader than traditional ideas of "service to the public." The contemporary representative wishes to meet these norms because he believes them to be just, but he also encounters powerful stimuli to responsibility from outside the government.

Pressure-group officials, leaders of public opinion, and especially members of opposition parties are the most important promoters of governmental responsibility to standards of public service. They define and develop the norms, and they determine when they have not been met. Moreover, they can penalize the governors by exposing their detected or suspected shortcomings to full view of the public. These "attentive elites" [13] normally have a vested interest, electoral or otherwise, in discovering and exposing failures to meet the norms.

The situation is similar with respect to the "nonpolitical" norms of governmental conduct. The governors are more or less dedicated to the standards of professional, technical, and personal excellence, but they are also held responsible by the built-in critics of representative government, who are as eager to expose instances of dishonesty and partiality as they are to discover omissions of positive policy.

The governors, for their part, wish to avoid these attacks. They attempt to prevent the omissions and abuses which lead to criticism, because their prestige depends to a great extent upon their service, competence, efficiency, and honesty, and also because they fear that their electoral fortunes will suffer when their shortcomings are brought to light. It is, of course, this possibility that motivates the government's critics to expose dishonesty, wastefulness, and bumbling. The people themselves therefore have a most important function to perform in keeping the representatives responsible to democratic standards of "good government."

Too much, however, must not be read into this function of the people. They do not determine the specific standards, nor do they detect failures to meet them. Electorates also have often re-elected men who have been held responsible for abuses as serious as peculation, although there is usually no evidence that these practices are specifically condoned by the electorates in question.* Finally, even when a party that has been the subject of a great scandal loses votes

---

* Where there is evidence that the electorate condones practices as flagrant as stealing from the public treasury, the conditions necessary for representative government are either not present or seriously weakened. This evidence consists primarily in the representatives' making no attempt to deny or excuse their dishonesty, and it is found in the fringe areas of the democratic state, such as the urban slums and rural backwaters of the United States.

in a subsequent election, it will usually be supported by a substantial proportion of the voters. It can at best be inferred that only a relatively small number of voters has "held the government responsible" for its behavior. If, for example, 70 per cent of the electorate votes both times, and the party receives 55 per cent of the ballots before the scandal and 45 per cent afterward, primary concern for honesty in government can be attributed to no more than 7 per cent of the electorate, and this calculation ignores all other possible motives for changes of preference.

Given these qualifications, the electorate exerts a real enough influence for responsibility to professional standards upon the representatives. Although most representatives are probably more sensitive to the opinions of their colleagues, the opposition, and leaders of public opinion, the tendency of at least a portion of their electorates to react unfavorably to moral and professional lapses is a factor that they certainly must consider. To put it another way, a representative government would suffer severely if its officials believed that their constituents were uniformly indifferent to incompetence, inefficiency, and dishonesty.

V

The pattern of political activity described above supplements the conclusions of previous chapters. In any operation as large and complex as government, it is natural that small groups of specialists initiate and execute all matters of significance. The democratic state differs from all others by possessing a large number of such groups, which are very often in competition with one another. The most striking features of the democratic state result from the competition of parties, parliamentary parties, pressure groups, editors of periodicals, and the rest. Nevertheless, this competition would be meaningless—indeed, the groups themselves would not even exist—if governmental officials were not selected by an electorate which chooses among alternative candidates.

This choice among candidates, as we have seen, does not imply that the electorate is responsible for selecting the best men or parties, no matter how "best" may be defined. The parties must nominate men with the will and capacity to operate the complicated and delicate mechanisms of representative government; every serious candidate must possess these characteristics to some degree. This does not mean that in every election one candidate is fully as good as another, but only that representative government does not depend upon the success of the candidate most likely to solve current problems. The history of democratic states illustrates this principle, and the ability of the parties always to nominate at least moderately capable and dedicated men explains it.[14]

Nevertheless, the electorate has a fundamental responsibility under representative government: it must elect only men who accept the constitutional structure of the democratic state. Uncoerced elections permit candidates to be nominated and campaigns to be waged by organizations determined to abolish representative institutions. If many of these candidates are elected, parliaments are unable to function properly; if they gain a majority in the parliament, representative government and the democratic state will very probably disappear. To choose only from among democratically committed candidates and parties is the single most important function of the electorate in the democratic state.

Finally, the people must participate in elections to the extent that these contests shall appear neither trivial nor farcical. Although the parties are primarily responsible for maintaining popular interest in elections—some of them almost always have something to gain by a reasonably large "turnout"—the electorate itself must be serious about the issues of the campaign and the general purpose of the electoral system. Absence of opposition to the democratic system is not enough; there must also be an absence of indifference.

VI

The realization that the electorate's major responsibility is to support democratic candidates dispels a great many misconceptions about the "common man" in the democratic state. As mentioned previously, the theory of the average democratic citizen has included a paradox. His governmental functions have been thought to require personal characteristics which he almost certainly does not really possess, yet somehow democratic states have managed to survive and in some cases to prosper remarkably. The solution to this problem is, of course, quite easy: the functions of the average elector are fewer and simpler than has customarily been supposed.

Traditional theory holds that some very interesting attributes are required of the common man. He must possess a habit of critical observation, an interest in the practical aspects of government, a desire to know what government has actually done in the near or distant past, a sense of the need for cooperation in the affairs of governing, and an appreciation of the complexity of political issues.[15] This list is obviously designed to provide the citizen with intelligent opinions that can serve as guides for governmental policy, and with attitudes that can aid him in apprehending governmental officials whenever they fail to meet their responsibilities. Since the electorate performs neither of these functions, its failure to possess the characteristics in question presents no problems for the analyst.*

Political theorists—in contrast to other political scientists—are apparently reluctant to admit that the great majority of the electorate have only the vaguest notion of what problems face their government and what it has done and is doing to meet them. Indeed, most people know very little about the structure and functioning of the government itself.[16] Apart from the fact that representative government operates quite well with an uninformed electorate, there is nothing particularly disgraceful or dangerous in this popular ignorance. The expansion of technology, population, and governmental activity has made life more complex and specialized; being shocked by political ignorance betrays a failure to recognize the necessity of this development. Furthermore, worrying about a "gap" between what government must do and what the people can understand indicates a failure to comprehend the reasons why the masses support a political system —even a system which requires their active participation.†

VII

Although the "average man" in the democratic state need not have the qualities of a political leader, he must possess some unusual characteristics in order to do his job. He must, first of all, be accessible to communication. Unless the candidates and parties presume that their arguments, claims, promises, and criticisms reach the electorate, representative government simply will not operate. This requires that the people be literate and have enough education and experience to be capable of understanding at least the major campaign issues, regarding both positive policy and the proper conduct of government. The remarkably high level of education and rate of literacy in contemporary democratic states meet this requirement. In addition, a competent electorate must have a familiarity with the types of problems dealt with by modern governments and a perspective which goes beyond the parochial. That is to say, although the voters need not be aware of, or even interested in, the specific problems requiring governmental attention, they must be sophisticated enough to understand that vital decisions have to be made regarding economic, social, military, and foreign affairs. Such sophistication results not only from democratic education but from the varied content of the mass media—newspapers, magazines, radio, cinema, television—and from the relative ease of geographical mobility. The first requirement,

---

* The "common" or "average" man in the democratic state is a symbol for the minimum capabilities possessed by a minimum proportion of the electorate, consistent with the proper operation of representative government.

† These reasons will be discussed in chapters 6, 7, and 8.

then, is that the people have a high enough degree of education and a wide enough range of experience to oblige the candidates and parties to presume that electoral choice can be motivated by preferences in governmental policy.

The second attribute required of the people is that they disapprove of their representatives' failure to be honest, efficient, and technically competent. This disapproval must be made concrete by the reasonably frequent defeat of representatives and parties with these deficiencies; aside from certain atypical cases, democratic electorates have generally behaved in this way. The "average man" is honest, and he respects and values competence and efficiency in any task. His attitudes are consistent with the legal and moral standards of his society, which, because of its economic and social structure, stresses the necessity of these virtues.

A representative government is dependent to an unusual extent upon popular confidence, and this confidence is the third and most important attribute of the electorate. Given that all the rules of the representative system are met—that elections are truly uncoerced, that the representatives have real control over the other organs of government, and that the specific requirements of the constitution are observed—the electorate must believe in the propriety of representative government, and it must support only those candidates who will work within and defend the system. The responsibility of the voter is not to identify antidemocratic candidates, since this is done by the other candidates, but to refrain from supporting them. The voter must not only understand the basic principles of representative government, he must also prefer them to all other alternatives. These attitudes are clearly within the competence of the "common man"; that he possesses them is fully established by the longevity of democratic states.

The reasons why the electorate supports representative government are obscure and complex, and they will be dealt with later in some detail. To anticipate briefly, the electorate comes to understand the fundamental principles of representative government through "political myths," which, although they only approximate the principles, adequately differentiate representative from nonrepresentative government. The electorate prefers the representative system because its results—welfare policy and civil liberties—are advantageous to the "Middle Class" which dominates the democratic state. These results are so strongly approved that the people actively participate in the democratic political process by voting in the periodic elections.

VIII

The electorate can choose from among at least two and usually not more than six parties. The democratic state thus exhibits a kind of "imperfect competition" among several large and powerful "sellers" of ideas about how government should be conducted. The restricted number of competitors naturally means that these ideas are restricted in both number and variety. The parties, as was indicated in chapter 3, can calculate tolerably well the welfare measures which their competitors will promise; consequently, they themselves promise only enough to hold their share of the electoral "market" or to increase it slightly.[17] This kind of restriction also occurs regarding standards of honesty, efficiency, and competence, for the criticisms leveled by the opposition parties against the incumbents may well be tempered by a tacit agreement on practices which appeal to all of them. When the parties are responsible for initiating new conceptions of public policy and for criticizing those in control of this policy, some very important ideas may never be suggested and some very pertinent criticisms may never be made.[18]

The parties' lack of imagination and their "collusion" may occasionally disappoint and even anger the observer of democratic politics. However, these drawbacks represent a price well worth paying. It was explained in chapter 2 how the parties are the great simplifiers of the electoral process, how electoral competition in a large constituency would be chaotic unless the parties reduced the number of candidates and issues. The positive proposals and the negative criticisms offered by the parties are concentrated, and their source is familiar and clearly identifiable. Although the Opposition's criticism may be softened by its desire to protect itself against the time when it is in office, the Government is always aware of a potential critic which has a vested interest in calling attention to official errors and oversights and which is able to attack with a minimum of wasted effort and with the assurance of full publicity for its statements. This concentration of criticism also makes the process of representative government more meaningful to the people, who would be lost in confusion without it. As their confusion increases, their confidence in representative government decreases. Irresponsible and unorganized criticism may be more thorough and imaginative, but it is certainly less effective.

It may be mentioned here that the parties provide another stimulant to the vital factor of popular confidence in representative government. One of the parties' most characteristic features is their ability to evoke the average citizen's loyalty, and loyalty in its turn creates a sense of responsibility. When a party is engaged in a vigorous campaign, and when its allied parliamentary party occupies the more important governmental offices, the voter who habitually identifies with it feels that he shares the responsibilities of campaign and office, even though he may be only vaguely aware of what is involved in both. The partisan's sense of responsibility, indefinite as it may be, should not be underestimated as an element of strength in the democratic state.[19]

The statement that the parties initiate new ideas about policy and level criticisms against officials does not, of course, imply that they monopolize this activity. The journalist, clergyman, and teacher, trained to criticize and to explore new alternatives, perform a most important function just because of their relative freedom from political commitments. Nonetheless, it must always be remembered that the parties make the final decisions about which policy alternatives are available, and that "perfect competition" is no more characteristic of the modern democratic polity than of the modern democratic economy.

IX

Those dissatisfied with the preceding account of the division of political labor between the general citizenry and the parties should remember that my intention was to describe as accurately as possible the functions which each performs in the remarkably vigorous political life of the twelve democratic states. Those who have found my implicit approval of this division of labor distasteful may well be assuming a conception of the ideal political position of the average citizen which has implications they have not always acknowledged.

Disappointment with the relatively passive role of the electorate probably comes, in the last analysis, from a comparison with pure democracy, where the citizens themselves are the "parliament." Political theorists have a tendency to consider pure democracy the ideal form of government; since it is not practically feasible, however, we must settle for representative government, the "second best" kind of government.[20]

The citizens of the modern democratic state have very few political functions compared to the citizens of pure democracy, but preferring pure democracy has two unsatisfactory implications. In the first place, it implies approval of a society which can produce citizens with the time and skill necessary for conducting governmental business. This society must either be very primitive or have a very restricted leisure class as its only citizens. Even in the small and uncomplex cantons of contemporary Switzerland, where the *Landsgemeinden* still operate, the democracy is far from pure, for elected representatives have the authority to amend and even reject the citizens' proposals.[21] Contemporary civilization in its least complex form requires specialization of function. Politics is no exception to this generalization.

In the second place, the preference for more political participation, even where pure democracy is possible, may be founded upon the assumption that every man knows his own interests best and therefore should participate in all decisions which affect them. This ethical assumption has two possible interpretations, neither of which is especially tenable. If it means that public policy should "reflect the interests of the people," it not only implies that the purpose of government is to satisfy everyone's selfish desires but also raises the insolvable "problem of the majority." If, on the contrary, the assumption means that the people would make good laws, they still must be proved capable of governing. The most lucid defenders of the common man claim only that he understands issues within the range of his direct experience and issues raising fundamental questions of democratic rights and justice.[22] It is pointless to argue that the people will become "good citizens" or "morally responsible men" through acting as their own legislators, unless their ability to legislate is first established.

X

Given that the average citizen cannot participate in representative government as much as he can in pure democracy, and that representative governments have prospered with the limited amount of popular participation described above, it might still be thought desirable to expand in some way the functions of the people. It is not easy, however, to determine where and how such expansion should occur.

The United States and Switzerland have adopted devices which give their electorates a larger share in government. The most important is the so-called referendum, by which parliamentary decisions can be submitted to the electorate for acceptance or rejection, but this has been generally unsatisfactory. The electorate has usually been badly informed about the issues involved; the need to decide on referenda, at least in the United States, has further confused an electorate already burdened with a "long" ballot; and there is no reason to believe that either the electorate or the government is improved when the former has given its "opinion" on proposed statutes.[23]

The American primary election has also expanded popular participation in politics. Primaries were introduced because it was thought that the selection of party nominees by loosely defined sections of the electorate would improve their quality and "representativeness." There may have been an immediate improvement, but subsequent experience has shown that conventions nominate candidates who are at least equally inspired and capable. In addition, the primary has had some positively unfortunate consequences. Like the referendum, it has increased the confusion of an electorate faced with many decisions, and it has seriously undermined the cohesion and consequently the responsibility of the parties.[24] If reform of the primary is contemplated, it should restrict rather than expand the political functions of the people.

Since any government must be operated by a relatively small number of specialists, it is useless to deplore the restricted role of the electorate. Government in the democratic state, however, requires a multiplicity of leadership groups, which are remarkably open to entry by the average citizen. Both the loosely organized and intermittent American parties and the "bureaucratic" and sometimes ossified parties of western Europe would profit from able new members, and they can probably absorb all those people normally interested in active politics. The parties have proven themselves the most efficient and effective instruments of democratic politics; those who desire a more active political life for the people should focus their attention upon the parties.

The parties at best can absorb only a small proportion of the democratic electorate. However, it is both possible and desirable to increase the ability of the larger part of the people to perform their modest functions. This can be done through education. The more thoroughly the electorate is educated, the more the parties will be motivated to improve the quality of their policy programs and the relevance and incisiveness of their mutual criticisms. The imagination and alertness of political leaders must increase with the expanding knowledge and sophistication of the audience before whom they perform. From the viewpoint of politics alone, the education which the citizens can profitably be given appears limitless.

Democratic education does not have to emphasize politics, economics, or "citizenship," and it does not have to include much beyond the normal "indoctrination" in democratic and national values now present in compulsory education.[25] The development of general intelligence suffices for most of the electorate. To attempt anything more would be nugatory, for most professors of political science themselves are unable to master the intricacies of taxation, national defense, and other areas of crucial governmental policy. Nevertheless, since so many people are needed to conduct the political life of democracy, special education in government and politics is vitally important. Unusual political information and skills are necessary for elected representatives at the central and local levels, members of large appointed governmental bodies, participants in political parties, officials in the numerous pressure groups, and politically unattached leaders of public opinion.

XI

In discussing the people's functions in representative government, we have seen how the traditional conceptions of self-government, government by the people, majority rule, and government responsible to the people are not accurate accounts of what the people really do. We have also seen that the problem of the common man's "rationality" is a false problem. Contemporary students of the democratic policy-making process have not so much rejected these ideas as they have simply ignored them.

Yet the traditional conceptions of the people's functions and attributes are not completely divorced from democratic reality. They are, rather, crude approximations and gross oversimplifications. After all, the general citizenry of the democratic state does participate much more fully in the governmental process than its counterparts in other states, and it must therefore have special aptitudes and attitudes. But the popularity and persistence of "government by the people" and the rest, which make them a primary datum of the democratic state, can be accounted for only in part by their simplicity and understandability. In chapter 7 it will be shown how they are related to the other primary data, through their status as the most important political myths of contemporary democracy.

6: THE "CONSENT" OF THE GOVERNED

One of the most popular phrases in democratic theory is "government by the consent of the governed." [1] Consent is always considered a necessary element in the democratic state, and often democratic governments are thought to be the only ones which receive consent. In the essay, "Of the Original Contract," Hume proved that the notion of consent cannot be taken literally, but writers have nevertheless continued to use it in the literal sense. Consequently, our first task is to demonstrate the meaninglessness of contemporary versions of the theory of consent. The introduction of the famous distinction between consent and "tacit" consent [2] may be an attempt to avoid the Humean criticism, but if so it is unsuccessful, for the arguments showing that consent is a fiction apply also to tacit consent.

Modern democratic theorists have very often used the terms "consent" and "tacit consent" to refer to certain attitudes presumably possessed by the citizens of the democratic state. Since consent is an act and not an attitude, this use of the terms is incorrect. However, there does exist a popular attitude of great political importance which seems to be what these theorists have in mind, especially in their conception of tacit consent. Our second task is to identify this attitude —which might well be called "hypothetical consent"—and to show why it alone satisfies the sense of "government by the consent of the governed."

The people of the democratic state have the attitude in question, but they are not the only ones who have it. "Consent," therefore, is necessary but not sufficient for the democratic state, and it may appear to have no place in the present analysis of democracy. However, "consenting" to a government is a function of the people, which they perform in a special and, indeed, unique way in the democratic state; understanding the democratic variety of "consent" depends upon an understanding of the concept of consent. In addition, the discussion of "consent" will disclose more of those common opinions about democracy which are themselves an important element of the democratic state.

I

To show that the concepts of consent by the governed are really fictions, it is necessary first to state very carefully what is meant by saying that a government is consented to. A dictionary will define the noun "consent" as "voluntary accordance with, or concurrence in, what is done or proposed by another." This meaning must be kept in mind, since political theorists can reasonably be requested to talk about consent only when they refer to a political situation wherein someone voluntarily agrees to something which someone else does. If the situation lacks any element of the act of consent, we can properly ask them to use another word.

There are several theories of consent which attempt to show that the governed perform, at one time or another, an act of voluntary accordance with, or concurrence in, the control which their governors exercise over them. The familiar theory of the social contract is a prototype of consent: the government's control has been consented to because its governed once voluntarily and expressly agreed (presumably in speech or writing) that the government would, in the future, have this control. If consent occurs in the modern democratic state, it must resemble the social contract in each of its essential espects: voluntariness, a specific act by the consenters, a specific action consented to, and specific agents who perform this action.

In contemporary political writing, consent is almost invariably linked with representative government, although some mention may be made of pure democracy. The latter need not be dealt with here, for most of the arguments against consent to a representative government also apply in the case of pure democracy. On the other hand, it is usually denied that consent occurs under nondemocratic regimes, although it may be thought that they can receive "tacit consent."

There is an obvious reason for the belief that only a representative government can be consented to. The unusual extent of popular participation in representative government has suggested to the theorists that, somewhere in this activity, the larger part of the democratic citizenry may perform an act of consent. Participation in elections has most often been thought to involve consent, but it has also been inferred from the nature of democratic constitutions.

II

It has been said that a representative government rests upon the consent of its governed because, at certain fixed periods, the policies of the government are submitted for the approval or disapproval of the governed.[3] According to this view, voluntariness is present because the elections are uncoerced; the action consented to is the past or future behavior of the candidates; the overt act is casting a ballot; and the consenters are the voters who supported the winning candidates.

This theory's first defect is that, except under proportional representation,* consent is given by only a small proportion of the population, and a substantial proportion always quite clearly dissents. The proof of a theory of consent does not depend on showing that everyone under a representative government's jurisdiction consents, but any such theory surely intends that at least the greater part of the electorate consents. When the occurrence of explicit dissent by as many as half the voters is added to this objection, the governed simply cannot be claimed to have consented by choosing among candidates.

In the second place, although genuine consent is given (by a part of the electorate) to the authority of the winning candidates, that which is being consented to is not fundamental enough to fit the customary sense of the theory of consent. After all, the voter at an election is faced with a *fait accompli* regarding the nature of the government: the most important aspect of the whole situation is the electoral system itself, and no one has given him an opportunity to approve of it. What is consented to is certainly intended to be something more than the "government" or the "administration"; the social-contract theory says that the governed consent to the entire system of government. To put this another way, membership in an association may be voluntary, but as long as one remains a member it is mandatory that he accept its authority.[4] The electoral system is an integral part of the association in question; hence, the authority of the association applies to it. A theory of consent must account for the voluntary acceptance of all aspects of the association's authority.

It might be denied that consent through elections is supposed to explicate the traditional theory of consent. If this is the case, the word "consent" has been unhappily chosen, for it naturally suggests that something more than an election has taken place. Everyone knows that governors are chosen by the electorate; it would not be clear that "consent" refers to nothing more.

Another theory of consent uses uncoerced elections in a different way. When the citizen participates in an election he accepts the general principles upon which the government is based, and from this acceptance it can be inferred that he accepts the specific governmental acts which control his behavior.[5] The man who votes is the consenter,

* This is the only argument in the present discussion that does not apply to proportional representation.

and his action is voluntary, not because he can support any candidate, but because he can refrain from voting if he so desires.[6] In other words, the voter is supposed to consent to the system of government, rather than to any individual governors or governmental policies.

Although this is a more sophisticated attempt to discover consent in the electoral process, it too contains a basic flaw. The voters do not consent directly to the "general order of the state" since it cannot be assumed that they consider elections as opportunities to approve or disapprove of the fundamental principles of representative government.[7] The theorist must infer acceptance of the system from the fact of voting in an election; that is, he must show a connection between the fact of voting and an overt but unobserved fact of consent. The "fact of consent" can only be the voter's explicitly saying to someone, or to himself, "I approve of the representative form of government."

This inference from voting to consent cannot be drawn because it is very improbable—no matter what evidence is presented—that any large numbers of people ever say explicitly that they approve of any system of government, and because the act of voting is not very closely connected with an attitude giving rise to consent. People may vote because they consider it a duty, or because they are interested in specific issues or candidates, or because they wish to conform to the behavior of their social group. These and other normal motivations for voting are not psychologically associated with an awareness of representative government as a system of government. The physical act of casting a ballot is also not likely to stimulate very many voters to reflect upon the system of which it is a small part.

In answer to this criticism, someone might object that the inference to be drawn from voting is not that each individual says, "I concur," but that he would consent if he happened to be asked. This is a reasonable retort, but it changes the subject. The present issue is whether acts of consent occur. Their probability is not increased significantly by stating that the voters would consent if they had an opportunity which they do not now have. The suggestion about "potential consenting" is important, however, and it will be taken into consideration later in the present chapter.

III

The preceding attempts to find consent have relied upon the uncoerced elections essential to representative government. First the voters for the winning candidates and then all the voters were identified as the consenters. These are the only possible ways for using elections as the act by which the governed consent to the government, but there are other phenomena which can be relied upon. The most important of these is a special type of constitutional system.

It has been said that the people, or a large number of them, expressly approve of a representative system because of their special relationship to the constitution of the democratic state: the governed both create the constitution and have the power to amend it. The power of creation and the power of amendment are distinct things, and it will be convenient to discuss them separately.[8]

If "creation" means that the people approve the constitution by plebiscite, then the theory is analogous to that which says consent occurs through the majority vote in particular elections; it also implies that one historical majority consents for all future generations. The theory in this form is only the traditional social contract rephrased.

However, the power to create a constitution, the "constituent power," is not merely the power behind the constitution's adoption; "the constituent group in the exact sense is to be understood as that part of the community which is capable of wielding the de facto residuary power of changing or replacing an established order by a new constitution." [9] This concept of constituent power quite correctly says that there are certain groups in every state which could change the form of government if they so desired, that every constitution has a certain pattern of political support. If a theory of consent is to be based on the constituent power, possessing this power must be shown equivalent to consenting, and the governed must be shown to possess it. Roughly speaking, the governed do possess constituent power in a democracy, but it cannot be established that by possessing it they consent to their government.

The governed possess the constituent power under representative government in the sense that the electorate must be depended upon to put into office men willing to preserve the system. By dividing the electorate into politically significant groups, each large enough to disrupt the system, one can avoid the assumption that the electorate as a whole is capable of political action. The American farmers, for example, by concerted action could seriously weaken and perhaps even destroy representative government in the United States, and circumstances can be imagined which would cause them to reject the existing constitution. Representative government is peculiarly sensitive to this type of group. A constituent power might well be attributed to each group of a given size and coherence, and the constituent power to all of them in conjunction. But it does not follow from this that they consent to the government.

The possessors of a power which by definition is capable of changing their form of government are, by their tolerance, consenting to the current form only if they are aware of their special position in the state's constitutional structure. If the "governed" consent, then the general membership of the principal economic or sectional groups —and not merely the leaders of organizations which may be drawn from them—must be aware of this position; in other words, the governed must consciously refrain from dissenting. There is, however, no reason to believe that this awareness is possessed by the larger part of the membership. Such "class consciousness," if it ever exists, does so only in the most unusual of circumstances—circumstances which are probably precisely the ones giving rise not to consent but to disaffection. Possessing the constituent power cannot be proved equivalent to consenting.

It might still be thought possible to discover consent in connection with the amending power. One might argue that through the amending process the governed have, at any time, a specific opportunity to change their form of government; since they do not take advantage of this opportunity, they behave in a way equivalent to consenting.

This argument cannot demonstrate the existence of consent because the process of constitutional amendment in democratic states does not consist solely of action by the electorate. National parliaments and organs of local government have equal or even exclusive powers, and saying that these agencies are elected by the people merely repeats the argument rejected above, that consent results from a majority's electoral decisions. Even if the power of amendment were given exclusively to the people, the majority-minority problem would remain. Finally, it cannot be assumed that the people are aware of their ability to change the constitution through the process of formal amendment.

To my knowledge, there have been no other attempts to demonstrate the existence of consent. The theories I have examined rely upon the institutions of the democratic state, which is not surprising: uncoerced elections and constitutions "popularly" amended are found only there, and the governed are not considered the constituent power in other modern states. It is unlikely that anyone would maintain that any nondemocratic governmental institutions imply the consent of the governed.

IV

Consent can no more be discovered by examining the behavior of individuals than by examining the behavior of groups. Consent implies voluntariness, and the association of almost every citizen with the government which controls him is clearly involuntary. The theory of consent says, if it says anything, that all individuals or groups are voluntarily under the control of a government; but the vast majority of people controlled by the most desirable government in existence were born into this condition. This criticism cannot be refuted by arguing that the political association is voluntary because any individual or group can withdraw from it, thus rejecting the mandatory nature of its control.[10] Although it is possible to emigrate voluntarily from many states and to choose a new state whose authority is to be accepted, simple withdrawal is not the central issue. An association is truly voluntary only when one can take himself beyond its control at any time whatever. After one has broken the rules, he can withdraw from clubs, lodges, political parties, labor unions, and professional organizations without having to incur the punishment—which is the essence of the type of control in question—always attached to breaches of authority. If the authority-breaker cannot escape the sanctions attached to rule-breaking, it is because the voluntary association's control is supported by the control of the government. There is no withdrawal from the government's control when one has broken the rules; therefore, there can be no consent to governmental regulation by those who have not consciously accepted it by means of voluntary immigration.

In brief, consent by an individual to governmental control can occur in two ways. He can voluntarily put himself within the area controlled by a government, as do voluntary immigrants and as the social-contract theory postulated for all citizens. Or, if he finds himself involuntarily subject to this control, he must be able at any time to remove from its jurisdiction. The overwhelming majority of the inhabitants of any state are in the latter condition, but at best they can withdraw from governmental control only when they are not subject to the sanctions supporting it. The law-breaker is kept under the control of government not by his own intentions but by the machinery of law enforcement. This is the feature that distinguishes the control exercised by government from the control exercised by other organizations or institutions that also direct human behavior, and it is this feature that makes the former involuntary.

The conclusion that consent does not and cannot occur in the association of a citizen with his government means that he cannot exhibit "voluntary accordance with, or concurrence in, what is done or proposed by" the personnel of government acting in their official capacities. Any attempt to save the situation by distinguishing between consent and "tacit" consent must also fail, for the necessary voluntariness can no more be silent or implied than it can be public and observable.[11] If "the consent of the governed" is taken literally, neither the democratic state nor any other contemporary state possesses consent.*

---

* It is often said that a representative government is one in which authority is delegated by the people to their governors, and one dictionary definition of "representative" is "one who is duly authorized to act and speak for others." When applied to government, these are theories of consent.

V

Although consent does not occur, there is a concrete difference between governments resulting from the presence or absence of a characteristic to which theorists have often given the name "consent." As I said above, this usage of the word is not entirely misleading, and the problem is to discover to what political phenomenon it most reasonably refers. The most convenient way to begin is by eliminating some common explications.

The first says that consent * is the opposite of force. All governments are supposed to lie on a continuum, the two poles of which are pure force and pure consent, although in practice no governments are at either extreme.[12] If this means that a government by consent rarely utilizes its monopoly of force, then it does not describe the seeming difference between consent and lack of consent. Some governments, at least in the past, have very strictly and thoroughly regulated the behavior of their people, who nevertheless appear to have given their consent. Governments of this type are usually called "paternalistic." Absence of restraint (the liberty of chapter 4) is clearly not the same thing as consent; force, in the sense of the presence of coercion, thus cannot be treated as the incompatible opposite of consent.

A variation of the contrast between consent and force is that governments "rely upon" or "rest upon" one or the other, or rather upon some combination in which one predominates. This theory concerns motivation for obedience: all governments use force, but in some states the people obey because they fear the consequences of disobedience, while in others their obedience does not depend upon this fear. Only the latter governments, it is said, are by the consent of their governed.

Consent, however, cannot be identified with obedience not motivated by the fear of force, because "consent" has normally been used with a more specific connotation. A person may obey because of habit, or because he has been told to obey by someone who has influence over him, or because he wishes to avoid the social opprobrium attached to the lawbreaker. These motives are neither singly nor in any combination what we have in mind when we think about the consent of the governed.

---

* Henceforth, the word "consent" will not be used in the literal sense of "voluntary concurrence in another's actions"; its meaning is to be determined. The best way to indicate this would be by placing the word always in quotation marks; but since their use would introduce an avoidable awkwardness, I have omitted them.

VI

Many attempts have been made to relate the vague but meaningful notion of consent to a specific reason why men obey their governments, but they have always been unsuccessful. In order to identify consent with a motivation for obeying the law, two conditions must be satisfied. First, the motivation must account for at least the larger part of the obedience given a government ordinarily judged to have the consent of its governed, and it must not account for the obedience to any government judged to be without consent. The possession by the governed of the motivation must be necessary and sufficient for the existence of consent. Second, the word "consent" must refer, at least roughly, to the presence of the motivation; it must have a meaning similar to "the presence of such-and-such a motivation." Neither of these conditions is met by the theories which say that consent is motivation for political obedience.

The most popular theory identifies consent with the motivation which comes from the people's "need and desire for the power of the state to restrain themselves." Most laws are enforceable, it is said, because most people want usually to keep them. They recognize that the laws are desirable, they realize that they themselves cannot always be trusted to act in accordance with the law, and they approve of the law's coercive element as a check upon their own tendency toward disobedience.[13] Motivation for obedience to the laws comes basically from the recognition by the governed that obedience is to their immediate or eventual advantage. One version of this theory emphasizes the appraisal by the governed of specific laws, and a second stresses their evaluation of the legal system as a whole.

Those who identify consent and this self-interested or "rational" motivation usually illustrate their thesis by referring to what are presumably the usual human reactions to governmental regulation of the least complex kind, such as traffic control.[14] It is probably thought that the very simplicity of the examples strengthens the argument that rational motivation for obedience is widespread, at least in the democratic state. But it actually weakens this argument; from the fact that only such simple examples readily come to mind, the most reasonable inference is that at best government gets obedience based upon rational agreement only regarding matters like the maintenance of "law and order."

When a person obeys a law because he believes it to be to his own advantage, he must understand and agree with the immediate and ultimate purposes of the law. In the case of traffic control, he must desire order, expedition, and safety; he must understand how

the traffic department is attempting to realize these ends by requirements and prohibitions; and he must believe that the means have
been properly chosen. It is very unlikely that enough people have these
attitudes even toward traffic control to warrant saying that the governed consent to laws regulating the speed and direction of vehicles.
When other areas of law are taken into consideration, the probability
is even smaller that enough people rationally agree to governmental
regulation so that the phrase "government by the consent of the
governed" becomes applicable.[15]

The theorists of consent as rational motivation cannot show that
the purposes behind each law, or even most laws, are communicated
to the governed, or that the governed understand and agree with those
purposes which are successfully communicated. For the reasons examined in some detail in chapter 3, it cannot be said that the governed
understand and thus that they agree with governmental purposes in
the difficult and complex areas of economic, military, and foreign
policy. Even less does any substantial segment of the governed comprehend the methods required for solving problems of modern public
policy. Under very simple conditions, perhaps both ends and means
can be understood and agreed to, assuming that such simplicity can
coexist with the necessary media of communication; but conditions,
especially in the democratic state, are no longer simple.

The search for specific evidence of rational agreement under
contemporary representative government immediately founders on
the fact of electoral disagreement. Personal contacts with the governed suggest—according to my own necessarily limited experience—
that, with respect to governmental actions touching upon matters
familiar to them, the governed disapprove at least as often as they
approve of both the government's intentions and its implementations
of these intentions. Allowing for the natural human propensity to
find fault, there is still no reason for concluding that these complaints
are exceptional or insincere; and there is no reason at all for supposing
that obedience to more than a very few laws is based primarily upon
rational agreement with their purposes.

VII

The second version of this theory holds that consent is the motivation for obedience that is based upon rational approval of the
government's ability to make regulations backed by the threat of
force, rather than upon rational agreement with the purposes and
methods of individual laws.[16] Obedience to specific laws does not
come from the citizen's agreement with their purposes, but from his
belief that obedience is to his own advantage, which he realizes may

not be apparent to him in every case. Or he may believe that the
government deserves support for the general function it is performing, although it may do things which he disapproves. Or, finally, he
may wish to do his part in preserving the government's ability to
issue mandatory regulations. All of these motivations for obedience
are supposed to come from the citizen's belief that the government's
power of mandatory authority is to his own interest; none adequately
accounts for obedience to governments ordinarily said to have the
consent of their governed; and, if any one or combination of them
did account for obedience to a government, we would not for this
reason alone say it had the consent of its governed.

This type of motivation is the sole or primary reason for political
obedience only under special circumstances. The citizen's belief that
governmental acts are always to his own advantage is characteristic
only of relatively primitive societies; more advanced societies distinguish between the authority of government and the successful use of
that authority.[17] It is unlikely, moreover, that many people believe
that their government deserves support because it solves foreign and
domestic problems as well as could be expected. Finally, people only
rarely obey because they are aware of their own interest in a strong
and effective central agency of control; on occasion, the desire to
avoid anarchy may justify the monopoly of force to a frightened
population, but the complete collapse of authority threatens only
infrequently. In short, this self-interested motivation clearly does not
underlie obedience to governments judged to have the consent of their
governed; the first condition for identifying consent with rational
obedience to the law is not met.

The second condition is that "consent" and "obedience because of
self-interested motivations" must be, if not synonymous, at least very
similar in meaning. The theory under consideration also fails to meet
this condition. Even if a government were recognized by its people
as eminently successful, or as doing a good job under the circumstances, or as standing between them and things they very much want
to avoid, or as doing all at once, we would definitely not for this
reason alone call it a "government by the consent of its governed."
We mean by the phrase something more than a popular attitude of
selfish calculation. The theorists who have persisted in maintaining
that obedience to representative government is motivated by rational
agreement, either to specific laws or to the government's general
function, have succeeded, I believe, only in strengthening the position
of those who argue that democracy is "impossible" or "false." The
moralists who have thought that the most desirable motivation for
political obedience is founded upon rational agreement, by consciously
or unconsciously implying the desirability of an artificial solidarity,

have clearly denied some of the most basic postulates of democratic ethics.*

In denying that consent is rational motivation, I have stated that self-interested agreement with the purposes of the laws or the whole legal system is practically never the principal motivation for political obedience. To show conclusively that consent is not motivation, let us examine the possible determinants of obedience to political control in any state, nondemocratic as well as democratic.

After considering some motivations for obedience—the recognition of the legitimacy of the law's source; the belief in the rationality of its contents; the feeling of obligation to the state; the fear of the sanctions involved in disobedience; the desire not to incur the obloquy of the lawbreaker; and the influence of self-interest, personal convenience, and inertia—Professor R. M. MacIver concluded that, despite the involvement of all these motivations in obedience, they are not sufficient to explain it. To them must be added the fact that "law-abidingness is a habit" which is "responsive to the totality of social conditions"; "law-abidingness is the pragmatic condition of and response to the whole firmament of social order." "All the ties that hold men together in any society, all the needs and all the hopes that depend on their society for realization, prompt them to law-abidingness." [18]

The hypothesis that men usually obey most of the laws because of a habit which cannot be separated from their "socialness" is inconsistent with any theory of consent as motivation for obedience. If habit is the basic motivation for the obedience of the citizens of every state, then a government which is by the consent of the governed cannot be distinguished from one which is not. If there are exceptions to this generalization, and the citizens of some states do not obey because of habit, the presence and absence of consent may well correlate with the presence and absence of the habit. But the correlation cannot be one of identity: in the language of political theory, the word "consent" surely suggests something more than being motivated to obedience by one's ties with his society.

VIII

I have argued that the word "consent" can refer neither to the opposite of force, nor to the absence of the fear of force, nor to any kind of motivation for obedience to the laws. When political theorists use the phrase "government by the consent of the governed" in

---

* It could also be shown how the doctrine of "rational consent" leads to the concepts of interest reflection, majority rule, and several of the others previously encountered. These are all different facets of the same theoretical approach to representative government and democracy, but any further comments on its defects would be gratuitous.

sentences which seem to convey meaning, they may have in mind a special attitude of the people toward their government. When, and only when, a reasonably large proportion of the governed take this attitude, their government has their consent. The attitude may motivate obedience, but it is normally not a principal motivation. This attitude is, most reasonably, the belief that the government has a moral right to receive obedience to its laws and a moral right to use force to help stimulate obedience. It is, as a matter of fact, found in conjunction with governments usually considered to be by consent, and it does not accompany those judged to be without consent. The primary difficulty of this interpretation is whether "consent" means something similar to "a belief in the moral right of the government to govern."

Let us call a government "legitimate" when most of its politically conscious subjects believe that it has this moral right to rule, whether or not they happen to be very law-abiding and no matter what motives may determine their actual obedience. Legitimacy can occur under any pattern of power underlying the government. The masses may be almost completely powerless, as under traditional monarchy or aristocracy, and still believe in the right of the monarch or the aristocrats to order their lives. Thus, those who consent do not necessarily possess the constituent power. Furthermore, the consenters do not always profit from governmental control; many people have been exploited by those whom they believed to be their rightful rulers.

In order that a government be legitimate, its presumed right to rule must be a moral right. The people must believe they have a moral obligation to obey their government, even though they do not always obey it, and even though fear may motivate many of their acts of obedience. Neither traditional political theory nor enlightened common sense attributes consent to a government believed by its people to have a nonmoral claim to rule—a claim based upon considerations of self-interest, rationality, or expediency.[19]

Legitimacy may be called "consent," or, better, "tacit consent," without too great a violation of accepted meaning; for belief in the government's moral right to rule may be described as the most important reason why the people would consent to its control, if they had the opportunity to give their voluntary accordance. This is why I used the expression "hypothetical consent" at the beginning of the present chapter. If the average man believed governmental control to be convenient, he might voluntarily agree to come under its control; if he believed it to be morally good, he very probably would consent to it. Evidence for this supposition must come from people already subject to the government's control, because immigrants are probably motivated primarily by considerations of expediency, and they have not been subject to the educational processes of their new society.

The concept of consent has been a part of political theory for many centuries despite its vagueness and despite the failure of most attempts to explain it. We have seen why these attempts have been unsuccessful. Either "consent" refers to a widespread popular belief in the government's moral right to rule—as Hume himself used the word [20] —or it has no meaning. I believe that it is meaningful; and, if the identification of consent and legitimacy has not discovered this meaning, I am unaware of any preferable alternative.

IX

It has been said that all human relationships are viewed in the light of "value-impregnated beliefs and notions," which determine, shape, and explain them.[21] To his position in the family, the neighborhood, the nation, the world, and the universe, man attaches value interpretations which have been called "myths." Special myths are associated with political relationships,[22] including the most important of all, the relationship between man and his government. The myths of this last relationship are expressed as reasons explaining why government has a moral right to issue regulations backed by force. They relate this right, more or less directly, with the other fundamental "value-impregnated beliefs and notions" which pervade the society. They are propagated by both official and unofficial agencies, by the government on the one hand, and on the other by philosophers, poets, journalists, and social scientists. Their appearance in the traditions of most societies is the primary evidence that governmental legitimacy is an almost universal phenomenon. Under representative government, under the several varieties of dictatorship, under the few remaining traditional aristocracies, and, to some extent, even under modern totalitarianism, one finds these moral reasons why people should submit to the control of their government.

Although it appears normal for men to create and believe in myths of governmental legitimacy, there are times when the governed can neither create their own myths nor accept those created for them. The consent of the governed is a function of the relationship between the way in which government is justified and the general socioeconomic character of the society in question. The more the myths conform to, and are outgrowths of, the experiences, histories, traditions, expectations, and values of all politically significant subgroupings, the more belief in them will be both widespread and firmly held. In addition to this general principle, there are certain objective conditions which indicate that consent is present. Some of these are the frequency and intensity of revolts by classes or areas against the

government; the frequency and severity of punitive measures taken
by the government for political reasons; * the number and intensity
of the sacrifices which the people are willing to make when their
necessity is obvious only to the government; the number of politically
inspired defections from the government's area of control; the degree
to which the people support the government when the latter is unusually unsuccessful in meeting its problems, such as those arising from
a war; and the readiness with which a people resubmits to a government returning to power after having, for some reason, been deposed.

X

It can now be seen that the democratic state is not alone in having
the consent of its governed. The theories which attempt to establish
that it is have been rejected because the aspects of representative
government upon which they rest, while unique, cannot properly be
called "consent." It is thus impossible to use consent to distinguish
between representative and nonrepresentative governments.

Representative government may have, however (as some writers
believe), more consent than any other government. No precise determination of the proportion of the governed that consents to a government can be made, but some rough comparisons appear possible.
Of all governments, that of the democratic state requires the largest
proportion of its citizenry to participate in political decision-making,
and it has the largest proportion of its social classes sharing the
constituent power.† These features suggest that the democratic state
requires the consent of a greater part of its people than does the
nondemocratic state. Well-established monarchies and aristocracies,
although they do not require such widespread consent, have apparently
been considered legitimate by large proportions of their subjects;
and modern dictators have had some success in legitimizing their rule
through direct appeals to the masses. However, monarchy and aristocracy appear obsolescent, and plebiscitary dictatorship seems at best
transient. In view of the political awakening of the masses, one might
conclude that a form of government which institutionalizes their
participation in government, by allowing them an uncoerced and thus
a more or less satisfying choice among alternative candidates, will
be most successful in the long run in retaining their moral support.

It has been shown why an overt act of consent occurs in no

---

* Neither a high rate of crime nor severe penalties for breaking the law
are evidence for a comparative absence of legitimacy. Their causes are not
disaffection with the government but objective social conditions, like an increase in mobility and a decrease in the family's cohesiveness, and prevailing
mores, like the acceptance of torture as a proper mode of punishment.

† By participating in the uncoerced periodic elections, the voters give us
reason to suppose that they would consent if they were given the opportunity
to do so. See the end of section II, above.

democratic state, and, a fortiori, in no nondemocratic state. Several popular attitudes which have been thought to satisfy both the scope and the sense of "consent" have been examined, and it has been argued that a belief in the government's moral right to rule is the only attitude meeting these requirements. Although this belief is not unique to representative government, the myths of the democratic state differ from those of all other states. It remains to identify these special myths and to show how they are related to the other primary political elements of the democratic state.

7: THE POLITICAL MYTHS OF THE DEMOCRATIC STATE

Although representative government is not the only legitimate government, it rests upon a special kind of "consent" because there are special political myths in the democratic state. The expression "political myth" refers to any moral justification of a government's right to direct human behavior and, if necessary, to use physical violence as an aid to this direction. When a person believes one or more political myths, he consents to his government, and a government "has consent" when its political myths are widely accepted. This usage of "political myths" conforms closely enough to usual practice; since only political myths are relevant here, they can be referred to henceforth simply as "myths."

Our analysis must first identify the special myths of the democratic state, which—like representative government, political parties, welfare policy, civil liberties, and popular participation—constitute one of its fundamental political elements. These myths must then be proved essential to the democratic state: they must be shown to be the reasons why the citizenry believes in representative government's moral right to rule; they must be shown to be operative only in the democratic state; and they must be related to the other principal political elements of democracy which have already been explained.

I

A "legitimate" government enjoys the consent of its governed; they believe it to have a moral right to rule them. Legitimacy is not the same thing as political authority; rather, it is a special kind of authority, which in practice is usually an element of the authority possessed by any government. In order to clarify the nature of legitimacy, some of the major elements of authority in general should be briefly examined. This will also aid in understanding the importance of legitimacy to the democratic state.

102

The word "authority" refers to several different types of relationship, which may or may not have some characteristic in common. We are here concerned only with the authority of governments; whether the expert, the parent, and the leader have the same kind of authority need not be considered.[1] Political authority in the democratic state is a phenomenon of organization; it is a direct result of "position," rather than of personal qualities, whether these latter are based on charisma or on expertise.[2]

It is generally accepted that representative governments "possess authority." They are very highly ordered and "structured," and thus very dependent upon position. Their prescriptions are issued in a highly formalized manner, and they emanate from relatively fixed and identifiable sources. These prescriptions, moreover, are followed most of the time by most of the people. There are three principal elements in this situation: the nature of the source of the directive, that is, the position itself; the quality of the communicated directive; and the motives for popular obedience. These three factors are very closely interconnected, but they can be separated for purposes of analysis.

To begin, certain facts are not relevant to an analysis of authority. First, if obedience to a prescription is motivated by the fear of force, either directly or through the medium of habitual response, the relationship is not one of authority. Second, authority is not consistent with an overt act of persuasion, whereby arguments appealing to reason, sentiment, value, or self-interest bring about obedience to a directive. Third, not all acts of obedience to a government which is judged authoritative need be accounted for. Since people obey the laws primarily as a matter of habit, the problem of authority concerns the factors giving rise to this habit, as well as those acts of obedience which are conscious and nonhabitual. Finally, the authoritativeness of individual directives is not dependent upon their always being obeyed. There is, of course, a fundamental connection between authority and obedience: an individual directive's authoritativeness depends on the government's general success in obtaining obedience to the entire body of its directives.[3] But the present investigation deals, by hypothesis, with a situation where the proper amount of obedience occurs.

When a citizen consciously obeys a governmental directive, he may be motivated either by the directive itself or by the source issuing it. If he views the directive as making good sense under the circumstances, authority will always be strengthened. If he conforms to the directive solely because of its reasonableness, the situation is not one of political authority. He must recognize something more in his own relationship to the directive—whether or not he happens to obey it. There is a most important difference between

receiving instructions in an emergency from a private citizen and
receiving them from an officer of the law, even when the instructions
are identically reasonable. Democratic political authority, as said
above, is a concomitant of a position—which implies an organized
hierarchy of positions—and an authoritative communication must
be connected, usually by means of a symbol, to one of the positions of
representative government. The motives for obedience, discussed in
the preceding chapter, which depended upon a "rational" appraisal
of individual laws thus cannot be parts of a relationship of political
authority.

Political authority depends upon the recognition by those
who receive the directives that the latter come from a particular
source—an "authoritative" source. Politically authoritative communications come only from sources accepted by the people at large as
properly possessing political power. In our discussion of consent,
several reasons for such acceptance were mentioned: the people may
believe that their government is in general very successful, or that it
does a good job given its problems, or that it stands between them
and things they desire to avoid. All these attitudes can create political
authority.

A second way in which the people accept their government as
a proper source of control is by believing it, and thus each of its
"official" members, to have a moral right to obedience. This is what
I have called "legitimacy"; it is authority based upon considerations
of morality, rather than upon calculations of expediency.[4] Legitimacy
is no more "irrational" than other varieties of political authority, for
it normally rests upon sound principles of value extending beyond
the sphere of the merely political. A belief in a moral obligation,
however, is usually less subject to conscious scrutiny than a belief
in a material interest. It can thus be compared with what I referred
to (in chapter 6) as the "rational" calculation involved in nonlegiti-
mate authority. Incidentally, defining a legitimate government as
one whose citizens believe it to have a right to rule does not imply
that the government is good by any other standard. It must be determined in each case whether the citizens are correct or mistaken.

The third important element in the relationship of authority is
the nature of the directive itself, but for our present purposes this
need not be examined. It will suffice to say that the directive must be
understandable to the recipient and consistent with his general experiences, expectations, and values. These qualities are necessary for
all kinds of authority.[5]

Although governmental authority usually consists of both expediency and legitimacy, it is possible to identify them separately and
thus to estimate the importance of legitimacy. No one would deny that

the West German Federal Republic in 1960 possessed an authoritative government. This government, however, is not legitimate, because too small a proportion of both the political elites and the general citizenry has thus far accepted the myths of democracy.[6] This lack of full legitimacy is the primary reason why there is doubt about the future of German democracy. The German case illustrates the fundamental place of myths in any state, and it shows why West Germany was not included in the "raw data" of the present study.

II

A legitimate government is, by definition, accompanied by certain political myths which the larger part of its population accepts as valid. In order to be accepted, the myths (as stated in chapter 6) must be consistent with the traditions, experiences, values, and expectations of the people concerned, but they must also be positively connected with the latter. The myths must emphasize those aspects of governmental organization and activity most meaningfully related to nonpolitical life. It follows from this principle that different states exhibit different myths; it also follows that states of the same general type have some myths in common. Myths, in short, may be divided into different types, which can be correlated with different types of governmental institutions and thus with types of policy, political elites, and the other principal political elements of a state. Myths are unique to any type of state for the same reasons that the other elements are unique. Our task here is to discover and explain the myths unique to the democratic state.

To illustrate the kind of thing we are seeking, let us look briefly at one of the most important studies of the political myth, J. N. Figgis' account of the seventeenth-century doctrine of the "divine right of kings." According to this doctrine, the monarchy is a divinely ordained institution, the monarch himself is accountable to God alone, and God enjoins nonresistance and passive obedience to the king's directives. The moral implications of the doctrine cannot be missed; yet it "fit the facts" of the early modern monarchies of England and France. In the first place, there was a single king who at least approximated the exercise of absolute power, and it was to many men's advantage that he did so, as a guarantee that the Pope would fail in his claim to universal sovereignty. This latter claim had familiarized the conception of "absolute freedom from positive law," which made the king's own claim to sovereignty meaningful. Furthermore, the seventeenth century was "an age in which not only religion but theology and politics were inextricably mingled," and the prevailing Christian sentiment considered subjection to government a religious duty. Finally, since the doctrine of divine right was an adaptation of a religious belief, it was consistent with "men's reverence for tradition" and their "instinctive sense that progress can never come by trampling on old institutions." [7] The myths of the democratic state must similarly be connected with institutions, practices, beliefs, and values.

The myths exhibited by all democratic states vary in their individual applications, but these variations are almost exclusively matters of emphasis. Each democratic state, however, has myths that it shares with none of its fellow democracies. This is true of every state, no matter what its type: each state has its own special myths derived from its own particular historical experiences and socioeconomic structure, as well as those myths which correspond to its political type. The most important special myths of the democratic state are connected with its community, which is, invariably, the nation. National myths depend upon the people's sense of belonging to an in-group, and they stress the origins, significant historical happenings, culture traits, and geographical locale of this group. For example, the government of the United States is legitimate because it is the current embodiment of the constitutional principles given by the Founding Fathers, which have served to promote the country's prosperity and which express the peculiar "American genius for ordered innovation."

The myths of the nation are found in all democratic states, but since they also occur elsewhere they are not relevant to the present discussion. However, the latent conflict between the myths of democracy and the myths of the nation should be noted. The former are universal and stress the values of individualism, while the latter are parochial and emphasize the solidarity of the group. Despite this conflict, national myths are apparently indispensable to the democratic state, since it always rests upon a national community.[8] The feelings of fellowship and fatherland appear to be among the most basic human sentiments, and it is instructive to remember that, when crisis threatens the democratic state, appeals to sacrifice are made primarily in terms of patriotism and only secondarily in terms of democratic values.

III

Political myths are to be found in the utterances of politicians, in the formal symbolism of government, in commentaries by leaders of public opinion (clerics, editors of periodicals, and officials of pressure groups), in the textbooks of the lower and higher schools, and in the writings of philosophers and social scientists. They are usually stated not as justifications of governmental control, but as objective descriptions of governmental organization and policy. Yet their moral overtones are unmistakable, and the obvious inference is that the writer or speaker approves of the government because it possesses these characteristics and that he expects his audience to share this approval.

The major political myths of the democratic state have already been discovered. In the order in which they have appeared, they are the reflection of interests, government by typical individuals, freedom and liberty, self-government, government by the people, rule by the majority, government responsible to the people, and government by the consent of the governed.[9] Because representative government has a certain structure (e.g., government by the people) and follows a certain policy (e.g., reflects the interests of the people), it is good government and should be obeyed.[10]

Although most of my examples of democratic myths were taken from the Anglo-American tradition, the myths are just as strong in continental Europe. After all, Rousseau was probably the greatest democratic myth-maker of all time. The strength of democratic mythology in continental thought is well illustrated by Don Luigi Sturzo's account of the presuppositions of Christian Democracy. Democracy must be government of the people, by the people, and for the people; it must possess a scheme of constitutionalism that will ensure a maximum of individual liberty; and it must guarantee to all an equal opportunity for well-being and betterment.[11]

In addition to emphasizing the Anglo-American tradition of democratic mythology, I have drawn my examples almost exclusively from the literature of social science and philosophy. These instances could easily be supplemented by quotations from other sources. Undoubtedly the most eloquent statement of the political myths of democracy, it must be remembered, was given at Gettysburg by President Abraham Lincoln.

Thus far, it has been shown only that these simplified descriptions of democracy are expressed by political activists in the manner and context necessary for genuine political myths. To go beyond this in order to show that the great masses of the modern democratic state accept these myths, we must necessarily rely upon indirect inferences. Both the myths and the people's behavior meet all the conditions for the "consent of the governed" discussed in the preceding chapter. The myths are credible, in the sense that they roughly approximate actual political conditions in the democratic state, and they are propagated by means of the democratic educational systems.[12] The people are capable of understanding the myths, and their behavior has generally corresponded to the specific objective indexes of consent: they show little political disaffection; they will support their governments in emergencies; and, after the liberation of Europe for example, they readily accepted the representative governments re-established in all former democracies.

There has been a tendency among writers to deny that France has maintained a solid belief in the legitimacy of democracy. Sometimes France is linked with Italy and Germany, rather than with Belgium and the Netherlands, as a state which "shows democratic tendencies." This appraisal ignores almost ninety years of democracy interrupted only by military defeat, and it must say that Fascism and Nazism were only accidentally absent from France.

All the evidence favors the vitality of the democratic myths in France. In the early days of the Third Republic, there was disaffection among the conservatives, but there are very good reasons to believe that a constitutional monarch and a more conservatively organized parliament would have satisfied them.[13] French democracy met the critical tests of World War I and the Great Depression. The rise of Hitler prompted some antidemocratic sentiment, but it has never been shown that more than a very small group of the French right disowned democracy.[14] There was no question that the constitution of the Fourth Republic was to be fully democratic. The dissatisfaction which has recently prompted 20 to 25 per cent of the French voters to support the Communists has been only in very small part a denial of democracy.[15] Finally, the constitution of the Fifth Republic is solidly democratic in intent. There is simply no evidence that more than a handful of Frenchmen reject the legitimacy of a government under the control of popularly elected representatives. The disagreement has centered about the questions of how democratic institutions should be constituted and how they should be used to deal with concrete social and economic problems.

Democracy requires political myths for the same reasons that almost all kinds of political authority involve legitimacy, and also for reasons specifically connected with democratic authority itself. Generally speaking, simple authority, based upon considerations of rational self-interest, does not suffice for any government. Legitimacy is required, because the average citizen simply cannot understand everything the government must do and is doing, because any government has great difficulty pleasing more than one special interest at a time, and because men apparently want to believe that the agency which has so much control over them is morally justified.[16]

The democratic state also must possess a fuller authority than most states, because it does not have the techniques of control normally available to governments. In the absence of regimentation and censorship, and with the great reliance upon the democratic commitment of the electorate, democracy would be chaos without authority. The democratic citizen, moreover, is relatively mobile and thus less influenced by those "ties with his society" which prompt law-abidingness. The complexities of representative government, democratic politics, and the democratic society surpass those of any autocracy; authority in the democratic state must thus include a substantial proportion of legitimacy.

It does not follow from these arguments that every citizen of the democratic state believes it legitimate, nor that all who consent do so with the same intensity and for the same reasons. Most of the people more or less strongly accept one or more of the myths of democracy.

IV

To show that the political myths of democracy are sufficient as well as necessary to the democratic state, it must be established that they do not and cannot occur in nondemocratic states. In general terms this is simple to do, because democratic myths, as we have seen, are simplified and approximate descriptions of unique democratic institutions and practices. The occasional occurrence of democratic myths in nondemocratic contexts is somewhat more difficult to explain. However, this discrepancy can be accounted for: nondemocratic governments are unable to persist in their use of the myths; and, in the special case of totalitarianism, the government often deliberately propagates myths that are inconsistent with prevailing political and economic conditions.[17]

Nondemocratic governments make genuine use of democratic myths only in the case of that group consisting of "government of the people," "typical governors," and, in the most frequent form, "government by men of the people." These myths are credible in the democratic state because it is a nation-state with no great barriers to movement from lower to higher social strata. Although the personnel of representative government are not "true samples" of the people, they never originate in a single clearly recognizable social stratum.

But the same situation characterizes most contemporary dictatorships. Where traditions of aristocratic rule have been broken and where the masses are acquainted with the democratic doctrine of the importance of the average man, political leadership is justified by the proper ability or "spirit," and never by a noble ancestry or a high degree of wealth or education. These myths are usually associated with national communities (or with leaders who are trying to construct them), but even totalitarianism, when it is concerned with legitimacy, can take advantage of having "men of the people" in ruling positions.

These variations of "government of the people" thus have no

special connection with the democratic state, where they occur, in fact, much less frequently than other myths more closely connected with the unique features of democracy. When they do occur, as pointed out above, they are usually linked quite frankly with patriotism, and they usually have no specific reference to representative government.

The second group of democratic myths consists of "government for the people" and "government which reflects the interests of the governed." It seems at first glance that they have been used frequently and even emphatically by nonrepresentative governments. All governments influenced by the Western tradition customarily maintain that they are protecting and promoting their subjects' interests. Again, the doctrine of the average man's importance has influenced nondemocratic politics, and "the interests of the people" now must be defined in terms of what the people themselves desire. "Government for the people" means, to any politically self-conscious people, government which does what they want it to do. Since it is impossible to say just what the people of any state want their government to do, nonrepresentative as well as representative governments can claim that in developing the economy or raising standards of health they are reflecting the people's interests. In many of these cases, there is no reason to suppose that the people are dissatisfied with governmental policy.

"Government for the people" and "government which reflects the interests of the governed" have, nevertheless, a special connection with the democratic state. This connection depends upon the general inability (as argued in chapter 3) of nonrepresentative governments consistently to pursue policies of material and social welfare. Contemporary nonrepresentative governments, in any event, have no positive reason to institute and persist in nationwide programs of "social security," and if they did so most of them would only undermine their own power. While autocracies may initially profit from claiming that they promote the welfare of their citizens, they are not able to continue the policies required to fulfill the claim. The only exceptions to this statement are dictatorships—such as that of Turkey's Ataturk—which consciously intend to make themselves eventually obsolete.

The preceding argument rests on the assumption that a government's claim to be operating in the people's interest is most meaningful when based upon the familiar experiences of material well-being and social deference. If this assumption is correct, only the democratic state (and those states moving in a democratic direction) can derive any long-term legitimacy from the myths of "reflection" and "government for the people." Since the special connection between them and democracy is only in the long term, and since dictatorships in their early stages can apparently obtain a favorable popular response by appealing to "national glory" without specific individual benefits, these myths are not as firmly connected to representative government as myths of democracy should be.[18]

<h2 style="text-align:center">V</h2>

The remaining group of myths found in the democratic state—self-government, government by the people, majority rule, government responsible to the people, and government by the consent of the governed—can occur only in conjunction with a representative system of government. Each of them is a variation of the fundamental myth which states: "representative government deserves to be supported and obeyed because it is a system in which the people govern themselves." This statement implies a degree of popular participation in government absolutely incompatible with a nonrepresentative government. Devices like plebiscites or "elections" of officially chosen "candidates" may be referred to as evidence that a ruling group has popular approval, but they can never be interpreted as actual governing or rule by the people. It goes without saying that a dictatorship which attempted to introduce any variety of "government by the people" would only be undermining its own foundations. Even totalitarianism does not propagate such ideas; rather, it emphasizes the role of elites which are supposed to function as "vanguards" of the working class or the *Volk*.

Including "government by the consent of the governed" in this last group of myths might seem a doubtful practice, and it is indeed unclear just what is intended by the remarkably frequent references to consent as a factor justifying representative government. "Consent" originally referred to a popular act, but when the political theorists failed to discover any relevant act, they used it to refer to certain popular attitudes. This sophistication cannot be attributed to those who normally call democracy "government by consent of the governed." The most reasonable conclusion is that the phrase refers only to choosing governors by popular elections, or, more generally, to the fact that many basic political decisions in the democratic state involve the participation of the whole citizenry. If "consent" is meant to refer to an attitude, the intention is probably to indicate no more than a general popular approval of the government. This usage, of course, implies no special connection between consent and democracy.[19]

Publicists often call representative government "free government" and the people of the democratic state "free people," and freedom and liberty are declared to be among the primary values of democracy. To one who has never reflected on political philosophy, "freedom" and "liberty" are probably synonyms which refer to an individual's being able to do what he wants to do. A free people consists of such individuals, and a free government allows them to follow their own inclinations. All this, of course, makes perfect sense to the people of the democratic state for, although only few appreciate the importance of civil liberties, most recognize that the government makes relatively few demands upon them.

Nonrepresentative governments are unable to permit more than a minimum of civil liberty, so the myths of "freedom" are not available to them. Some modern dictatorships have claimed that "true freedom" has no connection with civil liberty and that the individual's freedom results from the strength of the state or the nation. Such sophistication is difficult even for philosophers, and the argument probably makes very little sense to the average citizen of the dictatorship. In addition, the popular tendency to identify freedom and liberty makes it unwise for a dictator to talk too much about freedom. The myths of "freedom and liberty," like the several myths of "government by the people," are the exclusive property of the democratic state.

VI

Political myths serve two primary functions in the democratic state. They reinforce the authority of representative government by basing it upon considerations of moral right, and they provide the electorate with the information it must have to perform its vital task of supporting only those candidates dedicated to democratic goals and procedures. It was seen in chapter 5 that the voter must understand the fundamental principles of representative government; he gets this understanding from the myths, especially those which state that the people govern themselves. These two functions do not imply that each citizen accepts or even understands every myth. A myth's credibility depends to a great extent upon the experience and position of the person concerned. "Popular government" and "welfare government" may make more sense to the less privileged classes, while in order to appreciate "free government" a citizen probably needs a higher degree of education and a wider range of opportunity.[20]

To propagate the myths is not to delude the people, but to convey the essence of democracy to them in the most efficient manner. The myths are not noble lies, but indispensable oversimplifications. This interpretation of the myths does not assume that the people are incapable of understanding more accurate descriptions and explanations of the structure and results of representative government. The "average man" might even profit from exposure to the difficulties and subtleties that unavoidably attend the attempts of political scientists to give a precise analysis of democracy. The main problem is efficiency: everyone cannot be trained as a political scientist without seriously distorting the democratic educational system. The democratic polity no more than the democratic economy requires a popular understanding of its details and its intricacies. The most serious problem facing democracy is not ignorance of the complexity of modern life and modern politics, but disillusion resulting from an acute realization of this complexity. What must be reinforced is vigor and enthusiasm, not the powers of abstract political analysis.

The myths are not tools of "indoctrination," but expressions of the faith of the democratic community. The political scientists who so greatly fear dogmatism, who object to the regimentation implied by the concept of "making good citizens," nevertheless constantly use the slogans of "government by the people," "free government," and "government by consent of the governed," with obvious overtones of moral approval, and they would probably recommend more familiarity with the Gettysburg Address. If they did not do so, they would be shirking their responsibilities as political scientists and teachers. Democratic education does not, however, imply mandatory acceptance of these simple political values, and their difficulties and alternatives can and should always be presented and explained. The political scientist, like any other leader of public opinion, must present his own conclusions and preferences. Again, the articulate minority's propagation of the myths does not create an "opiate of the people" in the democratic state. There is no manipulation by a selfish and cynical elite, and civil liberty always provides an opportunity for the expression of dissenting opinions.[21]

VII

It has been shown why two groups of myths—"government by the people" and "government for the people"—are necessary and sufficient for the democratic state. The myths are found in the democratic state, and they are absent from all other states. Given that representative government must be legitimate, no other myths are available to it.

One of the most important facts of a political system is what its publicists say about it. When the most common statements about democracy are interpreted as political myths, their connections with democracy's other basic elements are made clear. Once again, it has proved most convenient to take the institutions and policy of representative government as the point of departure.

8: THE FOUNDATIONS OF THE DEMOCRATIC STATE

Enlightened common sense and political science have recognized that every political system has important connections with the social, economic, and communal relationships which accompany it. Consequently, they have recognized, at least implicitly, that as governments differ from one another so do societies, communities, and economies. Regarding the democratic state, the latter recognition has usually been explicit, for much attention has been paid to the so-called problem of democratic fundamentals. The democratic state not only tolerates competition and disagreement, but positively encourages these apparently divisive processes to such a surprising extent that most observers have realized that its governmental institutions must rest on unusually strong foundations. The source of this strength, however, has never been clearly determined.

The problem is to discover why political activists and electorates support the procedures and results of representative government. Its authority and legitimacy are necessary and vital to its strength and stability, but meeting the expectations of self-interest and political morality is not sufficient to account for its widespread acceptance. Behind the consent of the governed there are objective circumstances of human life. To support a government, people must not only be educated in and accustomed to its myths but must have expectations to which these myths correspond. From Aristotle's realization that any arrangement of magistracies is accompanied by its own structure of classes to John Stuart Mill's statement that behind a liberal government there must be a liberal society,[1] political science has searched for these objective circumstances.

The last and most difficult part of our analysis is to try to discover the community, society, and economy unique to the democratic state. We must show that this foundation exists in each of the twelve states upon which the inquiry is based, and only in these states; and we must explain why it is both necessary and sufficient for the democratic state. This latter task requires demonstrating how the special communal, social, and economic patterns are related to the other basic political elements of democracy already examined; and the institutions of representative government will once again serve as the focal point of the discussion.

I

Making authoritative policy through a representative system of government allows all organized and unorganized groups to express their grievances and to work for the realization of their policy goals. It further ensures that no group possessing quantitative or qualitative power will be badly discriminated against. The successful operation of representative government means that these groups are satisfied with its results and that they are willing to arrive at them by a method which requires open competition, mutual tolerance, self-restraint, and compromise.[2] Since it is very unlikely that many people prefer the method for its own sake,[3] the groups' support of the system must be based upon what they obtain from it. Nevertheless, their overt agreement is to the democratic "rules of the game," [4] for they differ in the policies they wish enacted and in the degree to which they are satisfied.[5] The results of the system which ensure their allegiance must, therefore, be connected with their long-term interests. The question is not only why the various groups exercise restraint but why they prefer the representative system in the first place.

Consensus on the democratic method must be shared by those relatively large segments of the electorate that can wreck representative government by selecting antidemocratic representatives, and by those relatively small organizations of political activists that can subvert democratic policy-making by intransigently using their direct influence upon elected and appointed governmental personnel and especially by refusing to cooperate in carrying out the latter's decisions. Representative government can tolerate some policy-aspiration organizations that do not follow the rules of compromise and self-restraint, and it can absorb the antidemocratic voting of some segments of the electorate, but these kinds of disaffection are definitely atypical phenomena.

The democratic consensus has been considered problematic because it has been assumed that self-restraint in human affairs requires explanation. Centrifugal forces might be expected to predominate at the level of the relatively short-term interests of the pressure groups, where inability to compromise could be attributed to selfishness and shortsightedness. Representative government allows them to influence policy to their own advantage, and they have proved themselves very willing to do so. The history of pressure-group activity in France and the United States is notorious; even in Great Britain, the most cohesive of the great democracies, the pressure groups frequently insist upon special treatment. Yet somehow disruption never occurs.

Centrifugal forces might also be thought likely to dominate the democratic state at the level of the general expectations of the large "social classes." [6] People obviously differ from one another in many respects, and these differences almost as clearly fall into a number of clusters, but political scientists have never been able to agree just which differences—occupation, social position, income, "ideology," and so forth—are relevant to politics, and just which and how many "classes" should be identified on the basis of these differences. Despite this uncertainty, even superficial descriptions of democratic politics require reference to the working class, the proletariat, the petty bourgeoisie, the middle class, the peasantry, or the farmers. Some theory of social stratification is always assumed, and, whichever it is, it implies that the different "life experiences" of the several classes give rise to different political attitudes and interests, which are "objectively" or "naturally" in opposition to one another. [7] This potential incompatibility might be expected to lead to a party system composed of antagonists capable at best of uneasy truces.

Since every organization is based upon some social stratum, these two levels of possible conflict are closely related. Although the attitudes and interests of an organization are not identical with those of its stratum, they are never radically different. A labor union or chamber of commerce, for example, has specific political aims not shared by all the workers or bourgeoisie, but these aims are refined and detailed expressions of general aspirations associated with the whole of the respective classes. The organization's goals, that is to say, must be based upon the experiences, values, and traditions of the class from which its members are drawn.

The problem of why all the classes and organizations support representative government has been approached in two ways. The first maintains that tolerance and self-restraint result from a "relatively equal distribution of power so that no one group, or combination of them, can dominate over the others." [8] The second suggests that all significant groups share some characteristics inclining them to restraint, no matter how power may be distributed among them at any time. The first approach requires an identification of the groups in so-called equilibrium; it thus depends upon a comprehensive theory of "classes." The other approach need only show that the given characteristics appear in each of the groups that, according to any class theory, could provide divisive tendencies. Since the second approach appears to have superior explanatory power, the foundations of the democratic state can be discussed in the absence of a precise theory of social stratification. It will be necessary only to recognize that certain characteristics are potentially divisive and, as a result, relevant to the question of representative government's support.

II

The first element of the democratic state's foundation is its principal community, the nation.[9] The restraint necessary for representative government depends upon the nation, but the nation alone does not suffice to create this restraint.

The nation is a geographical community coextensive with the boundaries of most modern states. Its essence is the people's identification with one another, their recognition that they all belong to a single group. All settled people are strongly influenced by familiar territory and its familiar inhabitants, and they naturally come to contrast their own villages or provinces with those of other people. As communications improve, this self-identification and self-consciousness can occur among human beings who are not directly known to one another but who inhabit a contiguous territory. The nation is an unusually large community of this type, which requires a quite advanced system of communications.[10] * Its members share certain characteristics, making it both possible and reasonable for them to think of themselves as one large group separate from other similar groups. These characteristics range from the compact area, excellent communications, centralized government, integrated economy, cultural and linguistic homogeneity, and the sharp consciousness of separation from foreigners of the British people, to the common belief in the ideals of "liberty" and "opportunity" of the heterogeneous, dispersed, and (at least originally) territorially indeterminate Americans.[11]

The nation also exhibits this territorial self-identification within all strata of its population. The politically, socially, and economically privileged consider themselves members of the same group as the underprivileged, and they are so considered by the latter. This differentiates the modern nation from the typical community of the Western feudal period, when the aristocracy believed itself to comprise a group quite distinct from the commoners, a belief which the commoners shared. The nation became possible only when the rulers recognized that all kinds of people were important, because they all could contribute to the state's political and economic strength,[12] and it will persist only so long as the privileged retain this primary identification with the masses.[13]

* The nations of the democratic state vary in population from 2,000,000 in New Zealand to 180,000,000 in the United States, the largest community thus far constructed.

All contemporary democratic states are nation-states. Although some contain sharp differences in language, culture, religion, manner of life, and economic behavior, their people think of themselves first as Swiss or Belgian or American and then as German Swiss or Catholic Belgian or Southern American. It is no accident that the democratic state has this kind of community; once people become familiar with the concept of the nation and its linkage of elites and masses, they are unwilling to admit the authority of a government whose personnel are not drawn from their own community. During the twentieth century, all nontotalitarian multinational states have collapsed, no matter how thoroughly autocratic they were. Representative government, with its exceptional reliance upon authority of all kinds, could obviously not operate without electors who believe themselves fundamentally related to one another. The national community is clearly necessary for the mutual tolerance required by the representative system of government.[14]

The national community is as clearly not sufficient for representative government.[15] Empirically, the two do not always coexist. The Italian, German, Spanish, and Portuguese nations in western Europe alone have been ruled by nonrepresentative governments during the twentieth century, and no one expects that when India, Ghana, and Nigeria, for example, develop a full sense of national self-identification, their governments will automatically become fully representative. The prospects for the new democratic institutions in Germany, Italy, and Japan do not depend solely upon the cohesiveness of the German, Italian, and Japanese nations. In fact, "revivals of nationalism" in these states would generally be considered unpropitious for the health of democracy.

The nation is no more than a group of people who identify more strongly with one another than with any other politically relevant group. This identification implies that they will be able to cooperate to some extent in their political life, and it makes possible a governmental legitimacy based on the myths of "government of the people." But there is nothing in the nature of the nation that implies any special distribution of power, institutions of government, or public policy. In this respect, the nation is analogous to the family, and families can be authoritarian or permissive, paternalistic or individualistic, hostile or amicable toward outsiders. Nothing in the composition of a family *ipso facto* prevents internal disagreements, disputes, intransigence, and irresponsibility.[16] Not only does the nation not imply the fundamental "agreement" which supports the centrifugal effects of representative government, but its existence provides no information about why the people of the democratic state positively prefer representative government to all possible alternatives. The nation is necessary but not sufficient for the democratic state.

III

In addition to a national community, the foundation of the democratic state consists of special social and economic relationships, which help to provide the stability required for representative government and which determine the positive preference shown it by both the political elites and the electorate. In the case of democracy, social factors appear to depend to a great extent upon economic factors, so it will be convenient to discuss the latter first.

It has long been recognized that there is an important connection between democracy and what is called the "middle class." The middle class is usually credited with a major role in the democratic state's development in western Europe, and it is often said that the present chances for democracy in underdeveloped areas depend upon the creation of a strong middle class. In these contexts, "middle class" usually refers to the bourgeoisie, the petty bourgeoisie, and the so-called independent professionals, although the importance of a landholding peasantry—and thus, where necessary, of land-reform programs—is frequently recognized. However, no one-to-one correlation can be found between democracy and any "middle class" defined in terms of occupations. Occupational groups other than the bourgeoisie, peasants, and professionals are loyal supporters of our twelve representative governments; the petty bourgeoisie and small farmers have periodically supported antidemocratic movements in Italy, Germany, and even France and the United States; [17] and the large bourgeoisie often has strong authoritarian tendencies.

If attention is turned from economic functions ("work situations") to material possessions or standards of living ("market situations"), a significant correlation can be discovered between modern representative government and a stratum of people which can reasonably be called a "middle class." This middle class, as Aristotle said, "possesses the gifts of fortune in moderation," [18] and to distinguish it from other groups I shall call it the "Middle Class."

In the modern democratic state, individuals from all occupational and social strata and from all localities belong to the Middle Class. Agrarians, proletarians, bourgeoisie, professionals, and black-coated and white-collared workers all possess the gifts of fortune in moderation; and all organized policy-aspiration groups of the democratic state, although they represent the special interests of labor, business, and agriculture, are drawn from and based upon the Middle Class. A comprehensive theory of social stratification is therefore not required in order to understand the foundations of democracy.

The Middle Class's possessions are both material and nonmaterial, but the latter are always translatable into the former. These possessions include the basic necessities of life; the requisites of a decent life, such as medical care and education; and luxuries such as mechanical means of transportation and household appliances. The nonmaterial possessions include money, job security, opportunity for occupational advancement, membership in organizations such as labor unions and business and professional associations, and expectations of income in the event of illness, unemployment, and superannuation.[19]

Material goods become possessions when an individual has a claim to receive and dispose of them which is backed by law and thus by the government's power and authority. This claim is never absolute, for property is always "a conditional equity in the valuables of the community";[20] but the degree to which receiving material goods is guaranteed, the degree to which their disposal is at the individual's pleasure, and the degree to which the conditions placed upon both are clearly defined and regularized are all enormously significant. "Possessing the gifts of fortune" implies a relatively high degree of each; it implies, that is, having a firm claim to the elements of what we now call a "standard of living."

The possessions of the Middle Class are "moderate" in quantity. Moderation in this context is relative to the needs and expectations of a society and to the distribution of possessions within it. In a mild climate, for example, the number of possessions meeting the standard of moderation is smaller than where the climate is extreme. Similarly, fewer possessions are needed to meet this standard in a society unaccustomed to lavishness: a bicycle in Asia, for example, is comparable to a motorscooter in western Europe, and both compare to an automobile in North America. Cultural preferences are also relevant to moderation: a people exacting about food and relatively indifferent to housing and clothing (as has been said of the French) can have a moderate standard of living with fewer total possessions than another Middle-Class group with reversed preferences. Finally, simple material comfort would not be moderate in a society where a very wealthy stratum was sharply and obviously separated from a modestly situated group. Such sharpness of contrast applies between societies as well, as evidenced by European dissatisfaction upon acquaintance with American affluence.

The relative nature of moderation in possessions depends primarily upon subjective factors. A person's level of material well-being is moderate when, after comparing himself with others, he believes it to be moderate. However, there is also an absolute element in moderation. A moderate standard of living implies both physical and social comfort; it is beyond bare subsistence on both counts. The person with a moderate number of possessions does not anticipate serious difficulty in meeting all his dependents' necessities or in meeting the minimum standards of what his society considers materially acceptable.

IV

All the principal occupational strata of the democratic state belong to the Middle Class. In nondemocratic states, on the contrary, the Middle Class is small and restricted to only a few occupations.

It is a commonplace that democratic states have the world's highest standards of living, and states which approach them in material well-being are ordinarily considered good prospects for democracy. This general knowledge is supplemented by the available relevant statistics. The most important of these are the figures for annual per capita incomes, which, as one authority has said, "reveal a fairly clear pattern of the contrast between abundance and scarcity." [21] In 1938, the annual per capita income of the democratic states ranged from $567 in New Zealand to $260 in France; in 1948, the range was from $1,525 in the United States to $418 in France. The group with the next highest incomes included those states operating democratic institutions at that time or showing some democratic potential. In 1938, their incomes ranged from $186 in the Union of South Africa and Argentina to $154 in Austria; in 1948, from $368 in Austria to $296 in Cuba.[22] * Omitting the United States, which is atypical even of democracies, the annual per capita income of the democratic states in 1948 was $669, while the income for the second highest group was $333. Two thirds of the world's states (and the overwhelming proportion of its population) had per capita incomes considerably lower than that of Austria, in 1938, and Cuba, in 1948. These figures give a rough measure of what I have called the state's "standard of living"; they indicate the pattern of distribution within the state.

Other statistics show the distribution of certain material possessions—particularly automobiles, telephones, and radios—which are closely associated with a high standard of living.[23] Although care must be taken in using these figures, since different cultures, even within the general democratic milieu, may prefer or require different patterns of consumption, it is significant that the democratic states have more of all three mechanisms per capita than any other states, and that the second group of states distinguished above has the second

---

* States included in 1938 were South Africa, Argentina, Czechoslovakia, Chile, Spain, Yugoslavia, Finland, Hungary, and Austria; in 1948, Austria, South Africa, Czechoslovakia, Uruguay, Venezuela, Argentina, and Cuba.

widest distribution, with the rest of the world coming far behind.[24]

The Middle Class results from an economy characterized by relatively high productivity and by a pattern of distribution that allows only rare instances of poverty, but it does not depend on any particular type of production. Manufacturing can predominate, as in Great Britain and Belgium; or the economy can be basically extractive, as in Norway and Canada; or it can be primarily agricultural, as in Denmark and New Zealand. The important point is that these different economies have raised the standard of living of all social strata to a level which the peasant, proletarian, and white-collar worker of central and southern Europe, for example, cannot begin to approach.

The only characteristic which seems necessary to the democratic system of production is that it be based upon a price system. The people must be confident that their labor and material goods will retain a more or less constant value over a medium-range period, because the security provided by a moderate level of possessions is absent when the government can shift at will the monetary value of labor and material goods or the real value of money. Property, as said above, is a right or claim to share in the community's valuables. The Soviet economy has provided the primary example of a non-price organization for production, and it has aided the Communists in keeping the people's standard of living at a low level.[25]

V

A man who possesses the gifts of fortune in moderation, said Aristotle, is "most ready to follow rational principle." This "rationality" is basically an attitude of prudence, for a moderate amount of property inclines the Middle-Class man to pursue a cautious course in all of his various activities. He can afford to jeopardize neither his modest material holdings nor his intermediate social position; he quite obviously has something to protect, and he does not have a great amount of power for the purpose. This Middle-Class attitude differs rather sharply from the predominant attitudes of both the very rich and the very poor, who, by the nature of their positions, are much less inhibited. The poor have neither material possessions nor social reputations to lose, and the rich feel secure in both respects no matter how they behave.

Because the security of the Middle-Class man requires protection, he usually remains unmoved by conflicts based upon abstract principles. Struggles over religious and other "ideological" matters appear to him dangerous or at least unprofitable. He takes a pragmatic view of the great issues of life, for he fears that any rigorous doctrine may have unseen implications which could affect his own position. He is concerned primarily with his own affairs, he is not interested in crusades to convert others to a point of view or manner of living, and he resists attempts by others to revise his own beliefs and practices.

Thus far, the Middle-Class man appears to be an unmitigated conservative, expending all his effort to preserve things precisely as they are. But the Middle-Class attitude has another facet. Moderate holdings give rise to moderate self-confidence and moderate expectations of improving one's position, and the Middle-Class man is willing to risk something to increase his standard of living. The gifts of fortune in moderation provide enough security and independence to stimulate adventures in quest of more security and independence, but they do not provide so much that the adventures become rash. In addition, the aspirations of the Middle-Class man are oriented toward the market, and they are thus based on the least dangerous and least violent of motivations. They are not normally directed toward increasing one's power over other men, but toward improving one's independence of them.[26]

According to the Middle Class, the proper condition of government is to be sufficiently strong to maintain the stability necessary for protecting a moderate amount of property, but not so strong that it might threaten these holdings. The Middle-Class man is also not averse to using government to improve his own position as well as to protect it. This implies some control over government, but to exercise extensive control is beyond the perspective of the Middle Class. The man with moderate possessions feels relatively independent of and detached from government, but he is certainly not indifferent to it.[27]

The typical attitudes of the very rich and the very poor regarding government are quite different. When the rich do not actively support autocratic government as a means of keeping the lower strata in their "proper" stations,[28] they are not greatly concerned about concentrated governmental power: they believe themselves strong enough to protect their interests from any autocrat, even when they realize he cannot be made their instrument.[29] The poor, on the other hand, when not simply politically apathetic, feel they have little to lose to any autocrat and possibly something to gain. They have traditionally been willing to support autocratic movements which promise programs of amelioration, no matter how unrealistic.[30]

The Middle-Class attitude of prudence can predominate in a society with rather striking material inequalities. When the society's values and beliefs are set by a dominant Middle Class, even the impoverished can share its prudence, provided that they believe improvement of their own positions is possible.[31] This belief need not be based on a careful calculation of their opportunities. If they consider themselves, on the basis of some actual examples of "rags to riches," eligible for unexpected strokes of luck, then their resentment toward the privileged and frustration at their own inferiority will be of secondary political importance.[32] A group can also drop from the Middle Class into poverty and still retain its habitual attitude of caution. This possibility was exemplified by the mild reaction of the democracies' peoples to the depression of the 1930's; but the duration of such a habit is no doubt limited, perhaps to a single generation.

When all social strata and policy-aspiration organizations share the attitude of the Middle Class, the restraint, tolerance, and willingness to compromise that are necessary for the operation of representative government are present. Even if the strata and the pressure groups do not grant their respective rivals' right to pursue their self-interest, which they may consider directly competitive, their action is still restrained by the naturally limited character of their own demands. Economic interests, moreover, are the simplest of all divisive factors to modify and compromise; the differences, so to speak, can always be split.[33] Finally, the Middle-Class attitude best provides the admiration for honesty, efficiency, and technical competence in governmental personnel, shown in chapter 5 to be a principal characteristic of democratic electorates.

The Middle-Class foundation of the democratic state is not a "power equilibrium" among strata or political elites. Occasionally a balance of forces may result from the Middle-Class political process, but it is not the basic cause of democratic restraint. If power is countervailed by power, the situation has occurred and persists only because of mutual tolerance. The check which labor and management exercise on each other, for example, is no more a result of their equal power potentials than the representation of minority parties on French and American legislative committees and the British guarantee of the Opposition's parliamentary rights are the results of an equilibrium of party strength.

The Middle-Class society exhibits a diffusion of power rather than an approximately equal distribution of power. This diffusion results from the Middle Class's tendency to personal independence and from the freedom of association and relatively easy access to points of decision-making which accompany representative government. But diffusion of power does not by itself imply the tolerance and willingness to compromise required by representative government; as has been said, a diffusion of power like that of the democratic state but including intransigent participants would certainly produce different results.[34]

Once the representative system of government has been established and accepted, the diffusion of power, encouraged by what has been called the "overlapping" of loyalties or interests,[35] has the highly significant effects described in chapters 3 and 4. Pressure groups in the democratic state may be able to exercise a veto over some items of public policy, but, even in the area of their most intense interests, they refrain from pressing their advantage to the limits of their power.[36]

VI

The argument has thus far been that the stability supporting the divisive propensities of representative government is provided by the Middle-Class society. It is more difficult to show why the Middle Class is sufficient, as well as necessary, for the democratic state; to prove that, when Middle Classes predominate, governments will invariably be representative.

The typical Middle-Class person, as said above, desires a government capable of protecting and promoting his interests, but not capable of wielding too much power. As a consequence, he is strongly predisposed to some kind of "constitutionalism," to some regularized restraint upon the actions of government. The ideal arrangement would seem to be pure democracy, where each individual can directly influence governmental action and guard against undue concentrations of political power. However, even in a polity small enough for pure democracy, the Middle-Class man prefers to devote his time to personal affairs and to leave the business of governing to "delegates" whom he selects from among his peers. Although he does not expect these "delegates" to be in complete sympathy with all his interests, he believes that his access to them is assured—at the very least through his franchise—and that they will be as wary of undue governmental power as he himself would be. He believes, in short, that he enjoys government of, by, and for people like himself.

The contemporary democratic state came into existence when small Middle Classes, composed of bourgeoisie and petty bourgeoisie, set up representative governments with restricted electorates and at least partially indirect elections. As economies became more productive and living standards rose, unfranchised social strata moved into the Middle Class and promptly began to agitate for the vote. Universal suffrage was achieved gradually, with modest property qualifications for eligibility expressing the recognition that representative government could be operated only by a Middle Class.[37] The newly enfranchised strata invariably gave their full support to the principles of democratic politics.

Despite constant fears of radicalism, the older sections of the Middle Class had good reasons to acquiesce in the political rise of the

newer sections. In order to resist the latter's demands for enfranchisement and, at the same time, avoid discontent of revolutionary proportions, proscribing even the mention of these aspirations would have
been necessary; but such censorship would have been incompatible
with representative government and eventually destructive of democracy, which the old Middle Class wanted to preserve. Furthermore,
there was really no point in denying a share in government to the
rising strata; although the power and prestige of the bourgeoisie
would no doubt be reduced to some extent, the rising strata belonged
or aspired to the Middle Class and had policy interests which were
basically economic and not difficult to satisfy. In addition, one or
more of the existing bourgeois parties usually hoped to enlist the
votes of these political newcomers—another example, incidentally, of
the parties' integrative function.[38]

The incorporation of the industrial proletariat into the Middle
Class is one of the great accomplishments of the democratic state.
Despite Marxist predictions, proletariats in all democracies have
become firm supporters of representative government, for their rising
standards of living have given them a large stake in prudent, efficient,
and limited government.[39] In addition to an unprecedented quantity
of material possessions, proletarians must now protect cooperatives,
family allowances, pension plans, guaranteed annual wages, unemployment and accident compensation, and the rights of their trade
unions. Although the aggressiveness of working-class parties and pressure groups reflects the relatively low material and deference positions
of their clientele, they nevertheless operate fully within the context
of the representative system. Being unable to anticipate new forms
of property, and failing to appreciate the potency of the gifts of
fortune in moderation, both Marx and Jefferson mistook the urban
proletariat as fundamentally undemocratic.

VII

Practically every politically influential group in the democratic
state belongs to the Middle Class, and whenever any group anywhere
becomes Middle Class, it also becomes a champion of representative
government. This Middle-Class democratic bias can be clearly seen
in the political history of certain nondemocratic states. The unsuccessful struggle for democracy in Japan, from 1853 until 1941, illustrates
particularly well how the several social strata of the modern state
support, oppose, and are indifferent to representative government.

When Japan was opened to foreign intercourse, she was strongly
influenced by French ideas of democracy and German ideas of authoritarianism. The ruling cabinet of nobles and soldiers, following

Bismarck's theory of strengthening autocracy, established a parliament which was elected but given little power. This action was intended to show the West that Japan was modern and strong and that therefore the disadvantageous treaties which she had been forced to accept should be revoked.[40] When the treaties were finally eliminated, official support of the Diet rapidly diminished. Preserving the Diet and expanding its functions then became principal goals of the several sectors of the Japanese Middle Class.

From 1890 until 1914, the Diet depended upon merchants, small industrialists, and landholders of modest proportions;[41] in 1898, for example, 70 per cent of its members were medium-sized farmers.[42] White-collar workers, teachers, and newspaper personnel soon joined the proparliament group and, in conjunction with the merchants and industrialists, gradually replaced the agrarians as the Diet's most numerous supporters. The Diet steadily increased its power until 1918, when (with an unprecedented war-occasioned prosperity) only a cabinet drawn from the parliamentary parties could maintain itself in office.[43] Until 1900, only 1 per cent of the total population was enfranchised; from 1900 until 1920, about 3 per cent; and from 1920 until 1925, about 8 per cent. In 1925, universal male suffrage was introduced through the initiative of the parties.[44]

During the early 1920's, the elected parliament had almost full control of all governmental policy, but democracy's chances were ruined by the Great Depression. Wartime prosperity had been accompanied by the concentration and partial cartelization of capital and industry,[45] which meant that most of the urban Middle Class had become wage-earners particularly susceptible to the reduction of economic activity at home and the world-wide movement to protectionist tariffs. The war had also brought about a consolidation of landholdings, which created large numbers of tenant farmers and agricultural laborers. These filled the ranks of the army, whose officers were almost exclusively rural in origin. The army was the most important antidemocratic element in the interwar period,[46] confronting the political parties and eventually triumphing when the latter's Middle-Class foundation crumbled.

To a great extent, the balance of power in the postwar struggle for democracy was held by the *zaibatsu*, the great family corporations and cartels which came to dominate the Japanese economy. During the prosperity of the 1920's, the *zaibatsu* were anxious to use representative institutions and democratic sentiment to check the strength of the military; they regularly gave large sums of money to the parties, and they even enlisted support for them from the working class and peasantry.[47] But, when the depression created an urban-leftist radicalism, the *zaibatsu* allied with the military and assisted the "patriotic societies" which served as the latter's hatchet men. This shift illustrates the indifference of the rich and powerful to representative government, as well as their belief that they are able to maintain themselves in an autocratic state. The undermining of the Middle Class and the defection of the *zaibatsu* put an end to Japan's first experiment in democracy.

The preference of the Middle Class for representative government and the destruction of both by the Great Depression are also exemplified in German political history. In explaining how Imperial Germany combined a modern economy with an archaic political system, historians stress the failure of the bourgeoisie, the Middle Class of the nineteenth and early twentieth centuries, to get control of the machinery of government.[48] When a representative government was finally realized after the Empire's disintegration, its principal initiators and most faithful defenders were the Socialist party and the labor unions, the spokesmen for the urban proletariat.[49] This very significant development resulted from the proletariat's entry into the Middle Class. Under the Empire, increasing industrial productivity, the excellent organization of the working-class movement, and Bismarck's program of social welfare had steadily raised the industrial worker's standard of living, until he came to possess the gifts of fortune in moderation.[50]

Another interesting example of the Middle Class's support of democratic government comes from Cuba. In the decade 1938–48, Cuba's per capita income relative to the rest of the world had doubled, putting her in the second most prosperous group of states.[51] In 1958, the dictatorship of Fulgencio Batista was overthrown by a movement led by Fidel Castro. One of the clearest accounts of this "revolution" states that the "most thoughtful and articulate supporters (and sympathetic critics) of Castro's movement [were] precisely among the groups that had the most to risk in a time of turmoil and anarchy." These supporters were the "professional and middle class"—retailers, small manufacturers, and especially doctors. Rotary officials maintained contact with the rebels, and country clubs "were frequently the rendezvous of rebel sympathizers. . . . Like their counterparts elsewhere in Latin America, the Cuban middle classes are in revolt against the whole tradition of government that has held the region in thrall. Graft, favoritism, police brutality, profligate waste of public funds, neglect of education, and rule by military and landed oligarchs —all these are the venerable afflictions which the emerging Latin middle class seeks to eliminate or at least moderate." [52] In Cuba as elsewhere, when an occupational stratum possesses the gifts of fortune in moderation, it initiates and supports movements against arbitrariness and for constitutionalism. Its ultimate goal is always representative government.*

VIII

To show more clearly that the political dominance of a Middle Class is always accompanied by a representative system of government (and not just that representative government depends upon a Middle Class), let us briefly examine the possibility that another form of government could as satisfactorily serve the needs and interests of the Middle Class.

The Middle Class's most important contemporary political problem is to maintain the protection and assistance that only a large complex of administrative hierarchies can provide, while ensuring that these governmental agencies do not themselves become a threat to its relatively vulnerable material, status, and power positions. The bureaucracy must not be left with final political decision, because its necessarily hierarchical structure would sharply limit the influence that could be exerted on any of its subordinate positions. To say this in another way, the bureaucracy's top officials would have too much power for the taste of the Middle Class. These officials might maintain high standards of efficiency and impartiality, but such responsibility is not the primary goal of the Middle Class. The Middle Class could not rely solely upon its organized pressure groups; without independent authority of their own, they would be obliged to wait on the bureaucracy's convenience.

The Middle Class must have some kind of regularized check upon the administrative agencies, and the only alternative to representative government seems to be a scheme which would give governmental authority to pressure groups. The most feasible arrangement would be some variety of "functional representation" or "corporativism," whereby the ultimate power of decision-making would be in the hands of a body chosen from social strata rather than from geographical areas. This kind of governmental system has not found favor with the Middle Class in the past, nor is it institutionally suited to a Middle-Class society.

"Functional representation" has, until now, been adopted only by dictatorships; its support has come from the entrenched rich, the underprivileged proletariat, or the declining petty bourgeoisie.[53] From an institutional point of view, the complexity and divisiveness of deciding which strata were to have how many seats in a "Chamber of Corporations" would prevent any Middle Class from embracing

---

* Castro's betrayal of his Middle-Class supporters in favor of a demagogic appeal to the least privileged provides a classical illustration of the risks involved in revolting for democratic purposes.

functionalism. Almost no one would believe that his interests were properly "represented." He would feel that his occupation's importance warranted a larger proportion of the chamber's seats, or that he had been improperly classified, or that his nonoccupational interests were more important. No scheme of "functional representation" is practicable in a complex Middle-Class society, for no group is willing to put all its political eggs into the single basket of its corporate deputies. Even if functionalism were instituted, it would be much too inflexible to meet the problems of a Middle-Class society.[54] Influence on a deputy would be restricted to those private citizens belonging to his occupational electorate; and, according to the organizability of the interests, the chamber would be either immobilized through intransigence or torn apart by dissension.[55]

There appear to be no other devices for controlling the bureaucracy which are not themselves hierarchical. Any kind of aristocracy is unthinkable, and the Middle Class is too conscious of degrees of ability to choose its governors by lot. It seems reasonable to conclude that only representative government meets the needs, interests, and expectations of the Middle Class.

IX

To function as the foundation of democracy, the national community and the Middle-Class society must be accompanied by a particular pattern of social deference. Deference, or "status" as Max Weber called it, is the degree of honor accorded a man by the norms of his society.[56] Different ways of life, systems of value, cultural traits, occupations, physical characteristics, and so forth lead to hierarchies of status in every society. There are definite degrees of status in the democratic state, but its status structure resembles the distribution pattern of its material goods in that the great majority of its people are accorded a moderate degree of honor. In a democracy, no significant groups are in an unapproachably superior social position, and no large groups are treated as pariahs. This implies that any individual can rise on his merits to a moderate position of honor.

Honor in moderation has precisely the same political implications as a moderate standard of living. Men who are neither aristocrats nor untouchables will follow rational principle; they will be willing to compromise, and they will desire an effective but restrained government. Again, those at the extremes will see no special threat in autocracy; they will believe either that they have little to lose or that they are incapable of losing.[57]

In most cases, the democratic pattern of social deference results from the predominance of the Middle Class. A person's deference is usually related to his standard of living and the importance of his economic role. The status of the proletarian, for example, rose as he became more important as both producer and consumer. While his increased political power also contributed to his enhanced social position, his enfranchisement itself was usually a consequence of his advance to the Middle Class. Nevertheless, deference does not always keep pace with living standards. Even in a prosperous national community, serious discriminations can be practiced toward occupational, religious, cultural, or ethnic groups; deference, therefore, must be treated as a variable independent, at least in the short run, of standard of living.

Although all groups in the democratic society are not given the same degree of honor, none is worshiped and none is despised. The principal exceptions to this generalization occur in the treatment of the European proletariat and North American racial minorities. Much of the discrimination against them, however, is mitigated by a kind of vicarious honor which they experience when individuals from their ranks are "accepted," for one reason or another, by the dominant social strata. The participation of European Socialist politicians and labor union leaders in their countries' highest political and economic decisions has done much to satisfy the social aspirations of the working classes; [58] and, in the United States, the pre-eminence of individual Negroes in fields like popular music and athletics has been a source of pride and self-esteem to the whole Negro population. Governments in the United States are presently attempting to increase the deference shown racial minorities by means of so-called civil rights legislation. It remains to be seen whether legally sanctioned honor will be as successful as legally created economic security.

Impregnable status differentials are incompatible with representative government because any kind of caste system would restrict the suffrage to the dominant status group, which would then eventually face the alternative of granting the vote to the lower groups or abandoning uncoerced elections. Since the lower groups cannot be kept ignorant of democratic principles without a degree of censorship inconsistent with representative government, they will sooner or later demand their own enfranchisement. The parties which compete for the votes of the dominant strata must be especially restrained, for they must maintain unanimity on the absolute political unfitness of the inferior status groups.[59] Finally, the continual frustration of the lower strata's demands for political influence will tend to make them less and less democratically inclined. Democracy is simply incompatible with a pattern of deference that does not permit all groups eventually to share in the business of government.

Even when universal suffrage has been established, social discrimination sometimes leads to antidemocratic behavior. There is evidence that the French and Italian proletariats vote Communist not only because of their poverty but also because they believe that the bourgeoisie find them socially unacceptable; occasionally very highly paid workers have been strong supporters of the Communists.[60] All democratic states must solve the problem of social discrimination as well as the problem of poverty. These are separate problems, although the elimination of poverty, and thus of personal and cultural differences, often goes far toward eliminating discrimination.

X

Representative government rests on the foundation of the nation and the Middle Class. The national community is necessary for the democratic state, but the Middle Class, which is politically dominant in all democracies and relatively impotent in all nondemocratic states, is both necessary and sufficient. Such a correlation cannot be drawn between representative government and any other politically significant phenomenon which could possibly serve as its foundation. Industrial, extractive, pastoral, and agrarian economies are found in both democratic and nondemocratic contexts. Democracies and dictatorships have been involved in the great interstate political struggles of the modern era, and both have been isolated from them. The "cultural tradition of the West" has prevailed in autocracies, and its absence does not warrant denying the possibility of democratic development.

Representative government and the Middle Class always occur in conjunction because the former is the best possible system of government by which the latter can enjoy helpful but limited political power. Once this kind of power is instituted, the conditions necessary for the remaining principal elements of the democratic state are created. Parties arise to conduct the elections, and their competition stimulates welfare policy and guarantees civil liberties. Representative government requires participation by the people, who come to have the requisite levels of education and sophistication. After the system has been established, the myths of government of, by, and for the people become customary and traditional, and the government possesses the consent of its governed.

Although this great superstructure rests on the foundation of the Middle Class, and although I have frequently spoken in terms of individual motivation, the argument does not assume that the citizens of the democratic state consciously desire all the specific results of representative government, nor does it assume that they are even aware of all of them. In the case of civil liberties, for example, the ordinary member of the Middle Class is concerned only with his own ability to pursue his own limited and probably pedestrian desires. He is probably more distrustful than tolerant of unrestricted discussion in science, art, religion, morality, and politics; yet he supports a system of government that provides a remarkable and unprecedented degree of civil liberty.

The democratic state thus possesses certain institutions of government, within which a special kind of leadership follows a given procedure to make decisions embodying a particular type of policy. The governed stand in a special relationship to their government; they have characteristic beliefs about it and attitudes toward it; and they have distinctive communal, economic, and social interrelationships. All these elements are parts of a complex and unique whole, the democratic state, and each is a necessary and sufficient condition of all the others.

9: THE PROSPECTS FOR THE DEMOCRATIC STATE

The political scientist, naturally enough, has a vested interest in his painfully acquired knowledge of the government and politics of democracy, and the citizen of the democratic state understandably has a practical commitment to his accustomed way of life. These interests by themselves make the future of the democratic state an issue of paramount importance, but this importance ultimately depends upon more profound considerations. Not only does the democratic state have the sole form of legitimate government capable of maintaining domestic peace and national independence under twentieth-century conditions, but, despite certain aberrations, it has been remarkably successful in realizing the traditional political values of Western civilization.

In examining the prospects for democracy, I shall attempt no prophecies. I intend only to use my analysis of the democratic state to try to identify the problems most likely to confront democracy and to estimate democracy's ability to meet them. It should be possible to say something about the future ability of democratic institutions to deal with their citizens' expectations, to maintain their own legitimacy, to meet the challenge of the emergent underdeveloped areas, to check undue concentrations of power within their own jurisdictions, to overcome restrictive parochialism, and to protect themselves from military defeat and internal subversion. Since democracy requires extensive popular political responsibilities, its viability also depends upon the future capabilities and attitudes of the people and their leaders.

All these problems have been raised before. The present chapter's primary purpose is to separate those which cast serious doubts on democracy's future from those which have been exaggerated. Despite current apprehensions, the pattern of things to come, rather than straining democracy beyond its capacity, may well prove its vitality.
134

1

In order to put our speculations about democracy's future in their proper perspective, it will be useful to review briefly the reasons why democracy is worth preserving. This review will also help us later to weigh the charge that the democratic state suffers from a so-called lack of faith.

A moral evaluation of the democratic state logically implies a complete system of ethics, including a detailed account of what constitutes a "good man" and what material, social, and personal conditions are necessary for his development. Such a system cannot be presented here; it must suffice to say that each man should fully realize his human potentialities, which means that his share of mankind's unique rational, spiritual, moral, and artistic capabilities should be utilized to its fullest in striving for the scientific, esthetic, and ethical ideals which make up the core of civilization. The successful utilization of these capacities depends upon, among other things, certain political conditions; the ideal political situation, that is to say, is instrumental to the higher ideal of personal human excellence.

What government does and fails to do is the immediate subject matter of political ethics. Evaluating the democratic state thus means concentrating upon the policy of representative government. However, since all governments are combined with special economic and social circumstances, an evaluation of the former necessarily implies a like evaluation of the latter. This ethical connection between representative government and the Middle-Class society has not always been recognized.

In Western ethical writing, the concept of "freedom" has included the indispensable conditions for realizing human potentialities. Generally speaking, a man is free when he is not impeded, by material or social or personal factors, in fully employing his uniquely human resources.[1] Western philosophers have long recognized that the use or threat of violence by other men is a very grave impediment to such behavior, and they have sought ways to limit and regularize it. Assuming (as I have done throughout) that government practically monopolizes violence, this aspect of freedom is identical with what I have called "civil liberties."

In chapter 4, it was shown how and why a representative government must allow the liberties of speech, press, association, and religion. It was also shown how and why no other modern form of government can permit them. Representative government thus meets the first criterion of political freedom.

It was apparently more difficult for the philosophers to recognize the second principal element of political freedom, the phenomenon called "positive freedom" by T. H. Green. The conscious will of other men is not the only potential impediment to the individual's self-realization; his social, material, and even psychological circumstances can also be powerful hindrances. When government is the only agency able to eliminate these restrictive circumstances, it has a moral responsibility to do so. Ignorance, poverty, illness, and economic insecurity have generally been accepted as restrictions that can be overcome only with the aid of government. As the productivity, economic organization, mobility, education, and communications of the industrial society have undermined the traditional pattern of small communities and tangible property, governments have taken on an increasing number of these responsibilities. This is the unavoidable price of the contemporary "open society."

The basic justification of the so-called welfare state is its provision of positive freedom. Security, welfare, and even the classic notion of political equality make sense only when seen as instrumental in eliminating undue restrictions upon men's opportunities to realize their potentialities. Europeans have tended to take the concept of equality quite literally, assuming it desirable that everyone have the same material possessions and social prestige. The American idea has usually been "equality of opportunity," [2] which more closely approximates the notion of positive freedom, for absolute equality is possible only where individual differences are as yet unrecognized or where totalitarianism has made all men equal in helplessness and insecurity. Nonetheless, strict equality of opportunity itself requires a regimentation incompatible with civil liberties.

By guaranteeing a minimum level of material and social well-being to all its people, representative government comes remarkably close to satisfying this second principle of political ethics. Neither absolute equality nor strictly equal initial opportunities are provided or sought, but only relatively few people find that a reasonable amount of effort fails to bring them the facilities necessary for their self-development. Despite accusations to the contrary, no representative government has ever consciously attempted to "level" its citizens or to force them into some kind of conformity.[3]

There has been a tendency, especially among Americans, to view material well-being as an end in itself. Green clearly saw positive freedom as instrumental to higher goals,[4] but the increasing comfort of life under democracy and the theoretical principle of the reflection of interests have combined to raise it to an ultimate value in human life. The principle of interest reflection emphasizes the positive or welfare aspect of democratic public policy, which it presumes incorporates the highest political desires of the people. Because it is generally held that representative government is good government and that democracy somehow should be "for all the people," this view naturally leads to the ethical position that the final goal of politics is to give the people "what they want." The result can very easily be a vulgar hedonism, recognizing no values higher than physical comfort.

Curiously enough, in their concrete manifestations, the political values of "positive" and "negative" freedom are incompatible in the short run. Whenever government's coercive power must be used to provide minimum standards of living and degrees of status, liberty is necessarily restricted. The foremost problem of practical democratic policy is to find the proper balance at all times and under all circumstances between the two freedoms. Any law can be judged in these terms, as can any failure to legislate. But, in the long run, liberty and welfare are absolutely dependent upon each other, for when the government is representative both are present, and when the government is not representative both are absent.

All other features of the democratic state are valuable insofar as they are instrumental to the great goal of political freedom. The honesty and competence of its officials, the efficiency of its institutions, the experience and talents of its professional politicians, its Government's "collective responsibility," its Opposition's "responsible criticism," and its citizens' sense of belonging and participation all are to be justified as means to the greater end.[5] There is no point in saving money and effort, no purpose in holding communities together, no object in keeping governors alert, unless liberty and opportunity are thereby enhanced. Normally, democracy's practical merits do contribute to the realization of freedom, but occasionally they may have to be sacrificed.

It has become increasingly popular in American political science to say that the final goal of political endeavor is the "democratic method." According to this view, the essential element of the democratic method is compromise, which is thus given value for its own sake. Apparently this judgment is motivated by a belief that democracy's supporters can agree only that compromise, conciliation, and adjustment should be used to arrive at policy upon which they cannot agree.[6]

Without some standards by which to judge the results of compromise, all compromises, no matter what their consequences, must be accepted as equally desirable. As has been said, "compromise as a *self-sufficient* principle divorced from considerations of truth and justice is simply, in the last analysis, the ancient Thrasymachian doctrine that might makes right." [7] The principal moral issue of contemporary America is racial discrimination, but, for the writers who consider compromise self-sufficient, the situation is meaningful only in terms of pacifying the Council of White Citizens and the National Association for the Advancement of Colored People. The demands of the two groups are to be adjusted and compromised, but no reason can be given why this action is desirable, and any adjustment is fully as good as any other. This is a very weak position. It seems clear that those discriminated against have a moral right to better treatment, because when stigmatized they are unable to realize their full potentialities. Whether racial discrimination is an infringement of political freedom and thus a matter for political action must be decided on practical grounds. If the decision is that government must intervene, then compromise may well be a useful instrument of alleviation. In general, the highest form of the "democratic method," representative government itself, is desirable only because it is the best way to accomplish what is worth accomplishing—including the elimination of racial discrimination. Moreover, academic idealists, who are "uncompromising" and thus rather dangerous, are not the only advocates of political freedom. Although there may be some vagueness about the purpose of freedom, the greater proportion of the democratic society certainly approves of it.

This very brief and incomplete evaluation has treated the democratic state as a type of state. The institutions, policies, and foundations of individual democracies leave much to be desired, and political reform is always necessary and usually possible. I have said only that the modern democratic state, while not ideal, is certainly preferable to any other kind of state now available. When judged by strict ethical standards, it emerges very well indeed. However, commending the democratic state would be rather hollow if it is destined for obsolescence. Although no definite predictions can be made, democracy's ability to meet its most likely immediate problems can at least be estimated.

II

Democracy's future depends upon the strength and adaptability of its institutions and the stability and capacity for growth of its foundations. Representative government must maintain its ultimate decision-making power, and it must arrive at and carry out certain necessary domestic and foreign policies. The people, for their part, must retain their Middle-Class approach to politics and their belief in the moral authority of representative government. The prospects for the democratic state are a function of both its "superstructure" and its "substructure."

A common fear is that the democratic political process will raise popular expectations and demands beyond representative government's ability to meet them. The belief is that electoral competition naturally favors politicians who promise their electorates the most comprehensive governmental benefits; these promises will eventually get too large to fulfill, and the government will become bankrupt and the people dissatisfied.

The electorate cannot itself devise policy programs. They must be suggested originally by the leaders of the several social strata— the politicians themselves—or by the leaders of pressure groups, who can work only through the politicians. We saw in chapter 3 how the democratic politician, by pitting policy aspirations against one another and by tacit agreement with his rivals, remains uncommitted to extravagant promises of governmental action. In any event, the Middle-Class nature of the average elector is inconsistent with the avidity apparently attributed to him. Recently, parties which promise less have been electorally more successful than their major opponents. The clearest instance has occurred since 1950 in Great Britain, which many consider an advanced case of *dirigisme*. The great issues of British politics in 1959 were modest increases in old-age pensions (which hardly implied an unrealizable demand) and the possibilities for greater economic expansion.[8] The Conservative party has at least held its own electorally by recommending less governmental action in all fields, including the expansion of the economy. Both theoretical principles and the facts of current democratic politics contravene the prediction that the democratic state will be inundated by popular demands and partisan promises.

This fear of excessive commitments is also countered by the fact that no contemporary representative government has yet even approached the capacity of its present organizational structure. Governmental activity could expand almost indefinitely in the area of so-called public works, and democratic "social welfare" programs are still sketchy and primitive.[9] Expansions and variations of the administrative machinery now available would be adequate for these familiar activities and others like them. Moreover, nothing suggests that democratic states will be unable to devise new instruments of administration to deal with unfamiliar problems, and even new arrangements of the elected branches of government if these prove too cumbersome. The evidence is rather for democracy's ability to innovate in both cases.[10]

Political problems, popular demands, and governmental institutions always form an integral whole in any political community not subject to serious class antagonisms. To fear that institutions will not keep pace is to make an artificial division between companion results of the same socioeconomic and historical-traditional context. The desires of democratic peoples and promises of democratic politicians do not occur in an abstract entity called the "democratic state," but in Sweden, Great Britain, the United States, and the rest. Although all the desires and promises are products of a Middle-Class society and handled according to the democratic method, they are also specifically Swedish, British, or American; hence, they are closely related to specifically national institutions designed for their resolution and fulfillment.[11]

That the democratic state can adapt and innovate is indicated also by the inherent flexibility of its institutions. Representative government can devise techniques to meet any contingency more easily than any other modern system of government—a statement which is the precise opposite of the cliché that democracy is inherently inefficient. When confronted by a problem, representative government can choose among and combine the basic sociopolitical processes of polyarchy, hierarchy, and bargaining.[12] * All political systems can utilize these processes to some extent, but only democracy can afford the dispersal of control necessary for a high degree of political and economic polyarchy, which, at the very minimum, makes possible the loyalty of the voter and the rationality of the price system. As I have argued throughout, decentralization of control, and even a large amount of individual decision-making, are basically incompatible with autocracy and totalitarianism. Autocracy is committed to hierarchy and bargaining; totalitarianism, to hierarchy alone. The remaining processes are not available to them. But the basic polyarchal principles of representative government—popular election of representatives and the representatives' control of administration—do not prevent it from utilizing hierarchy and bargaining to the full extent of their usefulness. So far, democratic states have used hierarchy most extensively for warfare, both for actual fighting and for producing and allocating men and materiel. Wartime hierarchy was remarkably efficient,[13] without in the least weakening representative government's essential polyarchal principles.

Democracy's use of hierarchy is often thought to be conditional upon an acute emergency, which creates a single purpose overriding all normal differences of opinion. War provides this purpose, but, it is believed, in peacetime the democratic state lacks the discipline necessary for hierarchical processes. This opinion is not necessarily well founded. Dahl and Lindblom have said that "rational social action does not require overriding purpose; on the contrary, it usually requires a carefully thought-out adjustment of potentially or actually conflicting actions aimed at a variety of purposes. It is

---

* This is Dahl and Lindblom's terminology. "Polyarchy" is a situation where nonleaders have "a high degree of control" over leaders; "hierarchy" is a situation where leaders cannot be displaced by nonleaders by peaceful voting and where leaders control their own patterns of consultation; and "bargaining" is a situation where leaders control one another.

probably not even true that economizing entirely through government hierarchies requires a single overriding purpose." [14]

If the people of the democratic state, through their pressure groups and politicians, "demand" more of the action that marks the era of the welfare state, there are good reasons to suppose that representative government can satisfactorily meet its increased responsibilities.

III

Another pessimistic view of democracy's future is based on the belief that its electoral process naturally selects politicians who are "soothing demagogues," [15] who advance only by flattery and bribery, and who normally choose the more popular and thus the softer and more self-indulgent policy.[16] Democracy exhibits a "declining capacity to govern," which casts serious doubt on its continuing viability.

The democratic politician, like all other features of the democratic state, is not flawless, but criticizing him for demagoguery is meaningless unless his functions are clearly understood and his performance is compared with that of his nondemocratic counterparts. Representative government's unique dependence upon popular confidence necessitates "soothing" the people fairly often and sometimes even flattering or bribing them. The successful democratic politician, however, is rarely a demagogue; normally, he is one who has obtained his electorate's trust. He may do this by telling them that they deserve and shall receive everything they desire, or by warning them of dangers to be met only by labor and self-discipline. Omitting all consideration of the conflicting pressures which converge on him and limit his ability and need to practice flattery, the successful politician gives an impression of genuine concern with the well-being of his electorate. American politicians, for example, seem to be most successful when they can make their electorates aware of a more or less serious problem which only they have the knowledge and determination to solve. No matter what form it takes, the impression of trustworthiness and interest is the personal characteristic most helpful to a politician; it is simply false that electoral success always comes to the soother and the flatterer.[17] There is no reason to believe that this situation will change in the future. Indeed, if problems become larger and more serious, this relationship between politician and elector should be strengthened.

The charge that democratic politicians, in order to please their constituents, tend to follow the most effortless and thus the most shortsighted policy ignores the necessity for popular understanding of and confidence in the broad aspects of public policy, as well as the need for popular approval of the men who make it.[18] These requirements can certainly impede decisions which take discipline and sacrifice, but the hindrance has been greatly exaggerated. The favorite example of democracy's presumed inability to make "hard" and provident decisions has been the period preceding World War II. Serious mistakes were undoubtedly made then, but the democracies were suffering their greatest internal crisis in the form of the Great Depression, the United States had not yet recognized her world-wide responsibilities, and totalitarianism was still too new to be clearly understood. Since that time the democracies have made a series of decisions—from the Marshall Plan, through the repression of Communist violence within France and toward South Korea, to the programs of aid to underdeveloped areas—which have been difficult, far-sighted, expensive, and appropriate.[19] The behavior of all the American politicians who in 1960 sought nomination and election to the presidency is a good illustration of the temper of current democratic politics. In aspiring to the most important elective office in the democratic world, they carefully and publicly emphasized the difficulties and sacrifices awaiting the American electorate in both domestic and foreign affairs.

Politicians of nondemocratic states may be more immune from popular pressure for short-term pleasure and long-term folly, but this possible advantage is offset by accompanying disadvantages. The modern autocrat is restricted because he is never sure that his decisions will be accepted as legitimate by the larger part of his subjects. If implementation of his policy does not depend upon popular support, his facilities will be too meager to enable him to make important decisions in the first place. To the extent that he does rely upon popular opinion, he becomes a captive of his own propaganda more often than the democratic leader, for his authority is, in large part, a function of his practical success. Under totalitarianism, the political leaders are almost completely unrestricted by popular attitudes. With regard to rational decision-making, this is as much a weakness as a strength: since they are isolated from much useful information, they can never assume any spontaneous popular support, and the whole governmental apparatus requires their direct and constant intervention.[20]

The prediction that democratic leadership will gradually become incapable of making the decisions required by contemporary domestic and foreign politics conflicts with both the principles and the performance of representative government. At the very least, its elected and appointed branches can make decisions as efficient, realistic, and rational as those made by any autocrat. At the very least, the record of democratic states in meeting the economic, social, and military emergencies of the twentieth century equals that of any autocrat.

IV

Another fear for democracy's future is that the elected branches of government will lose control over certain hierarchical organizations, either those within the government itself or those essentially private in nature, which direct vitally important parts of the economy and society. Great private interests—like corporations, labor unions, and trust funds—and powerful governmental agencies—especially those concerned with military affairs—may grow to the point where a few hundred overworked representatives, skilled only in carrying constituencies, cannot rationally regulate their activities. The current strength of these organizations reflects the complexity and scope of contemporary problems; and the expert knowledge, large-scale organization, concentration of direction and facilities, and (in the case of military matters) secrecy now required promise to become even more important in the future, when matters such as civil defense, "outer space," new sources of energy and food, and even the weather become principal objects of human effort. If representative government loses control of such decision-making, the "managerial revolution" will succeed and the democratic state will become a historical curiosity.

The state of technology even a few decades hence cannot be foreseen, and the political problems which it will raise cannot be predicted. A short-term projection of the technological and organizational developments of recent years is all that can be attempted. On the basis of this, it seems to me that the power of public and private bureaucracies can be properly contained, given the persistence of a Middle-Class society.

The military services provide the best test of the limits of democratic control, for they deal with crucial issues, manage enormous sums of money, and operate in an aura of glamour and mystery. Pertinent criticisms have recently been made of the military's influence on general democratic policy, the undue deference it receives from elected representatives, and the secrecy surrounding much of its activity. There may also be some justice in American complaints that it is in "collusion" with large corporations in awarding contracts for military materiel. Despite all this, presidents, prime ministers, secretaries of defense, and parliamentary committees presently exercise both general and detailed control over decisions made by the military services.[21]

Among democratic states, only France has had serious difficulty keeping the military subordinate, and the reasons for it (as for most of her difficulties) are instructive. J. H. Hobson pointed out many years ago that ruling an area populated by foreigners is incompatible with democratic institutions in the dominating country. Since this rule requires an autocratic government in the dominated area, a democratic government at home will eventually be weakened by unavoidable nondemocratic influences. Especially prominent among these are the emphasis on discipline and obedience connected with conquest and repression; the necessary denial of civil liberties and social equality to the subject people; and the direct challenge of colonial administrative hierarchies to the authority of elected officials at home, who do not "understand how to handle the natives" and who must not, by their uninformed and irresponsible criticism, "destroy the solidarity" of the mother country vis-à-vis the dominated people. In addition, these hierarchies are physically separated from the representatives and deal with issues unfamiliar to them and completely beyond the comprehension and interest of a very large proportion of the electorate. All these factors combine to weaken and, Hobson thought, eventually to undermine domestic democracy.[22]

Hobson was worried about the effect of a necessarily hierarchical element within a democratic government upon the latter's fundamental modes of thought and principles of superordination. During the Fourth French Republic, these fears were realized. The civil and military hierarchies in Algeria came to believe that they could not meet their governmental responsibilities while remaining subordinate to the representative bodies in Paris. The normal democratic chain of command was then broken, to be restored later only by the prestige and effort of General Charles de Gaulle.[23]

France's experience and Hobson's theories combine to emphasize that the factors which make rule of a foreign people a threat to democracy do not occur in the case of civil or military hierarchies operating within the democratic state itself. These organizations deal with issues which concern the practical interests of parties and pressure groups and which are generally meaningful to the average citizen; they are constantly subject to the normal influences of the democratic society and are spatially close to the source of representative government; the bureaucrats cannot claim that they alone understand local conditions; and, since all policy comes from and applies to a single community, the hierarchies' critics cannot be denounced as supporters of foreigners and thus as unpatriotic. Recent history also indicates that the elected branches of government can maintain control of the civil and military bureaucracies in future periods of "conventional" warfare, where disruption approximates that of World War II, and in future periods of "cold war," where the threat resembles that which has followed World War II. During the last twenty years, the democracies have passed some very severe tests.

I have been arguing that official bureaucracies will remain under the authority of the elected bodies because they cannot sufficiently detach themselves from the formal and informal processes of representative government. If the military, with its size, strength, and prestige, is unlikely to assert its independence, there is little chance that the civil hierarchies will do so. However, it is still possible that the bureaucracies' independence will be inadvertent, that their number, size, and complexity of organization and operation will cause them simply to drift beyond the supervisory competence of the elected organs.

Since an accurate estimate of the chances for this development is practically impossible, it will be best to make only some brief suggestions regarding the future course of bureaucracy. The problem is whether, given the belief by both bureaucrat and representative that the former is properly subordinate to the latter, this pattern of authority will nonetheless become physically impossible. To retain the democratic pattern, the scope of bureaucratic work must be kept within the span of control of the representatives, and its subject matter within their understanding.

Governmental functions requiring hierarchical treatment will no doubt increase in the future, but technologically they should not differ sharply from those currently undertaken. No matter how much of human life and the human environment comes to be regulated, the expertise required should not surpass that now used, for example, in the exploitation of nuclear energy. Since laymen representatives can currently acquire a high degree of specialized knowledge about given technical subjects, and since the final decisions in even the most "scientific" program are always policy decisions,[24] the likelihood is that bureaucratic activity will not become autonomous because of the representatives' inability to understand it.

It is more probable that democratic control will be undermined as a result of a sharp increase in administrative decisions and administrative personnel. Elected executives and legislatures may simply become physically unable to master the great quantity of details necessary to maintain representative government. Yet several general considerations suggest that this, too, can be avoided.

Often it is simply assumed that increasing human management of society and nature will be accompanied by proportionately increasing use of hierarchical organizations. If means are roughly adapted to ends, however, the natural limits to the usefulness of hierachy [25] should prevent it from eclipsing other forms of social action. On the empirical level, France again provides a valuable illustration. Both public and private administration have long been more centralized in France than in other democratic states, yet those who are presently trying to modernize her economy have found this centralization a handicap and are actively promoting schemes of decentralization.[26] The lack of flexibility, predominance of red tape, and overloading of certain decision-makers associated with hierarchy should naturally restrict its use. In other words, the principles of organization which have prompted the fear that representatives will lose control of hierarchies should operate to restrict the number, size, and scope of the hierarchies themselves.

In the second place, if a hierarchy works properly, its basic decisions are made by a relatively small number of people in executive positions, and the decisions they make (as said above) are generalized "policy" decisions about broad alternatives. Given these conditions, a future increase in the personnel and activity of representative government's administrative bureaucracies would not require a proportionate increase in the representatives' span of attention and digestion of details. If this concentration of decision-making is not present, the hierarchy itself is not functioning correctly, and there is no reason to suppose it will be permitted to continue long enough to reach undue independence.

Finally, the growth of hierarchy should be checked by the inherent distrust of governmental power which is one of the most characteristic attitudes of the Middle Class. A "managerial revolution" in government cannot occur when concentration of managerial discretion is incompatible with the political premises of the society itself.

Most of this reasoning applies as well to private hierarchies. They will probably remain responsible to democratic control because of the limits to their usefulness; the layman's continuing ability to understand their principal functions; their intimate spatial, socioeconomic, and value connections with the entire society; and the wariness of the Middle Class. The large business concern has the greatest potentiality for uncontrollable power,[27] but it is restricted by many nonpolitical factors as well as by its inferiority to government in both power and legitimacy.[28] While the political system rests on the suffrage of millions of citizens who do not identify themselves primarily with any private association, while it is directed by similarly detached political parties, and as long as the associations' officials themselves accept the legitimacy of representative government, the intentional or inadvertent breakdown of true democratic control is unlikely. As one expert has said, "so long as speech and thought are free, men will always rise capable of transcending the massed effects of any organization or group of organizations." [29]

V

Representative government, in addition to maintaining its formal constitution, must enact certain policies necessary for the future health of the democratic state. The most important of these concern the remaining underprivileged at home and the newly self-conscious people of the so-called underdeveloped areas. In both cases, the problem is to eliminate actual and potential disaffection by bringing these groups the Middle-Class standard of living and the Middle-Class political outlook. In both cases, governmental action is clearly required.

Domestic stability depends upon the belief of lower strata that they can advance to a moderate level of material well-being and social acceptance. A gradually expanding economy and increasingly comprehensive "social security" programs should provide for the former anticipation. The Middle Class has relatively modest material expectations, despite the remarkable affluence of some democracies, and it tends to be satisfied by a small increment for each generation. This kind of increase has been possible in the past and appears well within the future competence of democratic politics.

On the basis of past experience, it will be more difficult to eliminate undemocratic differentials of social deference. The critical groups are the American Negroes and the European proletariat; their social status must be raised, not necessarily to full acceptance by all other people, but at least to the point where they bear no stigma. To raise the degree of deference shown a group, its standard of living can be raised and legal penalties can be attached to discrimination against it. As a lower group acquires more property, its overt mode of life and its social and political attitudes come to resemble those of the groups above it; this naturally makes it more acceptable to them. Moreover, as the standard of living, education, and general sophistication of a superior-status group increase, it becomes more willing to accept people whom it previously considered inferior.[30]

The effects of legislating against discrimination are less well understood. American experience has suggested that, when overt discrimination is made illegal, the attitudes of the socially dominant groups will soften.[31] Whether or not respect can be created by means of law, the groups which the legislation is designed to help seem to derive satisfaction from it, and their leaders declare it very desirable public policy. To this extent, in any event, law can mitigate the undemocratic results of social discrimination.

Avoiding disaffection in the newly "awakened" underdeveloped areas is more difficult than expanding the Middle Class at home. The underdeveloped areas are problematic for the democracies because the latter can survive in the long run only if they have at least the tolerance of these vast numbers of people, and to gain such tolerance they must deal satisfactorily with the demands the "transitional societies" place upon them.[32] There are two basic facts of contemporary international politics: first, the coexistence of a small number of lightly populated but highly prosperous states and a large number of states containing most of the world's population living near the subsistence level; second, the patterning of the aspirations and ideals of the latter upon those of the former. Speaking roughly, the underdeveloped peoples want material well-being and social acceptance as states and as individuals. In their quest for these goals, they naturally turn for aid (if not satisfaction) to the democracies.

The democratic states cannot use their present military advantages to resist by force the aspirations of the underdeveloped peoples; to do so would mean aggressive war and domination of foreigners, both of which are incompatible with democracy.[33] Simply to ignore the underdeveloped areas would obviously be folly, since such great resources should not be allowed to come under hostile direction. The only reasonable alternative for the democracies is to help the underdeveloped states to achieve political and economic maturity, for the purpose of gaining their good will and encouraging them to opt for high living standards, and thus for democracy.[34]

The desires of the underdeveloped peoples, whether or not they realize it, are preponderantly Middle Class.[35] They are, therefore, completely understandable to the democracies. Curiously enough, they bring to mind an earlier critical period in the development of the democratic state, which saw the rise of the proletariat and its eventual absorption into the Middle Class and the political processes of democracy. As was shown in chapter 8, the Middle Class can resist the demands of those who aspire to political participation only by abandoning representative government. It is not too fanciful to describe democratic foreign secretaries as leaders of an international Middle Class, faced with a choice between preparing the poor for a share in political power or renouncing the principles of their own governmental system.

The underdeveloped areas are seeking international aid to raise themselves both materially and socially. In this quest, they naturally turn to those above them on both scales. Their requests of the democracies are generally in good faith; the principal difficulty is whether the democracies will recognize—as the bourgeoisie formerly recognized the challenge of the proletariat—that frustrating these requests will threaten their own existence. The contemporary situation is complicated by the physical separation of rich and poor and the consequent absence of the always powerful sense of community. This separation may prevent the democratic citizenry from becoming aware of the problems presented by the underdeveloped areas, or at least it may lead them to an imprudent indifference. There is, however, evidence against this possibility in the United States, which has relatively few connections with Asia and Africa and which must provide the leadership for the democratic states. American policy regarding both trade and so-called foreign aid has consistently shown an appreciation of the democracies' responsibilities; [36] the last three presidential campaigns have been conducted primarily on issues of international politics; and in the campaign of 1960, all the leading politicians explicitly supported the least popular aspects of America's foreign commitments.[37]

The relationship between the democracies and the underdeveloped areas is further complicated by international Communism. Since the democracies defeated totalitarianism in western Europe, the Communists have concentrated on promising to lead the underdeveloped peoples to material welfare and international prestige. To use my analogy, there is danger that the discontent of the "international proletariat" will be captured by an antidemocratic organization.[38] This Communist strategy has two effects on the democracies: it intensifies their problems, but it also stimulates them to search for solutions.

In general, the Middle-Class democracies' sense of self-preservation should make them capable of the proper policy decisions regarding underdeveloped areas. Whether they will make these decisions remains to be seen, but there is evidence that they recognize the nature and gravity of the difficulties confronting them.

VI

There are some substantial theoretical and practical reasons for being optimistic about the future of the democratic state's superstructure. After all, the problems so far examined are, in essence, only new forms of problems already successfully resolved. Turning to the prospects for the substructure of the democratic state, we encounter issues that are both more fundamental and more obscure. Changes in communal, economic, and social relationships are extremely difficult to predict. Even if they can be anticipated, their influence upon institutions and policy remains hard to assess. Nevertheless, certain potential weaknesses in the foundation of the democratic state can be identified, and some suggestions made on the possibilities of avoiding its sudden or gradual collapse. Much less optimism is warranted here, if only because we are so ignorant about these vital matters.

Since national parochialism is inconsistent with the common responsibilities of the democratic states, the community is a possible source of future weakness in the substructure of democracy. Although the democracies have recently done well in transcending their own narrow interests, their present degree of political independence makes a fatal breakdown in cooperation possible at any time, and the question arises whether the democratic community can be expanded to provide the foundation for larger democratic states. The simplest way to do this would be to combine two or more presently "sovereign" democracies.

The nation is distinguished from other communities principally by its great size; hence, there is nothing to prevent its expansion, given enough of the "building blocks" of common traditions, culture, and value systems. Democratic nations can be combined only with the voluntary acquiescence of each of them. The initiative for such combination must be taken by certain elites of the several nations who have come to believe in the desirability of a larger state, who are able to identify more closely with one another than with their own nations, and who can eventually convince their fellow nationals that the first loyalty of them all is to the "supranational" group. When the larger identification becomes primary, a new national community will be formed and a foundation provided for a larger democratic state.[39]

The experiences of the movement for "Western European Union" suggest that this kind of development is feasible. The initiative has been taken throughout by a small multinational group determined to end the continent's political fragmentation.[40] During the decade following 1945—when World War II, the enormous tasks of physical reconstruction, and the threat of Communism had all undermined faith in the viability of small states—this group was able to create a very general "moral" commitment to "Europe" within the so-called Six.* This commitment underlay the subsequent acceptance by the six states of several supranational organizations, although many different motives contributed to the ratification of the treaties which brought them into existence.[41] As the new institutions have exercised their supranational functions, they have gained in support. The various operations of the European Coal and Steel Community, in particular, have brought into being supranational parliamentarians, parties, bureaucrats, and pressure groups, all with vested interests in its continuing vitality.[42]

The idea of a greater Europe never caught the popular imagination in any of the Six, but little was done to disseminate it.[43] On the other hand, opposition to "Europe" has been fragmented and sporadic.[44] Although the people have been predominantly apathetic, potential receptivity to appropriate propaganda is indicated by the

* France, Belgium, the Netherlands, Luxembourg, Italy, and West Germany.

inability of the old nation-states to inspire enthusiasm,[45] the feeling
of impotence evoked by American and Soviet power, the internation-
alist traditions of Catholicism and Socialism, and the general non-
communal myths of democracy. As foreign and domestic pressures
have lessened, the enthusiasm for uniting Europe has waned, but the
experience has shown that where the creation of a larger democracy
is currently most feasible, the necessary steps in constructing one
democratic nation from several are all definitely possible. Whether
the democracies will actually combine, if combination becomes necessary for their survival, cannot be determined.[46]

VII

Democracy can persist only as long as it rests upon a numeri-
cally and ideologically dominant Middle Class. The durability of the
Middle Class is the most important single factor in the prospects for
the democratic state, but it is also the least predictable. There seem
to be two ways in which the Middle Class could disappear: it could
lose its modest material possessions, or it could increase them to the
point where its typical attitude of caution would be undermined.

Each section of the Middle Class has special antidemocratic
tendencies connected with its special occupational situation. Any
group can always find some reason to be dissatisfied with the methods
and results of representative government, but its occasional overt
antidemocratic behavior—usually voting for antidemocratic parties
or politicians—is the result of specific stimuli. Sometimes a flamboy-
ant politician arises to articulate the grievances of a particular group;
the antidemocratic behavior he evokes, however, rarely survives his
first personal misfortune.[47]

An overt threat to material or social position is probably the
most important stimulus to antidemocratic behavior, and a threatened loss of income makes the clearest impression on people who are
unable to anticipate impoverishment without actually experiencing
its beginnings. It has long been recognized that during economic
depressions the segments of the Middle Class may turn from the
democratic political process in an attempt to resolve their several
frustrations. War, the other catastrophe of modern life, has not
destroyed Middle-Class "rationality" in democratic states which have
been defeated and even devastated. Apparently, it is thought to be
beyond human control, and simply a burden that must be borne with
resignation.

In a depression, both skilled and unskilled proletarians tend to
support antidemocratic movements which advertise one form or another of the "proletarian revolution." These movements have been
pretty well absorbed by contemporary Communism, which promises

social and material security through a noncompetitive arrangement of human affairs. The Communists pay lip service to the anarchy of the traditional Marxist classless society, but no worker can miss the explicit claim that only the Communist party can bring about this utopia. Both this paternalism and the "automatic" security of the classless society are inconsistent with the democratic political process. The proletarian's insecure and subordinate occupational position, his appreciation of collective action, and his relatively low social status incline him in this particular antidemocratic direction.

The small businessman and small farmer—the "petty bourgeoisie" —tend to revert to an earlier political and economic order when faced by a loss of income.[48] Their occupations make them naturally suspicious and jealous of large and powerful organizations, whether business or labor or government, and in a crisis they support movements to curb the power of big business and big labor, to return control of the government from the parties to the "people," and sometimes to introduce corporate-type governmental institutions, apparently in order to guarantee the small enterpriser a voice in government. These movements are antidemocratic in their antilibertarianism and their emphasis upon the direct relationship between the people and the administration, with its corollary attack upon parliaments and politicians.[49]

The antidemocratic tendencies of nonmanual employees—the white-collared or black-coated workers—are less well understood. This group is strongly opposed to contemporary Communism and other antidemocratic movements based on the experiences of the proletariat, but it gives little support to the "populist" movements of the petty bourgeoisie.[50] The most reasonable supposition is that when a crisis occurs the white-collared worker tends to follow the lead of the highest social and income strata, with whom he usually identifies himself.[51] In an emergency, these highest groups incline to authoritarian autocracy, especially in reaction to antidemocratic movements of the proletariat and petty bourgeoisie.[52]

The remainder of the Middle Class consists of the so-called independent professionals—the engineers, teachers, doctors, lawyers, and so forth. Again, there is little evidence concerning their special antidemocratic tendencies. The best guess is that they either identify with whoever makes up their clientele or vaguely support some kind of "technocracy," which may include Communism as a supposed method of "social planning." Although many leaders of antidemocratic movements come from this group, it is probably too lacking in "class consciousness" to form a movement of its own.

The only linkage of economic depression and antidemocratic movements of critical proportions occurred within the German Weimar

Republic. The votes for the antidemocratic "left" and "right" went up and down together as economic conditions fluctuated, until they reached 51.6 per cent of the total poll in the first election of 1932. Such defection would have weakened any democratic state, and Weimar democracy was extremely fragile from the start. It had no sustained democratic tradition to rely upon, it arose out of military defeat and national humiliation, and it had just been through an astounding inflation. Even with these handicaps, however, after economic conditions had improved, the Nazis lost 4.2 per cent of the total poll in the second election of 1932. If the conservatives and authoritarians had not capitulated to Hitler, thus destroying uncoerced elections, his electoral strength might have disappeared as relative prosperity returned. In the better-established democratic states, representative government was remarkably successful in retaining its legitimacy during this period of economic paralysis.

Despite democracy's tenacity in the 1930's, its prospects will be much brighter if future depressions are avoided. In the last thirty years, electorates have come to hold their governments responsible for maintaining a Middle-Class standard of living. Although mild depressions will probably be tolerated, another great depression is most likely to provoke incompatible and uncompromisable demands from the several social strata and, eventually, disappointment and disaffection.

The ability of representative government to avoid future depressions is debatable. There are many devices available to mitigate the effects of depression, and, although it is hoped these will also create economic activity, no one can be sure that they will. Democratic states, it is true, can deal with depressions as well as any other state, but other states are not as sensitive to popular discontent.

VIII

The political effects of the Middle Class's moderate possessions may also be undermined by certain developments which could result from a rise in democratic standards of living. There are several ways in which both the production and the consumption of an affluent society could destroy the typical Middle-Class attitude of prudence.

In the first place, abundance is associated with a highly rationalized economic process, in which occupations become more routine and less time-consuming. The revolutionary potential of the job's decreasing importance has been recognized at least since Marx. The boredom of assembly-line work may lead to rash and violent reactions of frustration. The self-control and self-denial required by modern production techniques imply a high expenditure of nervous effort on physically and mentally nonarduous tasks, a situation which may create politically dangerous tensions.[53] But the principal threat of the system of mass production still seems to be the increasing inability of the machine-tender to understand how his work is related to the whole productive process and, as a result, how he himself is related to his fellow men.[54]

The routinization of work has been accompanied by a great increase in leisure time, during which the average man must supply his own discipline and goals. Since this time is no longer needed to revive oneself for the return to work, meaningless leisure may combine with satisfactionless work to weaken the caution which has characterized the Middle Class. David Riesman has written that Americans, who have been most thoroughly influenced by modern productive processes, cannot "resort to leisure as a counterbalance for the deficiencies of work"; as a remedy he can suggest only that "work flows could be redesigned to maximize the demands on the worker's intelligence. . . ." [55] There is a real possibility that most men are incapable of leading purposeful lives independently of the discipline of making a living.

The social, occupational, and geographical mobility inherent in the highly developed economy may also have an erosive effect upon Middle-Class attitudes. It has recently been said that, in the United States, the principle of mobility has destroyed the "sense of organic, recognized relationship between the individual and the community," which was formerly defined by the principle of status. The latter principle "affirms that a minor position may be worthy," while the former regards it "both as the penalty for and the proof of personal failure." [56] The need of the rational economy for mobility has been embodied in an unrealizable moral imperative. As long as the economy remains rational, this emphasis upon "getting ahead" will also remain, and those who have not done so will be looked down upon; yet "minor positions" can never be eliminated. The frustrations resulting from this discrepancy between expectations and actuality may outweigh the prudence of the Middle Class.[57]

Each of these conditions—the boredom, tension, and sense of meaninglessness resulting from routinized work; the unease of extended and aimless leisure; and the strain of unrewarded endeavor—is the concomitant of an economy organized for high productivity.[58] Although I have merely touched upon the problem, it is certainly possible that these conditions will intensify in the future and cancel the prudence and caution now connected with the Middle Class. Organizing the economy to provide a high standard of living may eventually destroy precisely the political effect that standard is supposed to provide. Here again, the prospects for the democratic state are impossible to estimate.

IX

In 1930, José Ortega y Gasset gave his classic description of the modern "mass man." The organization of production and control of nature, developed in the nineteenth and twentieth centuries, have led the masses to believe that their desires can be satisfied without limit and that the source of these satisfactions is nature itself. "The new masses find themselves in the presence of a prospect full of possibilities, and furthermore, quite secure, with everything ready to their hands, independent of any previous efforts on their part, just as we find the sun in the heavens without our hoisting it upon our shoulders." The mass man, said Ortega, possesses the outlook of the spoiled child, who believes that "everything is permitted to him and that he has no obligations." [59] He refuses to recognize any authority above himself; he is incapable of "submitting to anything or anybody." [60]

Walter Lippmann has supplemented Ortega's criticism by maintaining that contemporary democracy has no fundamental ethics in terms of which its leaders can make their decisions, no "public philosophy" which gives direction and meaning to democratic life.[61] The absence of such a philosophy leaves democracy's leaders floundering in a moral vacuum and unable to provide the people with a necessary sense of purpose.

If the Middle-Class man of the democratic state becomes the leaderless mass man of Ortega's description, the foundations of democracy will surely crumble. Whether this mutation will occur in the future cannot be predicted, but it seems to me that the strength of current democratic authority and responsibility has not been properly appreciated. In their overt behavior, the people of the democratic state respect the authority of their officials and institutions, especially regarding issues like foreign and military affairs, where no one is "quite secure, with everything ready to his hands." And they and their leaders probably have a better grasp of standards of political value than they have been credited with.

Our brief evaluation of the democratic state implied that an ethics of democracy has three levels, which concern, respectively, its method of making public policy, the kind of public policy it makes, and the kind of human being it helps to produce. The American tendency to justify the democratic state solely by reference to its procedure appears in political science as the identification of the "public interest" with the methods rather than the results of policy-making; it appears more generally as the attitude of the "organization man" who values the personal relationships necessary for action but who is relatively indifferent to the results of that action. I have argued throughout this book that the democratic method is intimately connected with desirable public policy, but to adopt this truncated ethics of procedure is to invite cynicism, complacency, and short-sightedness. A political elite which cannot rise above rules of order and compromise can hardly counteract antidemocratic tendencies on the part of the masses.

Despite this recent emphasis on procedure, the belief that government has a duty to allow every man to follow his own conscience and to guarantee a minimum level of security to everyone still occupies a powerful position in democratic thought.[62] The average man still believes in political freedom, although he may often compromise this belief when its implications seem to challenge his customary behavior and patterns of thought.[63] The belief is even stronger among the leadership of the democratic state, the teachers, lawyers, politicians, journalists, and ministers, whose "public philosophy" provides (as Lippmann realizes) the direction and purpose of every polity.

It is true, however, that the contemporary democrat has been puzzled at the third level of his ethics, the level which requires decisions as to why political freedom is necessary for the good life. Answers of earlier periods—that man must be free to do God's will, free to conform to the structure of the universe, free to recognize his human essence—are no longer completely satisfying, and no substitutes have been found. Yet, it is vitally significant that each former answer ultimately said no more than, "Man must do such and such because that is the way things are." Moreover, the psychologically important fact about these answers is that they postulated a standard of conduct not fully dependent upon the personal desires of the individual human being. Even though the leader of the contemporary democratic state may be unsure of the precise nature of this standard, he recognizes its necessity. In the absence of an ineffable dogma, this recognition should be enough to provide a sense of direction as democracy faces its great responsibilities at home and abroad.[64] It must be transmitted through the democratic educational system, while the unending search for the ethical foundation of human life continues.

NOTES

Introduction

1. When these interrelationships have been dealt with, usually only two or at best three of the elements have been considered. The following are among the better examples: the relationships between parties (and party systems) and electoral systems, in Maurice Duverger, *Political Parties*, trans. Barbara and Robert North (New York: John Wiley & Sons, 1954); the relationship between democratic leadership and the method by which it is chosen, in Joseph A. Schumpeter, *Capitalism, Socialism, and Democracy* (2nd ed.; New York: Harper & Bros., 1947), chaps. xxi–xxiii; the relationships between parties and the institutions of government, in E. E. Schattschneider, *Party Government* (New York: Farrar & Rinehart, 1942); the relationship between constitutionalism and governmental institutions, in Carl J. Friedrich, *Constitutional Government and Democracy* (rev. ed.; Boston: Ginn & Co., 1950); the relationship between parties and policy, in Anthony Downs, *An Economic Theory of Democracy* (New York: Harper & Bros., 1957); and the relationship between governmental institutions and interest-group activity, in David B. Truman, *The Governmental Process* (New York: Alfred A. Knopf, 1951).

Since this book was written, two studies on the general nature of the democratic state have appeared: Seymour Martin Lipset, *Political Man: The Social Bases of Politics* (Garden City, N.Y.: Doubleday & Co., 1960); and Henry B. Mayo, *An Introduction to Democratic Theory* (New York: Oxford University Press, 1960). Perhaps these indicate a growing interest in the type of problems I am here concerned with.

2. The group of states I have called "democratic" is restricted to these twelve, omitting such important countries as West Germany, Italy, and Japan, because there is some doubt that the latter possess all the characteristics possessed by the former, at least with respect to degree. This doubt is expressed, for example, by the question regarding their ability to "maintain democracy." It is safer to proceed by restricting the discussion to the given twelve. The results of this discussion will then provide criteria which should be helpful in diagnosing the health of democracy in Germany, Italy, and Japan. France is included in the list, despite her difficulties in maintain-

ing stable democratic institutions and despite recent doubts about her democratic future. She was clearly a democratic state from the 1880's until the 1950's—a long time to go without a change in basic political form—and the fundamentals of democracy persist in France despite the proven inadequacy of her institutions. See chapters 7 and 8.

3. Cf. Karl A. Wittfogel, *Oriental Despotism* (New Haven: Yale University Press, 1957), a study basically similar in intent to the present one. Wittfogel's work is, however, much more detailed. This is necessary because he must marshal a great amount of evidence to support his theses, since oriental despotisms are both historical and, as he points out, relatively neglected. Such a problem does not arise with contemporary democratic states. Furthermore, while Wittfogel devotes a major portion of his work to the several varieties of oriental despotism, the present work is more modest and will not examine the various types of democratic states.

Chapter 1

1. Studies of the backgrounds of representatives have shown that they come from groups which are atypical of the general population in every quality which could possibly be thought politically relevant. They originate in groups which have more money, higher social prestige, and more education; before their election they belong to atypical occupations; and the proportion of them coming from the dominant racial and religious types is larger than the proportion of these types in the general population. For a summary of, and references to, these studies, see Harold F. Gosnell, *Democracy, the Threshold of Freedom* (New York: Ronald Press, 1948), chap. xii.

2. Perhaps the best alternative is the term "polyarchy," as used in Robert A. Dahl and Charles E. Lindblom, *Politics, Economics, and Welfare* (New York: Harper & Bros., 1953), p. 275. However, it has the disadvantages of being unfamiliar and referring to only one element of the government, namely, the relations between elected leaders and ordinary citizens; see p. 276. "Representative government" does not necessarily have this latter restriction.

3. Cf. David Easton, *The Political System* (New York: Alfred A. Knopf, 1953) p. 153.

4. Although these two elements are obviously essential, the emphasis on the kind of policy made by representative government has probably contributed to the absence of any detailed analysis of them. There has even been a strong tendency to consider these structural aspects to be relatively unimportant variables. The following is an example: "Representative government is a government that makes great use of devices to ensure representation, *such as* the election of officials" (Alfred de Grazia, *The Elements of Political Science* [New York: Alfred A. Knopf, 1952], p. 145; emphasis supplied). De Grazia is clearly speaking of the government of the democratic state.

5. See Joseph P. Harris, "Elections," *Encyclopaedia of the Social Sciences* (New York: Macmillan Co., 1935), V, 452. See also Karl A. Wittfogel, *Oriental Despotism* (New Haven: Yale University Press, 1957), p. 104, for an account of elections under oriental despotisms.

6. See Herman Finer, *The Theory and Practice of Modern*

Government (rev. ed.; New York: Henry Holt & Co., 1949), pp. 386–90, on the duration of elected legislatures. Also see p. 388 on the special conditions under which the duration of a British House of Commons can be extended.

7. See V. O. Key, Jr., *Politics, Parties, and Pressure Groups* (3rd ed.; New York: Thomas Y. Crowell, 1953), pp. 648–51. The secret ballot was adopted in Britain in 1872 and generally in the United States by 1900. There is no reason to believe that before its adoption British and American government, despite electoral abuses, was not representative. For the early history of the secret ballot, see John H. Wigmore, *The Australian Ballot System* (Boston: Boston Book Co., 1889), pp. 1–56.

8. It should be remembered here that in the most extreme case of a one-party area, the southern United States, competition for office has been shifted from the general election to the primary.

9. France under the Second Empire is a good example (see Peter Campbell, *French Electoral Systems and Elections, 1789–1957* [New York: Frederick A. Praeger, 1958], pp. 67–68; and Brian Chapman, *The Prefects and Provincial France* [London: Allen & Unwin, 1955], pp. 32–36). Latin America provides an example of elections in which some of the candidates are "sponsored" by the government (see William W. Pierson and Federigo G. Gil, *Governments of Latin America* [New York: McGraw-Hill Book Co., 1957], pp. 222–23). In the United States, Huey Long's success in subverting the process of democratic elections depended upon his control of a local government in a federal system.

10. For example, the presence of Huey Long in the United States Senate, despite the fact that a great amount of his power rested on coercion at the polls, did not change the basic nature of American representative government. On Long's tactics, see V. O. Key, Jr., *Southern Politics* (New York: Alfred A. Knopf, 1950), pp. 156–64; and Harnett T. Kane, *Louisiana Hayride* (New York: William Morrow, 1941), chap. iv. If Long's power had spread to other constituencies, as it was threatening to do, representative government would have been at least seriously weakened.

11. For example, Sidney Hook, *Reason, Social Myths, and Democracy* (New York: John Day, 1940), pp. 285–86. Hook goes further and says that for real "representation" or "democracy" the policy views and programs of the winning candidates or parties must be put into practice after they assume office.

12. That American parties are indistinguishable from one another in their policy stands and that they are even incapable of putting what programs they possess into action have been challenged by some writers. For example, Julius Turner, "Responsible Parties: A Dissent from the Floor," *American Political Science Review*, XLV (1951), 143–57.

13. See the following: H. G. Nicholas, *The British General Election of 1950* (London: Macmillan Co., 1951), chaps. v, vi, viii, ix; D. E. Butler, *The British General Election of 1951* (London: Macmillan Co., 1952), chaps. vi, vii, ix; and Butler, *The British General Election of 1955* (London: Macmillan Co., 1956), chaps. iv, v, vi.

14. This is a thesis of two influential books on American gov-

ernment and politics: Pendleton Herring, *The Politics of Democracy* (New York: W. W. Norton, 1940); and Arthur N. Holcombe, *Our More Perfect Union* (Cambridge, Mass.: Harvard University Press, 1950).

15. For example, Anthony Downs, *An Economic Theory of Democracy* (New York: Harper & Bros., 1957).

16. Finer, *The Theory and Practice of Modern Government*, pp. 230–36. Swiss males, however, seem to be relenting (see *The Economist*, February 14, 1959, p. 583).

17. For a summary account of this development, see Gosnell, *Democracy, the Threshold of Freedom*, chap. iii.

18. See chapter 8 for the explanation of these attitudes.

19. See Carl J. Friedrich, *Constitutional Government and Democracy* (rev. ed.; Boston: Ginn & Co., 1950), chap. xv, for a description of the several electoral systems.

20. Sweden has the only indirectly elected chamber with extensive governmental authority, although there are some indirectly elected members in the "upper" chambers of Switzerland, Belgium, and the Netherlands. The constitution of the Fifth French Republic provides for an indirectly elected senate.

21. Swedish parties, policy, and attitudes toward civil liberties, despite the indirectly elected chamber, are fundamentally identical with those of the other democratic states. See Dankwart A. Rüstow, *The Politics of Compromise* (Princeton: Princeton University Press, 1955).

22. "Representative Government," in *Utilitarianism, Liberty, and Representative Government* (London: J. M. Dent & Sons, 1910), p. 228.

23. Minor exceptions to this generalization occur in Belgium and the Netherlands regarding the positions of their respective monarchs. See Jan-Albert Goris (ed.), *Belgium* (Berkeley: University of California Press, 1946), p. 90; and Bartholomew Landheer (ed.), *The Netherlands* (Berkeley: University of California Press, 1943), pp. 94–96.

24. There has been a tendency in modern political science to suggest that, with the increasing size, complexity, and discretionary power of the administrative branch of representative government, the elected branches have lost or are in serious danger of losing their positions of ultimate control. The evidence, however, is to the contrary. Through the use of devices such as the question hour, the legislative investigation, and the personal supervision by elected executive officials, the "bureaucracy" has been kept under control. The situation is usually thought to be most serious in France, with its traditionally "weak executive," but the assembly and cabinet have maintained control over the bureaucracy; see David Thomson, *Democracy in France* (London: Oxford University Press, 1946), pp. 170–71; Finer, *The Theory and Practice of Modern Government*, p. 536; Finer, *Governments of Greater European Powers* (New York: Henry Holt & Co., 1956), pp. 438–41; and, for a special case in point, Edward G. Lewis, "Parliamentary Control of Nationalized Industry in France," *American Political Science Review*, LI (1957), 669–83. For the situation in Britain, see Hiram Miller Stout, *British Government* (New York: Oxford University Press, 1953), pp. 82, 143. In

Big Democracy (New York: Alfred A. Knopf, 1945), Paul Appleby has strongly emphasized the ability of the elected branches of government to control the bureaucracy. See also chapter 9 below.

25. Mill also approached the position of the elected body from a somewhat different point of view, when he said that it was supported by the strongest political forces in the community and that this constituted its position of pre-eminence ("Representative Government," p. 229). What these strongest forces are and why they support a representative government will be the topics of chapter 8.

26. Friedrich has called this the "functional" meaning (*Constitutional Government and Democracy*, pp. 123–24).

27. *Ibid.*, pp. 28–33.

28. Friedrich distinguishes five methods by which the administrative branch of government can be held responsible: the promotional measures, the disciplinary measures, financial measures of control and audit of expenditure, judicial measures, and finally the spirit of craftsmanship (*ibid.*, pp. 398–409). The financial and judicial measures are completely formal, and the promotional and disciplinary measures must be formalized if they are to remain consistent with the goals of the democratic state. Only the spirit of craftsmanship is basically nonformal.

29. See R. T. McKenzie, *British Political Parties* (New York: St. Martin's Press, 1955), *passim*.

Chapter 2

1. Cf. V. O. Key, Jr., *Politics, Parties, and Pressure Groups* (3rd ed.; New York: Thomas Y. Crowell, 1953), p. 222.

2. Cf. Bertram M. Gross, *The Legislative Struggle* (New York: McGraw-Hill Book Co., 1953), pp. 62–63. E. E. Schattschneider states that making nominations is a necessary condition of a party, but he does not say that it is also sufficient (*Party Government* [New York: Farrar & Rinehart, 1942], p. 64).

3. Key, *Politics, Parties, and Pressure Groups*, pp. 351–53.

4. The best source of information on primary elections under "one-party" conditions is V. O. Key, Jr., *Southern Politics* (New York: Alfred A. Knopf, 1950), *passim*.

5. *Ibid.*, pp. 23–24.

6. *Ibid.*, p. 33.

7. On this and other matters regarding the direct primary under "multiparty" conditions, see Key, *Politics, Parties, and Pressure Groups*, pp. 411 ff.

8. See C. A. Berdahl, "Party Membership in the United States," *American Political Science Review*, XXXVI (1942), 241–62.

9. See V. O. Key, Jr., *American State Politics* (New York: Alfred A. Knopf, 1956), especially pp. 127–28.

10. See James M. Burns, *Congress on Trial* (New York: Harper & Bros., 1949), p. 157. The member of the House of Commons is inhibited from breaking party lines because of "his knowledge that the party can deny him renomination, and that an appeal to the local party association against the Central Office would almost always be in vain." Cf. R. T. McKenzie, *British Political Parties* (New York: St. Martin's Press, 1955), pp. 585–86: "the parliamentary leaders

can be virtually certain that the withdrawal of the whip by the parliamentary party or expulsion from the mass organization [the party proper] will result in the political death of the apostate concerned." See also Leon D. Epstein, "Cohesion of British Parliamentary Parties," *American Political Science Review*, L (1956), 360–77.

11. The position of the British M.P. in relation to his local party is generally quite weak—at least in the Conservative party. See Allen M. Potter, "The English Conservative Constituency Association," *Western Political Quarterly*, IX (1956), 363–75. This, combined with the American situation, suggests a negative correlation between the centralization of a nationwide party and the power of the individual representative in his local party organization.

12. Maurice Duverger, *Political Parties*, trans. Barbara and Robert North (New York: John Wiley & Sons, 1954), pp. xxiv–xxx.

13. This has happened periodically with the French Radical Socialist party. Herman Finer puts groups of the Radicals in three unconnected positions in a spatial diagram of the February, 1956, distribution of party strength in the National Assembly (*Governments of Greater European Powers* [New York: Henry Holt & Co., 1956], p. 403).

14. Duverger, *Political Parties*, pp. 182–202. See pp. 392–421 for a discussion of the different roles played by parliamentary parties.

15. See McKenzie, *British Political Parties*, chap. x, on the history of the British Labour party. The ascendancy of the parliamentary leaders over the party leaders is primarily the result of the power and prestige which the former derive from being the "Government" or the potential "Government."

16. See F. A. Hermens, *Democracy or Anarchy?* (Notre Dame, Ind.: University of Notre Dame Press, 1941), pp. 354–55; and Ben A. Arneson, *The Democratic Monarchies of Scandinavia* (New York: D. Van Nostrand Co., 1949), chap. viii.

17. For example, Sigmund Neumann, "Toward a Comparative Study of Political Parties," in Neumann (ed.), *Modern Political Parties* (Chicago: University of Chicago Press, 1956), p. 396. Parties "are concerned with the control of governmental power," and they "compete for popular support with another group or groups holding divergent views." One might compare their competition in certain cases to that between freetraders and gangsters.

18. This thesis is expressed most clearly by H. McD. Clokie, "The Modern Party State," *Canadian Journal of Economics and Political Science*, XIV (1949), 139–57.

19. There are many studies of party voting in the United States Congress. See, for example, A. L. Lowell, "The Influence of Party upon Legislation in England and America," *Annual Report of the American Historical Association*, I (1901), 321–51; Julius Turner, "Responsible Parties: A Dissent from the Floor," *American Political Science Review*, XLV (1951), 143–57, and *Party and Constituency: Pressures on Congress* (Baltimore: Johns Hopkins University Press, 1951); Roland Young, *Congressional Politics in the Second World War* (New York: Columbia University Press, 1956), Appendix B; and, for a summary account, Key, *Politics, Parties, and Pressure Groups*, pp. 706–7. For the manner in which informal party programs

are drawn up, see Hugh A. Bone, "An Introduction to the Senate Policy Committees," *American Political Science Review,* L (1956), 339–59.

20. The clearest statement of this technique of Stalinist rule is given by Barrington Moore, Jr., *Terror and Progress—USSR* (Cambridge, Mass.: Harvard University Press, 1954), chap. i. See also Merle Fainsod, *How Russia Is Ruled* (Cambridge, Mass.: Harvard University Press, 1953), pp. 208, 284.

21. See Karl O. Paetel, "The Reign of the Black Order," in *The Third Reich* (New York: Frederick A. Praeger, 1955), *passim,* especially p. 643.

22. See Hannah Arendt, *The Origins of Totalitarianism* (New York: Harcourt, Brace & Co., 1951), p. 258; Renzo Sereno, "Italy," in Taylor Cole (ed.), *European Political Systems* (New York: Alfred A. Knopf, 1953), p. 408; and Taylor Cole, "Italy's Fascist Bureaucracy," *American Political Science Review* XXXII (1938), 1157. Since this chapter was written, Dante L. Germino, *The Italian Fascist Party in Power* (Minneapolis: University of Minnesota Press, 1959), has argued strongly for the totalitarian nature of the Fascist party.

23. Duverger, *Political Parties,* gives the most useful single account of these differences among the several types of "party."

24. On the origin of political parties, see Duverger's "Introduction," *ibid.*

25. It is generally recognized that parties occur when the voters become too numerous for more than a few of them to be personally acquainted with the candidates. This should not obscure the fact that a party can come into existence when there is a relatively small electorate, given that the party has an issue of major importance. For example, in 1791, Jefferson's party was strongest in North Carolina, where the suffrage was relatively broad, in New York where it was moderately restricted, and in Virginia where it was very restricted. See S. E. Morison and H. S. Commager, *The Growth of the American Republic* (rev. ed.; New York: Oxford University Press, 1937), I, 122–24, 130.

26. Too frequently, analysts of the democratic state do not go beyond this point, perhaps assuming that "accepting the rules of the game" is self-explanatory. However, such acceptance, not only by the political parties but by the society as a whole, has its causes, and these must be explored. Chapter 8 of the present work is an attempt to discover these causes.

27. See Duverger, *Political Parties,* Bk. I, secs. 1 and 2.

28. The best account of the motivations of members of totalitarian groups is in Gabriel A. Almond, *The Appeals of Communism* (Princeton: Princeton University Press, 1954).

29. Cf. Schattschneider, *Party Government,* pp. 50–53. F. A. Hermens has stressed the confusion of multiparty systems and the loss of popular morale associated with it. See *Democracy or Anarchy?* and *Europe between Democracy and Anarchy* (Notre Dame, Ind.: University of Notre Dame Press, 1951).

30. Cf. Joseph A. Schumpeter, *Capitalism, Socialism, and Democracy* (2nd ed.; New York: Harper & Bros., 1947), pp. 288–89; and Charles E. Merriam and Harold F. Gosnell, *The American Party System* (3rd ed.; New York: Macmillan Co., 1940), p. 126. Merriam

and Gosnell single out the following characteristics required of party leaders: sensitiveness to the strength and direction of social and industrial tendencies, facility in group combination and compromise, facility in personal contacts "with widely varying types of men," and ability to express dramatically the sentiments of large groups of voters. Robert A. Dahl and Charles E. Lindblom, *Politics, Economics, and Welfare* (New York: Harper & Bros., 1953), p. 304, make a similar statement.

31. There are obviously exceptions to this statement. Reinhard H. Luthin, *American Demagogues—20th Century* (Boston: Beacon Press, 1954), gives summary accounts of demagoguery and other abnormal practices in the United States. It should be noticed that almost all these exceptions occur in areas where the parties are weak or nonexistent.

32. See Key, *Politics, Parties, and Pressure Groups*, pp. 563–64.

33. Even within the limitations of organizational effectiveness, success in elections is not correlated with the quality of organization. This comes out most clearly in Britain, where the parties are relatively very well organized but where the party with the inferior organization in a constituency often has the greater electoral success. See H. G. Nicholas, *The British General Election of 1950* (London: Macmillan Co., 1951), pp. 40–41; D. E. Butler, *The British General Election of 1951* (London: Macmillan Co., 1952), pp. 30–31; and Butler, *The British General Election of 1955* (London: Macmillan Co., 1956), p. 205.

34. The implications of this relationship among parties will be developed in chapter 5.

Chapter 3

1. On Portugal, see Paul Johnson, "Behind Salazar's Façade," *New Statesman*, November 2, 1957, pp. 553–54; Kingsley Martin, "Fascism in the Name of Jesus," *New Statesman*, March 2, 1957, p. 268; and Oswell Blakeston, *Portuguese Panorama* (London: Burke Publishing Co., 1955), chaps. vii, xi, xii. For a general statement of the existence of welfare policy, see Harold Zink, *Modern Governments* (New York: D. Van Nostrand Co., 1958), pp. 785–86.

2. For Argentina, see George I. Blanksten, *Perón's Argentina* (Chicago: University of Chicago Press, 1953), chap. xi. Cf. Robert J. Alexander, *The Perón Era* (New York: Columbia University Press, 1951), p. 147. On Egypt, see E. V. Lawrence, *Egypt and the West* (New York: American Institute of International Information, 1956), pp. 24–26; Claire Sterling, "Can Nasser Ransom Himself from the Russians?" *The Reporter*, May 1, 1958, pp. 11–12; and especially Hal Lehrman, "Egypt: Potemkin Village on the Nile," *The Reporter*, May 3, 1956, pp. 30–34. For a theoretical account, see Willard Range, "An Interpretation of Nasserism," *Western Political Quarterly*, XII (1959), 1005–16.

3. For a summary account of the low Soviet standard of living, see William Ebenstein, *Today's Isms* (2nd ed.; Englewood Cliffs, N.J.: Prentice-Hall, 1958), pp. 39–57. For a specific statement of the attitude toward the Soviet worker, see Mark G. Field, *Doctor and Patient in Russia* (Cambridge, Mass.: Harvard University Press, 1957),

chap. ii. On the Soviet program of "qualified medical care to all," see *ibid.*, p. 224, where Field says that in some cases this principle "assumes the proportions of a macabre farce." See Hannah Arendt, *The Origins of Totalitarianism* (New York: Harcourt, Brace & Co., 1951), p. 333, for the farcical nature of Soviet unemployment benefits; and Jerzy Gliksman, "Recent Trends in Soviet Labor Policy," *Problems of Communism,* V (July–August, 1956), 20–28, for an account of how the Soviets use social insurance as a tool of labor discipline.

4. See Blanksten, *Perón's Argentina,* Part III, and Frank Owen, *Perón—His Rise and Fall* (London: Cresset Press, 1957), chap. vi, on Perón's *descamisados.* For a general statement, see George W. F. Hallgarten, *Why Dictators?* (New York: Macmillan Co., 1954).

5. Milovan Djilas, *The New Class* (New York: Frederick A. Praeger, 1957), has most strongly emphasized this aspect of Communist dictatorships.

6. See William P. Tucker, *The Mexican Government Today* (Minneapolis: University of Minnesota Press, 1957), chap. xxiii. Russell H. Fitzgibbon, "A Statistical Evaluation of Latin-American Democracy," *Western Political Quarterly,* IX (1956), 607–19, uses social-welfare legislation as a criterion of democracy; its development correlates with those states we generally consider fairly democratic —Uruguay, Costa Rica, Chile, Mexico, and Brazil.

7. See Gwendolen M. Carter, John H. Herz, and John C. Ranney, *Major Foreign Powers* (3rd ed.; New York: Harcourt, Brace & Co., 1957), pp. 503–4.

8. The idea of interest reflection is expressed very clearly by Alfred de Grazia in *The Elements of Political Science* (New York: Alfred A. Knopf, 1952), a book which is of special value as a clear summary of prevailing hypotheses and opinions: "Representation is a relation between an official and a citizen that exists whenever an action of the official accords with the desire of the citizen. Representative government is a government that makes great use of devices to ensure representation, such as the election of officials" (pp. 144–45). Other expressions are in Carl J. Friedrich, *Constitutional Government and Democracy* (rev. ed.; Boston: Ginn & Co., 1950), p. 267; Arthur N. Holcombe, *Our More Perfect Union* (Cambridge, Mass.: Harvard University Press, 1950), p. 188; Stuart A. Rice, *Quantitative Methods in Politics* (New York: Alfred A. Knopf, 1928), pp. 193–94; J. S. Mill, "Representative Government," in *Utilitarianism, Liberty, and Representative Government* (London: J. M. Dent & Sons, 1910), p. 241; and Harold D. Lasswell and Abraham Kaplan, *Power and Society* (New Haven: Yale University Press, 1950), p. 165. Locke says that "the legislative has the declaring and, as it were, the keeping" of the single will of society; Herman Finer considers this to be a definition of representative government (*The Theory and Practice of Modern Government* [rev. ed.; New York: Henry Holt & Co., 1949], p. 221). A variation is given by W. D. Handcock, "What Is Represented in Representative Government," *Philosophy,* XXII (1947), 99–111: his answer is special interests, rather than those of all the people.

Samuel H. Beer calls the idea of interest reflection the "Radical Theory of representation" and considers it one of the most important conceptions of democratic government in the Anglo-American tradition ("Representation of Interests in British Government," *American Political Science Review*, LI [1957], 613–50). Joseph A. Schumpeter calls it the "classical conception of democracy" (*Capitalism, Socialism, and Democracy* [2nd ed.; New York: Harper & Bros., 1947], chap. xxxi). I have found it assumed by a large proportion of professors of and students in political science.

The popularity of interest reflection may well come from a simple but erroneous process of reasoning. In "genuine democracy," all policy is made directly by the citizens themselves. In representative government or "representative democracy," direct control of policy is "delegated" by the citizens to a small group known as "representatives." The inference is that somehow the representatives make the same kind of policy as is made under "real democracy" by the citizens themselves. It is often unclear, however, whether a writer who accepts this conception of the reflection of interests intends it to apply to the actual operation of representative government, or whether it only expresses an ideal of "representation" which should be approached by governments in order that the state they govern be "truly democratic."

9. The reflection-of-interests concept is normally not connected with the notion of majority rule. For some exceptions where the will of the majority is identified with the will of the people, see Beer, "Representation of Interests in British Government," p. 633. For a more extended analysis of the people's possession of interests, see C. W. Cassinelli, "Some Reflections on the Concept of the Public Interest," *Ethics*, LXIX (1958), 48–61.

10. A classic example is given by Schumpeter. Under what was undoubtedly a military dictatorship, Napoleon as First Consul arrived at his famous religious settlement, which, says Schumpeter, was definitely wanted by the French people, "if ever there was any justification at all for holding that the people actually want something definite" (*Capitalism, Socialism, and Democracy*, pp. 255–56). It is difficult to see upon what grounds one could refute this analysis of the situation; in any event, as will be seen, the evidence for this statement is as good as that for any reflection of interests in a democratic state.

11. Schumpeter has attacked the idea that the acts of a representative government are "in accord with the desires of the people," by arguing that the people do not possess the relevant desires (*ibid.*, pp. 250–64). In order to be reflectable, the will of the people "must be something more than an indeterminate bundle of vague impulses loosely playing about given slogans and mistaken impressions." For the popular will to be more than this, each individual will must be definite and based upon adequate intelligence, information, and ability to draw logical conclusions. It is highly unrealistic to attribute such characteristics to the masses of the democratic state; hence, the "classical theory of democracy" must be rejected.

However, one can accept Schumpeter's argument that the general citizenry is usually ignorant of the issues upon which its government is acting, without accepting his conclusion that the concept of interest reflection must be rejected. I assume that no defender of the concept would deny that the people of the modern democratic state, at least because of unavoidable ignorance, are incapable of possessing a will on most of these issues. Those writers concerned with establishing the political competence of the common man usually say that his opinions are politically relevant only regarding issues within the range of his direct experience and those which raise fundamental questions of democratic rights and justice; for example, Carl J. Friedrich, *The New Image of the Common Man* (Boston: Beacon Press, 1950), pp. 28–37. The conclusion to be drawn here is that the theory of interest reflection cannot claim that every act of a representative government is in accord with the desires of the people; but the theory is not committed to such a claim. The scope of reflection need merely be restricted to include only certain types of governmental actions or a certain quantity of them.

12. Since writers who subscribe to the concept of interest reflection almost never attempt to state it with any precision, this version may not prove acceptable to them. In any event, it is much more reasonable than the very general accounts which they themselves give, and also better than the crude version attacked by Schumpeter.

13. See Cassinelli, "Some Reflections on the Concept of the Public Interest."

14. I have heard this argument frequently in conversation, but I have never discovered it in writing—an indication, no doubt, of its weakness.

15. The empirical studies of voter motivation are referred to, and summarized in, the following: V. O. Key, Jr., *Politics, Parties, and Pressure Groups* (3rd ed.; New York: Thomas Y. Crowell, 1953), chap. xx, with reference to the United States; Sten Sparre Nilson, *Histoire et sciences politiques* (Bergen: Chr. Michelsen Institut, 1950), Part I, with reference to the United States and Europe; and Harold F. Gosnell, *Why Europe Votes* (Chicago: University of Chicago Press, 1930), chap. vii.

16. Friedrich, *Constitutional Government and Democracy*, p. 267; cf. Rice, *Quantitative Methods in Politics*, pp. 193–94.

17. This position is stated explicitly by some authors; see Marie C. Swabey, *Theory of the Democratic State* (Cambridge, Mass.: Harvard University Press, 1937); and A. L. Lowell, *Public Opinion and Popular Government* (New York: Longmans, Green & Co., 1914), p. 240. Variations occur in Holcombe, *Our More Perfect Union*, and Mill, "Representative Government."

18. For a summary of, and references to, the studies of the make-up of parliaments, see Harold F. Gosnell, *Democracy, the Threshold of Freedom* (New York: Ronald Press, 1948), chap. xii.

19. The following show how this condition occurs in modern dictatorships: Hans Gerth, "The Nazi Party: Its Leadership and Composition," *American Journal of Sociology*, XLV (1940), 517–41; Harold D. Lasswell and Renzo Sereno, "Governmental and Party Leaders in Fascist Italy," *American Political Science Review*, XXI (1937), 914–29; and G. K. Schueller, *The Politburo* (Stanford, Calif.: Stanford University Press, 1951).

20. For the interesting and well-known example of the changes

experienced by "proletarian" politicians, see Robert Michels, *Political Parties*, trans. E. and C. Paul (Glencoe, Ill.: Free Press, 1949), pp. 205–14.

21. There is a variation of this argument, which says that, rather than acting as the people want them to act, the typical representatives act as the people *would*, if the people themselves had the opportunity to make official policy (see Holcombe, *Our More Perfect Union*, and Rice, *Quantitative Methods in Politics*). This statement is probably a direct outgrowth of the concept of interest reflection. However, even granting the typicalness of the representatives, the statement tells us nothing about the kind of policy which is made, and therefore is of no scientific value.

22. It has occasionally been thought that the democratic electoral system is only one of several methods by which "political representation" is obtained. De Grazia, *The Elements of Political Science*, refers to elections as an example of "devices" which "ensure representation" (see note 8, above). In another place (*Public and Republic* [New York: Alfred A. Knopf, 1951], p. 7), he suggests that selection of governors by lot would be another such device. See also "Representation," *Encyclopaedia Britannica*, Vol. XXIII, where it is maintained that both the parliament and the jury are representative bodies. The factors common to these devices are not made clear. There would be, for example, many basic differences between a state in which the governors were selected by lot (a "device" which others besides De Grazia may have in mind) and one where they are selected by election. In the former, there would be no political parties, no popular participation in government to the extent found under the latter, no desire by the governors to improve their chances of retaining their jobs, and no vested interests in the protection of civil liberties. All of these features, as will be shown, are absolutely essential to the twelve contemporary democratic states.

23. E.g., Anthony Downs, *An Economic Theory of Democracy* (New York: Harper & Bros., 1957), chap. ii. This recent book is a very good illustration of the point I wish to make: that one cannot account for the policy of a democratic government by reference to the representatives' desires to do what their constituents want them to do. Downs begins with the "vote maximizing" hypothesis, but he is obliged to introduce so many qualifications as he proceeds that the hypothesis is, in effect, abandoned by the conclusion of the book. It seems to me, moreover, that, by means of careful and persistent logic, Downs has demonstrated the great crudeness of the "economic" conception of rational self-interest as a basic tool of political analysis.

24. The classic statement of this hypothesis is by E. E. Schattschneider, *Party Government* (New York: Farrar & Rinehart, 1942), pp. 94–96. An interesting study in support of it is Samuel P. Huntington, "A Revised Theory of American Party Politics," *American Political Science Review*, XLIV (1950), 669–77. The difference of opinion under consideration is probably not intended to apply fully to the situation under proportional representation, because of PR's tendency to encourage specialized appeals to minority groups in the constituency. See F. A. Hermens, *Democracy or Anarchy?* (Notre Dame, Ind.: University of Notre Dame Press, 1941), chaps.

ii–iii; and Maurice Duverger, *Political Parties*, trans. Barbara and Robert North (New York: John Wiley & Sons, 1954), pp. 245–55.

25. This figure of 80 per cent seems to be the normal maximum reached by victors in "one-party" constituencies under the winner-take-all electoral systems of Britain and the United States. See H. G. Nicholas, *The British General Election of 1950* (London: Macmillan Co., 1951), pp. 320–22; D. E. Butler, *The British General Election of 1951* (London: Macmillan Co., 1952), pp. 267–68; and Butler, *The British General Election of 1955* (London: Macmillan Co., 1956), p. 168. For the United States, see *The 1952 Elections—A Statistical Analysis*, published by the Republican National Committee (Washington, D.C., 1953), Table 1, showing that, save for Mississippi and South Carolina, the Republican candidate for the presidency received at least 17 per cent of the popular vote in every state, in both 1948 and 1952; and Table 16, showing that in 1948, 1950, and 1952, in every state except eight in the South, Republican candidates for the House of Representatives received at least 25 per cent of the state-wide vote.

26. In modern mass politics, as in large-scale action of any kind, initiative and leadership in ideas and proposals must be taken by a minority. See C. W. Cassinelli, "The Law of Oligarchy," *American Political Science Review*, XLVII (1953), 773–84.

27. See J. D. Stewart, *British Pressure Groups* (Oxford: Clarendon Press, 1958), especially chap. ii; David B. Truman, *The Governmental Process* (New York: Alfred A. Knopf, 1951), chap. xvi and *passim*; and Robert A. Dahl, *A Preface to Democratic Theory* (Chicago: University of Chicago Press, 1956), chap. v.

28. As one example, see Richard Hofstadter, *Social Darwinism in American Thought, 1865–1915* (Philadelphia: University of Pennsylvania Press, 1944), pp. 86–91, and *The Age of Reform: From Bryan to F. D. R.* (New York: Alfred A. Knopf, 1955), pp. 149–52, for descriptions of the Protestant clergy's influence upon programs of social welfare.

29. See Herman Finer, *Governments of Greater European Powers* (New York: Henry Holt & Co., 1956), pp. 89–92, on Britain; Alexander Brady, *Democracy in the Dominions* (Toronto: University of Toronto Press, 1947), chaps. v, ix, xiii; Julius Turner, *Party and Constituency: Pressures on Congress* (Baltimore: Johns Hopkins University Press, 1951), p. 23, and "Responsible Parties: A Dissent from the Floor," *American Political Science Review*, XLV (1951), 143–57; Leslie Lipson, *The Politics of Equality: New Zealand's Adventures in Democracy* (Chicago: University of Chicago Press, 1948), chap. ix; Louise Overacker, *The Australian Party System* (New Haven: Yale University Press, 1952), chap. x; Arnold J. Zurcher, "The Political System of Switzerland," chaps. iii–iv, in James T. Shotwell (ed.), *Governments of Continental Europe* (rev. ed.; New York: Macmillan Co., 1952); Philip Williams, *Politics in Post-War France* (London: Longmans, Green & Co., 1954), chaps. xxii–xxiii. For a summary of the studies of American parties, see Neil A. McDonald, *The Study of Political Parties* (New York: Doubleday & Co., 1955), pp. 69–75. When coalition governments are normal, party influence tends to be even stronger. For a detailed discussion of

the example of Belgium, see Carl-Henrik Höjer, *Le régime parlementaire belge, de 1918 à 1940* (Uppsala: Almqvist & Wiksells, 1946), especially chap. xi.

30. It must be remembered that there are many other qualifications to this relationship between the governors and the governed in the democratic state. The representative need not fulfill all his promises; he may vote against the welfare of his constituency on the basis of an overriding issue of the "national interest"; very often it is impossible for him to translate into law welfare programs of great benefit to his electorate; and his appeals are usually modified by his calculations regarding the extend to which he is obliged to outbid his rivals. The competition in an election is "monopolistic," and this fact narrows, to a greater or less extent, the scope and intensity of the appeals which need be made by any individual candidate or party. When the electoral process is correctly described, very little indeed remains which can be called "the reflection by the government of the interests of the governed."

31. This has been recognized by Downs, *An Economic Theory of Democracy*, p. 273: "abstention does not harm those who are indifferent because . . . parties still cater to their interests so as to get their votes next time."

32. If certain groups persistently abstain from voting, and it is recognized that they do so, the influence of their franchise may be considerably weakened. See Key, *Politics, Parties, and Pressure Groups*, p. 581.

33. Franco's regime in Spain is typical. See S. Grover Rich, Jr., "Franco Spain: A Reappraisal," *Political Science Quarterly*, LXVII (1952), 378–98.

34. This undermining of dictatorship has been occurring in Latin America during the past decade. See William W. Pierson and Federigo G. Gil, *Governments of Latin America* (New York: McGraw-Hill Book Co., 1957), pp. 318–20. Also see chapter 8 of the present work.

35. This statement of the goals and methods of totalitarianism obviously cannot stand by itself. The argument necessary to support it, however, would require another book. It must suffice to say that I would follow the general outlines of the conception of totalitarianism presented by Hannah Arendt in Part III of *The Origins of Totalitarianism*. The present hope that the "new middle class" will temper the arbitrary nature of the Soviet regime illustrates my general proposition.

Chapter 4

1. E.g., Harold J. Laski, *The Rise of Liberalism* (London: Allen & Unwin, 1936), especially chap. ii; and Frederick Watkins, *The Political Tradition of the West* (Cambridge, Mass.: Harvard University Press, 1948), chap. v.

2. See David Easton, *The Political System* (New York: Alfred A. Knopf, 1953), pp. 293–305, for a discussion of this theory and references to its exponents.

3. One of the primary weaknesses of the theory of interest reflection is its failure to account for the coexistence of liberty and welfare in the democratic state; by its exclusive emphasis upon the

latter, it has, I believe, actually impeded our understanding of the former.

4. For an example of this usage of the phrase "civil liberty" appearing in a textbook, see James M. Burns and Jack W. Peltason, *Government by the People* (3rd ed.; Englewood Cliffs, N.J.: Prentice-Hall, 1957), p. 142.

5. M. Searle Bates, *Religious Liberty: An Inquiry* (New York: Harper & Bros., 1945), pp. 546–47; also see Part I for religious liberty in contemporary nondemocratic states. The nondemocratic states in the first category were Brazil, Chile, Czechoslovakia, Eire, Uruguay, China, Cuba, Ecuador, Estonia, Guatemala, Honduras, Liberia, Nicaragua, Panama, and Salvador. In the second category were the Weimar Republic, Bulgaria, Costa Rica, the Dominican Republic, Haiti, Hungary, Argentina, Bolivia, Latvia, Paraguay, Venezuela, and Yugoslavia.

6. For an analysis of the role of religious liberty in the development of the democratic state, see Laski, *The Rise of Liberalism*, chap. ii.

7. See also Maurice Duverger, *The French Political System* (Chicago: University of Chicago Press, 1958), chap. ix, for a similar statement about the normal situation in France.

8. Zechariah Chafee, Jr., *Free Speech in the United States* (Cambridge, Mass.: Harvard University Press, 1941), p. 150.

9. Milton R. Konvitz, *Fundamental Liberties of a Free People* (Ithaca, N.Y.: Cornell University Press, 1957), p. 275.

10. The Party has a definite membership, it continues to publish newspapers, and it "makes noises that one associates with life —or at least with existence" (*ibid.*, p. 336).

11. *West Virginia Board of Education* versus *Barnette*, 319 U.S. 624 (1943), the case in which the Supreme Court declared compulsory saluting of the flag inconsistent with the Bill of Rights, is a classic example.

12. The large corporation's right to fire at will has been increasingly questioned, even by the corporations themselves. See Adolf A. Berle, Jr., *The 20th Century Capitalist Revolution* (New York: Harcourt, Brace & Co., 1954), chap. iii.

13. See the survey of censorship in the *Senior Scholastic*, LXXI (February 7, 1958), 8 ff. The survey concludes that restrictions on news originating within these states are severe and harsh, and that they are often even more severe on news coming from outside the state in question. There is, of course, some censorship in the democratic states, but it falls within the limits already specified in the text. See also "The Gagged Press," *The Economist*, April 18, 1959, pp. 242 ff., a report of the findings of the International Press Institute.

14. See Caroll Binder, "The Shadow of Global Censorship," *Saturday Review*, March 24, 1951.

15. Chafee, *Free Speech in the United States*, p. 29.

16. See John P. Roche, "American Liberty: An Examination of the 'Tradition' of Freedom," in Milton R. Konvitz and Clinton Rossiter (eds.), *Aspects of Liberty* (Ithaca, N.Y.: Cornell University Press, 1958), p. 157. Roche gives major credit in the defense of American civil liberties to these "civil liberty elites," and especially to the professors of law.

17. See Herbert Tingsten, *The Problem of South Africa* (London: Victor Gollancz, 1955), especially chap. viii.

18. Cf. E. E. Schattschneider, *Party Government* (New York: Farrar & Rinehart, 1942), p. 48. For a summary account of the extension of the suffrage, see Harold F. Gosnell, *Democracy, the Threshold of Freedom* (New York: Ronald Press, 1948), chap. iii.

19. Perhaps the most notorious exception to this mild definition of subversion was the internment of Japanese-Americans during World War II. This event occurred when the normal processes of representative government had been partially suspended, and when a threat from without had caused an unnatural degree of indifference to domestic politics. Many of the injustices caused by this action have been rectified (see *The Economist,* July 4, 1959, p. 38).

20. The story about General Franco's telephoning the most important members of the "Family" before making any decision, whether or not it is true, is certainly based upon a real possibility.

21. "The exaltation of the ruler is characteristic of all autocracies, in whatever form the claim is actually expressed" (Diana Spearman, *Modern Dictatorship* [London: Jonathan Cape, 1939], p. 190). George W. F. Hallgarten takes as one of the defining characteristics of dictatorship the claim that it is the dictator's vocation to rule (*Why Dictators?* [New York: Macmillan Co., 1954], p. 4).

22. Much has been written about the "safety valve" technique of Communism, whereby people are encouraged to criticize lower governmental functionaries. Even if this is a method by which to prevent popular disaffection—and its primary function is most probably to keep the functionaries insecure—it has nothing to do with countering the effects of liberty of speech and the press.

23. For example, Joseph A. Schumpeter, *Capitalism, Socialism, and Democracy* (2nd ed.; New York: Harper & Bros., 1947), pp. 240–43. On p. 271, Schumpeter says, "the democratic method does not necessarily guarantee a greater amount of individual freedom than another political method would permit in similar circumstances."

24. It should be remembered that civil liberties occur earlier than welfare policy in the development of the democratic state, because, while the very operation of a representative government requires the former, the latter occurs only when competition for the votes of the masses becomes necessary.

Chapter 5

1. There are, however, instances of its use as a supposedly meaningful concept in serious contexts; see, for example, H. W. Percival, *Democracy Is Self-Government* (New York: World Publishing Co., 1952); and Laurence Stapleton, *The Design of Democracy* (New York: Oxford University Press, 1949).

2. Note the title of a popular and well-written textbook on American government, James M. Burns and Jack W. Peltason's *Government by the People* (3rd ed.; Englewood Cliffs, N.J.: Prentice Hall, 1957).

3. See David Spitz, *Patterns of Anti-Democratic Thought* (New York: Macmillan Co., 1949) pp. 103–10.

4. This is not to claim that the representative is an expert on

all the complex issues facing contemporary representative governments. The argument that government should be left to the expert
is a separate one, and beyond the scope of the present inquiry. It
can be said here, however, that representative government does at
least as well in solving these technical problems as does any other
kind of government. See Robert A. Dahl and Charles E. Lindblom,
Politics, Economics, and Welfare (New York: Harper & Bros.,
1953), chaps. xiv–xv. Also see chapter 9 of the present work.

5. For example: "The denial in absolute terms of democracy
as majority rule . . . is subject to the crucial objection that the
only alternative to majority rule is some form of minority rule. On
the other hand, the simple equation of democracy with majority
rule . . . is subject to the equally decisive refutation that majority
rule may prevail in even the most dictatorial of governments"
(Spitz, *Patterns of Anti-Democratic Thought*, p. 271).

6. Samuel Lubell's interviews of American voters have presented strong evidence for the democratic electorate's mixed motives. For an instance of the same policy preferences leading to
support of different candidates, see his interviews preceding the
elections of 1958, published in the *Capital Times* (Madison, Wis.),
September 29 to October 30, 1958.

7. Cf. Robert A. Dahl, *A Preface to Democratic Theory* (Chicago: University of Chicago Press, 1956), chap. v, a critique of
the notion of "majority rule."

8. Spitz, *Patterns of Anti-Democratic Thought*, p. 107.

9. Often it is said that "it is better to count heads than to
break them." Since this allows for no third alternative, it is no
justification of decision-making by the majority.

10. The best example is found in Rousseau. The popular assembly is not asked to accept or reject a proposal brought before
it; they are asked whether it is or is not "in conformity with the
general will, which is *their* will." This is the point on which the
citizen expresses his opinion when he votes, "and from the count-
ing of the votes proceeds the declaration of the general will. When,
therefore, a view which is at odds with my own wins the day, it
proves only that I was deceived, and that what I took to be the
general will was no such thing. Had my own opinion won, I should
have done something quite other than I wished to do, and in that
case I should not have been free" (*The Social Contract* [New York:
E. P. Dutton & Co., 1913], Bk. IV, chap. ii). This theory fails completely to explain why the minority is "deceived," why it "really"
wishes to do what the majority overtly desires. While the Rous-
seauan doctrine assumes constant unanimity, the doctrine of the
original contract assumes only an initial unanimity which includes
an agreement henceforth to be bound by majority decision (see
Locke's "Second Treatise on Civil Government," chap. viii, par. 97,
in *Of Civil Government* [New York: E. P. Dutton & Co., 1924]).
This latter theory is no justification, since it gives no reason why
majority rule was agreed to in the hypothetical contract.

11. For example, R. M. MacIver, *The Modern State* (London:
Oxford University Press, 1926), pp. 201–2.

12. See Carl J. Friedrich, "Public Policy and the Nature of
Administrative Responsibility," in Friedrich and Edward S. Mason

(eds.), *Public Policy* (Cambridge: Harvard University Press, 1940), p. 12.

13. Gabriel A. Almond, *The American People and Foreign Policy* (New York: Harcourt, Brace & Co., 1950). Almond agrees that these attentive elites provide the criticism of governmental action.

14. The argument has been that it is not a responsibility of the people to choose among the several democratic candidates; that is, it makes no difference to the system of representative government which democratic candidates are successful. It is assumed that there will always be enough supporters of a minority party to maintain at least the necessary two parties. The reason for this assumption is that in a democratic society (to be explained in chapter 8) a majority party which threatens to destroy its rivals electorally will become too large and heterogeneous to preserve its own unity; this means, incidentally, that it will never be strong enough to suppress its rivals forcefully, even if its leaders had this unlikely inclination. On these latter points, see E. E. Schattschneider, *Party Government* (New York: Farrar & Rinehart, 1942), chap. iv.

15. This list combines the statements of Ramsey Muir, *National Self-Government* (New York: Henry Holt & Co., 1918), p. 7, and Arnold Bennett Hall, *Popular Government* (New York: Macmillan Co., 1921), pp. 39–43.

16. Most of the concrete evidence on popular political ignorance is drawn from the United States. See William Albig, *Modern Public Opinion* (New York: McGraw-Hill Book Co., 1956), pp. 231–32, where there are also references; Martin Kriesberg, "Dark Areas of Ignorance," in Lester Markel *et al.*, *Public Opinion and Foreign Policy* (New York: Harper & Bros., 1949); and James L. McCamy, *The Administration of American Foreign Affairs* (New York: Alfred A. Knopf, 1950), pp. 311–18. There is every reason to believe that data from the other democratic states would support the same conclusion. See Gérard Herberichs, "Is There No European Opinion?" *Prod Translations*, III (December, 1959), 3–9.

17. Cf. Schattschneider, *Party Government*, chap. iv.

18. The competition among parties roughly resembles that among the economists' "oligopolists," as stated, for example, in Joe S. Bain, *Pricing, Distribution, and Employment* (New York: Henry Holt & Co., 1948), pp. 200–6.

19. See chapter 8 for other aspects of the elector's identification with a party.

20. An unusually clear statement of this opinion is by James Hogan, *Election and Representation* (Oxford: B. H. Blackwell, 1945), p. 114.

21. See William E. Rappard, *The Government of Switzerland* (New York: D. Van Nostrand, 1936), p. 37.

22. Carl J. Friedrich, *The New Image of the Common Man* (Boston: Beacon Press, 1950), pp. 28–37.

23. See Christopher Hughes, *The Federal Constitution of Switzerland* (Oxford: Clarendon Press, 1954), pp. 100–2. Hughes says that the referendum has been "not unsuccessful" as a device to increase a sense of responsibility among the Swiss; but he also says that "a House of Lords which acted as irresponsibly as the Swiss people did in the years before 1914 would not deserve to last six

months." For a general statement, see Herman Finer, *The Theory and Practice of Modern Government* (rev. ed.; New York: Henry Holt & Co., 1949), pp. 562–64, where he says that experience with the referendum has left states "no better off and probably worse off."

24. See V. O. Key, Jr., *American State Politics* (New York: Alfred A. Knopf, 1956), chap. iv.

25. See chapter 7 for a discussion of democratic "indoctrination."

Chapter 6

1. A slightly different version of this chapter appeared in the *Western Political Quarterly*, XII (1959), 391–409. The material is presented here with the kind permission of the *Quarterly*'s editors.

2. For example, Guido de Ruggiero, *The History of European Liberalism* (London: Oxford University Press, 1927), p. 409. Locke's statement occurs in chap. viii, par. 119, of the "Second Treatise on Civil Government," in *Of Civil Government* (New York: E. P. Dutton & Co., 1924).

3. Sidney Hook, *Reason, Social Myths, and Democracy* (New York: John Day Co., 1940), p. 285. Almost all the arguments for both consent and tacit consent which I shall examine are at least suggested in chap. viii of Locke's "Second Treatise"; it is their contemporary expression which concerns us here.

4. See Robert Bierstedt, "The Problem of Authority," in Morroe Berger *et al.* (eds.), *Freedom and Control in Modern Society* (New York: D. Van Nostrand, 1954), p. 80.

5. "The exercise of the right to vote is an implied acceptance of the general order of the state. By that act each voter affirms the principle that what the majority determines shall stand as the policy of the whole state, while his right remains effective to work for the triumph of the policy which is his own" (R. M. MacIver, *The Modern State* [London: Oxford University Press, 1926], p. 199).

6. This theory cannot apply to any democratic state which has adopted compulsory voting.

7. Cf. Hume, "Of the Original Contract," in Ernest Barker (ed.), *The Social Contract* (London: Oxford University Press, 1947), p. 221.

8. This theory is stated by Carl J. Friedrich, *Constitutional Government and Democracy* (rev. ed.; Boston: Ginn & Co., 1950), pp. 135–36, 266.

9. *Ibid.*, p. 136.

10. See William S. Livingston, "Emigration as a Theoretical Doctrine during the American Revolution," *Journal of Politics*, XIX (1957), 591–615, for a summary of the traditional views on withdrawal from governmental control.

11. No doubt consent through failure to emigrate is supposed to be tacit consent, although the intention is usually not made explicit. Cf. Hume, "Of the Original Contract," p. 223.

12. For example, James Hogan, *Election and Representation* (Oxford: B. H. Blackwell, 1945), p. 119.

13. A. D. Lindsay, *The Modern Democratic State* (New York:

Oxford University Press, 1947), I, 206. See also Leslie Lipson, *The Great Issues of Politics* (New York: Prentice-Hall, 1954), p. 57: "People want certain results from their government and they are willing that their officials have the means of bringing those results to fruition."

14. Lindsay, *The Modern Democratic State*, I, 206.

15. The defenders of "rational" motivation as consent recognize that no government can operate without relying to some extent upon the fear of legal punishment. Only the anarchist denies this proposition. As a consequence, in the discussion of the several motivations supposed to serve as the consent of the governed, the existence of a certain amount of the fear of punishment will always be assumed.

16. See Lindsay, *The Modern Democratic State*, I, 206. In this passage he appears to say both that people desire compulsory regulation regarding specific matters which they understand, and that they desire "the power of the state" in general. Lipson, *The Great Issues of Politics*, p. 57, speaks of "consent to the general body of law," a phrase which may have reference to the government's possession of force rather than to any individual use of this force.

17. See Max Weber's summary in *From Max Weber: Essays in Sociology*, trans. and ed. H. H. Gerth and C. Wright Mills (New York: Oxford University Press, 1946), p. 249. Bierstedt, "The Problem of Authority," pp. 70–72, suggests that this attitude is connected not with the ordered relationship of authority but with the dominance-submission relationships of leadership. An early stage in the transition from leadership to authority would no doubt retain much of this belief in the ultimate success of those in authority, a success which would probably be required to prove itself periodically.

18. R. M. MacIver, *The Web of Government* (New York: Macmillan Co., 1947), pp. 76–77.

19. Franco's regime in Spain is a good example. Although Franco's supporters—the army, the church, the Falange, and the aristocracy—accept his position of authority, even they do not believe him to have a moral right to rule. The masses more or less heartily concur, although they are reported to feel that his stabilizing influence justifies his rule. This lack of a moral right makes Franco a ruler without the consent of his governed. It is interesting to notice how disaffection has been growing in Spain as memories of the anarchy of the civil war fade.

Another useful illustration is the situation in a state under "occupation" by a military conqueror. The defeated people may consider that the victor has a right to rule, because of one expediency or another, but they will probably not consent to this rule.

20. The people "consent, because they think, that, from long possession, [the prince] has acquired a title . . ."; and "they consent; because they apprehend [the prince] to be already by birth, their lawful sovereign" ("Of the Original Contract," pp. 221, 225).

21. MacIver, *The Web of Government*, pp. 4, 447–48.

22. Cf. William Y. Elliott and Neil A. McDonald, *Western Political Heritage* (New York: Prentice-Hall, 1949), p. 7.

Chapter 7

1. On the general problem of authority, see Carl J. Friedrich, "Authority, Reason, and Discretion," in Friedrich (ed.), *Authority* (Cambridge, Mass.: Harvard University Press, 1958).

2. Cf. Robert Bierstedt, "The Problem of Authority," in Morroe Berger *et al.* (eds.), *Freedom and Control in Modern Society* (New York: D. Van Nostrand, 1954).

3. See Hans Kelsen's discussion of the "efficacy" and "validity" of the law, *General Theory of Law and State* (Cambridge, Mass.: Harvard University Press, 1946) pp. 39 ff.

4. This usage of the terms "authority" and "legitimacy" is adopted by Hannah Arendt (p. 83) and David Easton (p. 180) in essays in Friedrich, *Authority*.

5. Students of administration have stressed this aspect of authority. The fundamental works are Chester I. Barnard, *The Functions of the Executive* (Cambridge, Mass.: Harvard University Press, 1938); and Herbert A. Simon, *Administrative Behavior* (New York: Macmillan Co., 1947). Carl J. Friedrich has argued that the directives must be "capable of reasoned elaboration" in order for the confidence of the recipients to be retained ("Authority, Reason, and Discretion").

6. On the German masses, see Richard Hiscocks, *Democracy in Western Germany* (London: Oxford University Press, 1957), *passim* and especially chap. xi. On the elites, see *ibid.*, chap. ix; and John H. Herz, "Political Views of the West German Civil Service"; Gabriel A. Almond, "The Politics of German Business"; and W. Phillips Davidson, "Trends in West German Public Opinion, 1946–1956"; all in Hans Speier and W. P. Davidson (eds.), *West German Leadership and Foreign Policy* (Evanston, Ill.: Row, Peterson, 1957).

7. John N. Figgis, *The Divine Right of Kings* (2nd ed.; Cambridge, Eng.: Cambridge University Press, 1914), pp. 11, 45, 95, 175.

8. See chapter 8.

9. See Marie C. Swabey, "The Leading Myths of Our Time," *Ethics*, XLIX (1939), 168–86. The author also calls attention to beliefs that are connected with democratic political myths, such as equality, fraternity, the inalienable rights of the individual, the rationality of the common man, and the moral precedence of the individual over society. We have already seen why these beliefs are associated with the democratic state.

10. It is curious to see that L. S. Amery maintains that the government of Great Britain is government *of* and *for* the people, but not *by* the people (*Thoughts on the Constitution* [2nd ed.; New York: Oxford University Press, 1953], p. 21). This statement expresses the Conservative attitude of government by the elite for the benefit of the masses. Yet the Conservative party has supported the doctrine of the "mandate," whereby a Government is supposed to go to the country before initiating any new policy program. See Byrum E. Carter, *The Office of Prime Minister* (Princeton: Prince-

ton University Press, 1956), pp. 282 ff. The "mandate" is fully in the democratic tradition of "government by the people."

11. Luigi Sturzo, "The Philosophical Background of Christian Democracy," *Review of Politics*, IX (1947), 3–15. Cf. Jacques Maritain, *Man and the State* (Chicago: University of Chicago Press, 1951), p. 25.

12. It has been my experience—admittedly covering only a very small sample—that college freshmen almost unanimously reply to the question, "What is democracy?" in terms of our myths. They usually stress that the citizens of the democratic state govern themselves to their own advantage. Although these freshmen are atypical of the general population, they are products of the same primary and secondary education, and they know little about American government and politics.

13. See D. W. Brogan, *France under the Republic* (New York: Harper & Bros., 1940), especially Bk. II, chap. ii. The dispute between right and left at the start of the Third Republic concerned institutional variations, whether to have a constitutional monarch, and later whether to have a president and an upper house. The growth of the "liberal empire" before 1870 is often overlooked in evaluating French devotion to democracy (see Theodore Zeldin, *The Political System of Napoleon III* [London: Macmillan Co., 1958], especially chaps. ix, xi). The history of nineteenth-century France can be read, without too much distortion, as a continuing attempt to find a viable representative government.

14. Charles A. Micaud, *The French Right and Nazi Germany* (Durham, N.C.: Duke University Press, 1943), does not show that more than a few were willing to give up democracy. Moreover, "the dilemma of the Right was not limited to France; the same picture of hesitation and confusion could be found in other Continental countries and even in Great Britain, the stronghold of placid liberalism" (p. 229). James Christopher, in E. M. Earle (ed.), *Modern France* (Princeton: Princeton University Press, 1951) p. 57, can say only that "at least a fraction of the bourgeoisie" went Fascist. It is instructive that, on p. 45, Christopher states that "both men of property and would-be men of property took the bourgeois outlook"; even some proletarians shared this spirit. (See chapter 8 of the present work.)

The Vichy regime was backed only by a minority, who had taken the initiative because of the Third Republic's military defeat; it never found sympathy with the great majority. See Dorothy M. Pickles, *France between the Republics* (London: Love & Malcomson, 1946), chap. ii. "A conscious faith in democracy was undoubtedly far and away the most important factor in resistance [to Vichy]" (p. 53). Cf. Gordon Wright, *The Reshaping of French Democracy* (New York: Reynal & Hitchcock, 1948), chap. iii.

David Schoenbrun has succinctly summarized the French performance: "France is the only major power on the Continent of Europe that has remained loyal to its democratic traditions in this century of totalitarianism" (*As France Goes* [New York: Harper & Bros., 1957], p. 15).

15. Public-opinion polls of Communist voters have shown only a few to be antidemocratic. See Maurice Duverger, *The French*

Political System (Chicago: University of Chicago Press, 1958), p. 11; also see E. Drexel Godfrey, Jr., "The Communist Presence in France," *American Political Science Review*, L (1956), 321–38. Cf. Schoenbrun, *As France Goes*, pp. 88–89. The Communists, incidentally, have always had to protest their adherence to both democratic and national values and ideals: they present themselves as the *true* democrats and the *true* nationalists.

16. The Soviet experience following the death of Stalin is instructive here. Even a regime with a minimum dependence upon popular support found it necessary to try to invoke some sense of legitimacy. The revival of the Communist party as the vehicle of proletarianism and the memory of Lenin as the author of the revolution is the primary manifestation of this development.

17. See Hannah Arendt, *The Origins of Totalitarianism* (New York: Harcourt, Brace & Co., 1951), pp. 382–83.

18. The evidence that modern people respond more favorably to programs of social welfare than to those of individual material sacrifice for the benefit of the group is found primarily in the behavior of the political leaders most closely associated with the largest and least-favored occupational and social groups of the modern state. Labor unions and Socialist parties have usually been concerned with very practical matters of living standards and social acceptance, even when these issues have been expressed in terms of the proletarian revolution. It is reasonable to suppose that, if the "masses" could be more easily appealed to by means of doctrines stressing a Spartan-like caste system for the purpose of augmenting the strength or purity of the nation, the unions and parties which sought popular support would have utilized such doctrines. This general statement is not inconsistent with an occasional flurry of jingoism within the lower classes, or with their support of the nation in emergencies, such as the famous voting of war credits by European Socialist parties prior to World War I.

19. "Consent" could possibly refer to a popular approval of government, which is manifested neither in popular action nor even in popular attitudes. This usage resembles the concept of the General Will. "Consent" and "will" are, after all, words with roughly similar connotations.

The vagueness surrounding the notion of consent is well illustrated by the following quotation from Harold J. Laski. The doctrine of consent "emphasizes, what needs continual iteration, that the end of the state is fundamental. It throws into relief the striking fact that while the government of the state must endure, if its own existence is to be possible, its purpose is at each stage subject to examination." The state "must exist not less for our welfare than its own" (*Authority in the Modern State* [New Haven: Yale University Press, 1919], pp. 34–35). Laski realizes that "consent" cannot be understood literally, but it is not easy to see how he arrived at his nonliteral interpretation. For another illustration of the difficulty in determining just what is meant by "consent," see David Spitz, *Democracy and the Challenge of Power* (New York: Columbia University Press, 1958), chaps. ii, xii.

20. See Samuel A. Stouffer, *Communism, Conformity, and Civil Liberties* (New York: Doubleday & Co., 1955), p. 57. A sur-

vey showed that the proportion of "community leaders" willing to tolerate nonconformism was more than twice as great as that of a "national cross-section." See also C. H. Smith, "Liberalism and Level of Information," *Journal of Educational Psychology*, XXXIX (1948), 65–82. However, J. N. Perryman, "On the Meaning of 'Democracy,'" *Public Opinion Quarterly*, XVII (1953), 47–60, found that labor-union members frequently cited "freedom of expression" as a democratic essential. Perryman's sample, incidentally, showed remarkable agreement between the ordinary citizen and the "public personality" on the meaning of "democracy." The most frequent responses to the question, "What is democracy?" were: the selection of one's governors; the freedoms of expression, economic opportunity, and religion; and the freedom from discrimination.

21. On the problems of education in democracy, see the Committee for the Advancement of Teaching, of the American Political Science Association, *Goals for Political Science* (New York: William Sloan, 1951), chap. ii. An interesting statement of the function of education "ideally to make political scientists of all" is given by William H. Harbold and Dell G. Hitchner, "Some Reflections on Method in the Study of Politics," *Western Political Quarterly*, XI (1958), 753–73. Perhaps the most instructive example of democratic "indoctrination" was the performance of the public-school teachers of the Third French Republic, which certainly played a major role in the strengthening of French democracy. See Dorothy M. Pickles, *The French Political Scene* (London: Thomas Nelson, 1938), pp. 28–30.

Chapter 8

1. Aristotle, *Politics*, trans. Benjamin Jowett (New York: Modern Library, 1943), Bk. IV; John Stuart Mill, "On Liberty," chap. iv, in *Utilitarianism, Liberty, and Representative Government* (London: J. M. Dent & Sons, 1910).

2. Political scientists often answer the question regarding the foundation of democracy by reference to the attitudes needed to operate representative institutions. Schumpeter says "Democratic Self-Control"—obeying undesirable laws, being honest and tolerant of differences of opinion, refraining from irresponsible opposition —is a major condition "for the success of the democratic method" (*Capitalism, Socialism, and Democracy* [2nd ed.; New York: Harper & Bros., 1947], pp. 294–95). The same kind of answer is given by Ernest S. Griffith, John Plamenatz, and J. Roland Pennock, "Cultural Prerequisites to a Successfully Functioning Democracy: A Symposium," *American Political Science Review*, L (1956), 101–37. Such answers, in effect, only restate the question.

3. Cf. Robert A. Dahl and Charles E. Lindblom, *Politics, Economics, and Welfare* (New York: Harper & Bros., 1953), p. 297. The only exception to this statement seems to be political scientists themselves. See chapter 9, below.

4. This phrase has been used by many writers; see, for example, David B. Truman, *The Governmental Process* (New York: Alfred A. Knopf, 1951), pp. 512–13. There is a frequent tendency to consider "agreement on the rules of the game" to be an explana-

tion of democracy's foundation, whereas it, too, simply restates the question.

5. Cf. Carl J. Friedrich, "Democracy and Dissent," *Political Quarterly,* X (1939), 571–82.

6. The problem of democratic cohesion could be seen as one of coordinating, into a pattern of self-restraint and cooperation, millions of *individuals,* each of whom has a remarkable leeway in determining his own affairs. The difficulty could be considered to stem from human selfishness or perversity, or simply from the difficulty of coordinating such vast numbers or from a combination of both. But this level of abstraction has little theoretical utility in the present context.

7. Reinhard Bendix, "Social Stratification and Political Power," in Bendix and S. M. Lipset (eds.), *Class, Status, and Power* (Glencoe, Ill.: Free Press, 1953), 596–609, argues that we cannot *predict* political action from a theory of "classes," but grants that it "identifies major elements of the struggle for power."

8. Description by David Easton, *The Political System* (New York: Alfred A. Knopf, 1953), p. 293.

9. I use the term "community" to refer to any group characterized by the common self-identification of its members. A community has traditionally been thought of as a geographical phenomenon, but men identify themselves with nonregional groups as well—economic "classes," and religious, racial, and cultural groups. This usage resembles that current in social science, although it is somewhat narrower. E. C. Lindeman defines a community as a group which is aware of its mutual interdependency. ("Community," *Encyclopaedia of the Social Sciences,* IV, 102–5). See also Gordon W. Blackwell, "Community Analysis," in Roland Young (ed.), *Approaches to the Study of Politics* (Evanston, Ill.: Northwestern University Press, 1958), p. 309.

10. The best treatment of the nation is Karl W. Deutsch, *Nationalism and Social Communication* (New York: John Wiley & Sons, 1953). My description is based on his analysis.

11. See Deutsch's discussion of the "building blocks of nationality" (*ibid.,* chap. ii). On the United States, see Hans Kohn, *American Nationalism* (New York: Macmillan Co., 1957), pp. 8–9, 224–25.

12. Deutsch, *Nationalism and Social Communication,* p. 153.

13. It is significant that modern totalitarianism has abandoned the national community, basing its political organization on an "international" elite considered inherently superior to the average man. This practice points up the restraining influence of the national community upon political power. See C. W. Cassinelli, "Totalitarianism, Ideology, and Propaganda," *Journal of Politics,* XXII (1960), 68–95.

14. This has been recognized by many authors. See, for example, the Royal Institute of International Affairs, *Nationalism* (London: Oxford University Press, 1939), p. 198; Mill, "Representative Government," in *Utilitarianism, Liberty and Representative Government,* pp. 360–61; Ramsey Muir, *National Self-Government* (New York: Henry Holt & Co., 1918), pp. 7–8; and Carl Mayer, "Democratic Nationalism," in Max Ascoli and Fritz Leh-

mann (eds.), *Political and Economic Democracy* (New York: W. W. Norton, 1937), p. 296.

This does not imply that a democratic state cannot be founded when only political elites have this sense of community. The movement toward unification of western Europe after World War II could result in a single democratic state of "The Six," when only certain leadership groups were "good Europeans," but for the state to persist the masses would very soon have to think of themselves as Europeans first, and Italians, Frenchmen, and so forth second. Ernst B. Haas, *The Uniting of Europe* (London: Stevens, 1958), discusses the factors which can give rise to a larger sense of community. Also see chapter 9, below.

15. See the Royal Institute, *Nationalism,* p. 198, where nationalism is said to provide "a line beyond which opponents will agree not to differ."

16. This indeterminacy caused much confusion in the late nineteenth and early twentieth centuries, when the relationship of democracy and nationalism was a major theoretical issue. See the Royal Institute, *Nationalism,* p. 54: "Since 1871 there has been a constant debate between political theorists whether nationalism should properly be regarded as an attribute of democracy or of absolutism, of progress or of reaction."

17. See chapter 9.

18. "Now in all states there are three elements: one class is very rich, another very poor, and a third in a mean. It is admitted that moderation and the mean are best, and therefore it will clearly be best to possess the gifts of fortune in moderation; for in that condition of life men are most ready to follow rational principle" (*Politics,* 1295b, 1–6 [p. 190]).

19. For an account of the expanding nature of what is relevant to material possessions, see Walton H. Hamilton and Irene Till, "Property," *Encyclopaedia of the Social Sciences,* XII, 528–38.

20. *Ibid.*

21. W. S. and E. S. Woytinsky, *World Population and Production* (New York: Twentieth Century Fund, 1953), p. 395. The figures, of course, are not strictly comparable. In comparing the standards of living of states with widely differing social and economic structures, A. J. Brown concludes that, since a large part of incomes is spent on goods not traded internationally, the states with lower industrial productivity do not have standards of living as low as their per capita incomes suggest. American incomes, for example, will not buy almost three times as much as British incomes, but only about twice as much, and the real purchasing power of Indian incomes is a tenth or twelfth of American incomes, rather than a twentieth or a thirtieth (*Introduction to the World Economy* [London: Allen & Unwin, 1959], pp. 85–86). Even given this adjustment, the "contrast between abundance and scarcity" remains.

22. The source of the figures is Woytinsky, *World Population and Production,* pp. 389–90, 391, 399–400.

23. These indexes of wealth are used by S. M. Lipset in "Some Social Requisites of Democracy: Economic Development and Political Legitimacy," *American Political Science Review,* LIII (1959),

69–105. With minor variations, Lipset's argument connecting democracy with a high living standard is similar to mine.

24. In 1954, the ratio of automobiles to population in the democratic states ranged from 1 to 3.3, in the United States, to 1 to 31, in Norway. The Netherlands' ratio was 1 to 48, a clear exception to the general pattern. The ratio for all democracies was 1 to 5.3. In the second group of states (those with the second highest per capita incomes in 1948), the range was from 1 to 23, in South Africa, to 1 to 76, in Austria; with a ratio of 1 to 41.7 for them all. The ratio of telephones to population in the democracies ranged from 1 to 3, in the United States, to 1 to 14, in France; with a composite ratio of 1 to 4.3. The range in the second group of states was from 1 to 14, in Austria, to 1 to 57, in Venezuela; with a composite ratio of 1 to 21.4. The ratio of radios to population in the democratic states ranged from 1 to 1.3, in the United States, to 1 to 4.7, in France; with a ratio of 1 to 1.9 for them all. In the second group of states, the range was from 1 to 4.2, in Austria, to 1 to 28, in Venezuela; with a ratio of 1 to 8.1 for them all. All figures calculated from Tables 135, 143, and 181 of the United Nations *Statistical Yearbook, 1955*. (No figures for Czechoslovakia were available.)

25. The per capita income figures for the highly productive Soviet Union were $105 in 1938 and $181 in 1948 (Woytinsky, *World Population and Production*, pp. 389–90, 391, 399–400). See Harry Schwartz, *Russia's Soviet Economy* (2nd ed.; New York: Prentice-Hall, 1954), pp. 430–33, 628–31; on the revaluation of the ruble as a method for eliminating private savings, see pp. 478–80, 510.

26. It is interesting to notice that, as the standard of living in Great Britain has increased during the 1950's, the parties (and thus presumably the electorate) have become much less restrictive and protectionist. See the account of the Labour party's program in "Forward from Socialism," *The Economist*, November 29, 1958, pp. 763–65.

27. The Middle Class is "least likely to shrink from rule, or to be over-ambitious for it" (Aristotle, *Politics*, 1295b).

28. Lipset has explained this attitude very clearly. When a society has a very low absolute standard of living, the upper classes are under pressure to treat the poverty-stricken masses "as beyond the pale of human society, as vulgar, as innately inferior, as a lower caste. The sharp difference in the style of living between those at the top and those at the bottom makes this psychologically necessary. Consequently, the upper strata also tend to regard political rights for the lower strata, particularly the right to share in power, as essentially absurd and immoral. The upper strata not only resist democracy themselves, but their often arrogant political behavior serves to intensify extremist reactions on the part of the lower classes" ("Some Social Requisites of Democracy," pp. 83–84).

29. Cf. José Ortega y Gasset, *The Revolt of the Masses* (Mentor ed.; New York: New American Library, 1950), chap. xi, p. 73.

30. George W. F. Hallgarten has summarized this tradition in *Why Dictators?* (New York: Macmillan Co., 1954), Part II, "The 'Ultra-Revolutionary' Dictatorships." The American experience has

been summarized by Reinhard H. Luthin, *American Demagogues— 20th Century* (Boston: Beacon Press, 1954).

31. Fritz Lehmann has said that large inequalities do not necessarily lead to disaffection because people are "more interested in getting a higher share for themselves than in getting equal distribution for all" ("Distribution of Wealth," in Ascoli and Lehmann, *Political and Economic Democracy*, p. 165). Cf. John K. Galbraith, *The Affluent Society* (Boston: Houghton, Mifflin, 1958), pp. 85–87. Distribution was rather unequal in Great Britain before 1945; for the figures, see Gwendolen M. Carter *et al.*, *Major Foreign Powers* (3rd ed.; New York: Harcourt, Brace & Co., 1957), pp. 11–12.

32. For an illustration, see Katherine Archibald, "Social Orientations among Shipyard Workers," in Bendix and Lipset, *Class, Status, and Power*, pp. 395–402.

33. Lipset, "Some Social Requisites of Democracy," p. 84, links political tolerance with the existence of "enough wealth in the community so that it actually does not make too much difference if some redistribution does take place."

34. David Easton, *The Political System*, p. 300. Some theorists have suggested that the essential attribute of democratic government is its specific "technique for the functioning of the interests" (Arthur F. Bentley, *The Process of Government* [Chicago: University of Chicago Press, 1908], p. 320; and Truman, *The Governmental Process*, p. 264). This attribute is certainly unique, but it is not causally fundamental, for the interaction of the pressure groups occurs within the context of the Middle-Class society.

35. "The evidence available suggests that the chances for stable democracy are enhanced to the extent that social strata, groups, and individuals have a number of cross-cutting politically relevant affiliations. To the degree that a significant proportion of the population is pulled among conflicting forces, such groups and individuals have an interest in reducing the intensity of political conflict" (Lipset, "Some Social Requisites of Democracy," p. 97).

36. See David Riesman, *The Lonely Crowd* (New Haven: Yale University Press, 1951), p. 255. See also A. A. Berle, Jr., *The 20th Century Capitalist Revolution* (New York: Harcourt, Brace & Co., 1954), chap. ii: the corporation "must tell the truth, and so conduct itself that it retains the confidence of its customers, its labor, its suppliers and the sector of the public with whom it deals" (p. 60).

37. For the history of the expanding suffrage in Great Britain, see Hiram Miller Stout, *British Government* (New York: Oxford University Press, 1953), pp. 202–5; in the United States, V. O. Key, Jr., *Politics, Parties, and Pressure Groups* (3rd ed.; New York: Thomas Y. Crowell, 1953), pp. 600–4; in Sweden, Dankwart A. Rüstow, *The Politics of Compromise* (Princeton: Princeton University Press, 1955), pp. 44–45; in Denmark and Norway, Ben A. Arneson, *The Democratic Monarchies of Scandinavia* (New York: D. Van Nostrand, 1949), pp. 28–29, 37; in Canada, Australia, and New Zealand, Alexander Brady, *Democracy in the Dominions* (Toronto: University of Toronto Press, 1947), pp. 63, 131, 245; in Belgium, Felix E. Oppenheim, "Belgium: Party Cleavage and Compromise," in Sigmund Neumann (ed.), *Modern Political Parties*

(Chicago: University of Chicago Press, 1956), p. 156; in the Netherlands, Bartholomew Landheer (ed.), *The Netherlands* (Berkeley: University of California Press, 1943), p. 84. French history is somewhat different: universal manhood suffrage was introduced in 1848, but voting was unofficially restricted and controlled throughout the Second Empire. See Peter Campbell, *French Electoral Systems and Elections, 1789–1957* (New York: Frederick A. Praeger, 1958), pp. 67–68.

38. It is instructive that the history of the spread of the franchise has nothing to do with an "equilibrium" among political forces.

39. Only France has experienced serious proletarian disaffection. However, taking the French working class to number eight million and assuming that their proportion of voting equaled the national average in 1951 (80 per cent), only about 2.2 million or 34 per cent voted for the Communists when the latter received 25.6 per cent of the total ballot (calculations based on figures given in Herman Finer, *Governments of Greater European Powers* [New York: Henry Holt & Co., 1956], pp. 347, 401–2). There is no reason to believe that all these supporters of the Communist party are antidemocratic (see E. Drexel Godfrey, Jr., "The Communist Presence in France," *American Political Science Review*, L [1956], 321–38). There is some reason to believe that the poorest sections of the proletariat vote Communist, especially those with the worst housing facilities (see François Goguel, *France under the Fourth Republic* [Ithaca, N.Y.: Cornell University Press, 1952], p. 97). Remember that France has had the lowest per capita income of the twelve democratic states, and that in the last few decades "for the first time in two centuries the gross national product has remained almost stationary from one generation to the next" (Henry W. Ehrmann, *Organized Business in France* [Princeton: Princeton University Press, 1957], pp. 476–77). It is no accident that France has had the greatest tendency to political instability of all the democratic states.

40. See Nobutaka Ike, *The Beginnings of Political Democracy in Japan* (Baltimore: Johns Hopkins Press, 1950). For the influence of Bismarck's idea of strengthening authoritarianism by means of elected assemblies and for the influence of French democratic theory, see Chitoshi Yanaga, *Japan since Perry* (New York: McGraw-Hill Book Co., 1949), pp. 150, 168.

41. For the growth of these groups see Edwin O. Reischauer, *Japan—Past and Present* (New York: Alfred A. Knopf, 1946), p. 98. E. Herbert Norman has characterized the Japanese landlord as "a modest Cobden" (*Japan's Emergence as a Modern State* [New York: Institute of Pacific Relations, 1940], p. 171). See also Robert A. Scalapino, *Democracy and the Party Movement in Prewar Japan* (Berkeley: University of California Press, 1953), especially chap. vii.

42. Yanaga, *Japan since Perry*, p. 227.

43. *Ibid.*, p. 325.

44. Norman, *Japan's Emergence as a Modern State*, pp. 189–90.

45. Yanaga, *Japan since Perry*, p. 396.

46. See E. Herbert Norman, *Soldier and Peasant in Japan* (New York: Institute of Pacific Relations, 1943).

47. Yanaga, *Japan since Perry*, p. 491.

48. See Werner Burmeister, "Western Europe," in Burmeister (ed.), *Democratic Institutions in the World Today* (London: Stevens, 1958), p. 10. How they were kept out of power is explained by Thorstein Veblen, *Imperial Germany and the Industrial Revolution* (New York: B. Huebsch, 1918), *passim* and especially pp. 78, 82–83, 169–70, 224, 244–45.

49. For the history of this period, see Koppel S. Pinson, *Modern Germany* (New York: Macmillan Co., 1954), chaps. xiv–xvi. "The Majority Socialists were sincerely devoted to the cause of democratic and parliamentary institutions . . . [they] rejected any and all forms of dictatorship, including the dictatorship of the proletariat . . . [they] retained a horror of violence and bloodshed and a sense of the dignity of the individual . . . ," and as early as 1919 they "clearly saw what was going on in Bolshevik Russia and recognized the calamitous threat to liberty, democratic institutions, and human rights created by the Soviet regime . . ." (*ibid.*, p. 373). The working-class organizations remain the strongest supporters of the Bonn Republic. See Richard Hiscocks, *Democracy in Western Germany* (London: Oxford University Press, 1957), chap. x; and Otto Kirchheimer, "West German Trade-Unions: Their Domestic and Foreign Policies," in Hans Speier and W. Phillips Davidson (eds.), *West German Leadership and Foreign Policy* (Evanston, Ill.: Row, Peterson, 1957).

50. See Carl E. Schorske, *German Social Democracy, 1905–1917* (Cambridge, Mass.: Harvard University Press, 1955), especially chap. xii. During the period 1848–78, the working-class movement was fully committed to democracy, and the Erfurt program of 1891 was basically evolutionary; the trade unions always supported "revisionism" under the Second Empire (*ibid.*, pp. 2–3, 6, and chap. iv). For the unions' "social welfare" program, see *ibid.*, pp. 13–14. For Bismarck's "social" legislation, see Elmer Roberts, *Monarchical Socialism in Germany* (New York: Charles Scribner's Sons, 1913), chaps. iv, v.

The German standard of living has always been the most hopeful factor in the attempt to create a democratic Germany, while the lack of well-founded myths of democracy has been the most discouraging. Interestingly, these factors are reversed in the case of Italy. In 1938, the German per capita income was $335, higher than the Netherlands, Denmark, Belgium, and France. In the 1950's, the standard of living was comparable to its prewar position. For Italy, the per capita income in 1938 was under $150, compared to $260 for France, the poorest democratic state; in 1948, it was $225 compared to France's $418 (figures from Woytinsky, *World Population and Production*, pp. 391, 399–400). For the Italian tradition of democracy, see C. J. S. Sprigge, *The Development of Modern Italy* (London: Duckworth, 1943), *passim* and especially chap. xi. It is instructive that Joseph G. LaPalombara assumes a standard-of-living definition of the middle class in discussing the prospects for democracy in post-World War II Italy ("Left-Wing Trade Unionism: The Matrix of Communist Power in Italy," *Western Political Quarterly,*

VII [1954], 202–26: "only if the criterion used were the availability of running water, heat, undamaged living quarters, three meals a day, and the like, could Italy be said to have much of a middle class" (p. 212). The Japanese per capita income has been only about one-third of the French, but it is almost twice that of Ceylon, the next highest Asian country (Woytinsky, *World Population and Production*, pp. 391, 399–400). Given Asian standards, it is not unrealistic to say that Japan comes close to being a Middle-Class state.

51. Cuba's 1938 per capita income was about one-third of the French. In 1948, it had risen to 70 per cent (Woytinsky, *World Population and Production*, pp. 391, 399–400).

52. Karl E. Meyer, "Who Won What in Cuba?" *The Reporter*, February 5, 1959, pp. 20–23. Cf. John J. Johnson, *Political Change in Latin America* (Stanford, Calif.: Stanford University Press, 1958), especially chap. i.

53. It is interesting that, in 1904, Thorstein Veblen thought that American trade unionism was endeavoring "to construct an institutional scheme on the lines imposed by the new exigencies given by the machine process," that is, a kind of "functionalism" (*The Theory of Business Enterprise*, chap. ix [Mentor ed.; New York: New American Library, 1958], p. 160). When the laborer joined the Middle Class, he was no longer interested in movements like technocracy, guild socialism, and syndicalism.

54. The best example of functional representation in a democratic state is the Economic Council of the Fourth French Republic. The members of each of the several occupational groups on this body maintained an intransigent solidarity because they saw their job as protecting the single interest for which they were supposed to speak. See Ehrmann, *Organized Business in France*, pp. 254–56; Philip Williams, *Politics in Post-War France* (London: Longmans, Green & Co., 1954), pp. 297–300; and Harry Seligson, "An Evaluation of the Economic Council of France," *Western Political Quarterly*, VII (1954), 36–50.

55. For the basically antidemocratic nature of functional representation, see Norman L. Stamps, *Why Democracies Fail* (Notre Dame, Ind.: University of Notre Dame Press, 1957), p. 105. Corporativism is a technique of dictatorships "because a chamber representing different interests can possess no inherent cohesion and because any unity of action which it may attain is likely to be an imposed unity." "Occupational representation is a divisive rather than an integrating element because it treats men on the basis of how they are different rather than on the basis of how they are alike." It is interesting to reflect that if the theory of political equilibrium were correct, the corporate state would be the most likely institutional result.

56. See *From Max Weber: Essays in Sociology*, trans. and ed. H. H. Gerth and C. Wright Mills (New York: Oxford University Press, 1946), pp. 186–87.

57. Aristotle seems to have been aware of the political influence of deference. See *Politics*, 1295b, 6–8, 15, 21–22 (pp. 190–91); here he refers to the factors of birth, being in disgrace, friendship, and fellowship.

58. The French workingman apparently does not experience

much vicarious status from the power of his trade-union leaders. See Val R. Lorwin, *The French Labor Movement* (Cambridge, Mass.: Harvard University Press, 1954), p. 164. This is no doubt a result of the general weakness of French trade unionism.

59. The American South solved this problem by adopting a one-party system of relatively issueless politics which was not supposed to have influence on, or be influenced by, the party struggles in the remainder of the country. See E. E. Schattschneider, "United States: The Functional Approach to Party Government," in S. Neumann, *Modern Political Parties*, pp. 201–2. In South Africa, where the situation is national rather than sectional, there seems to be a movement toward a "one-party" system.

60. According to Panfilo Gentile, relatively properous northern Italian workers have supported the Communist party and trade union because of their frustration by the rigid Italian social structure ("Italy's Greatest Problem Is Lack of Hope," *New York Times Magazine*, December 7, 1952). Also see Angelo Rossi, *A Communist Party in Action*, trans. and ed. Willmoore Kendall (New Haven: Yale University Press, 1949), p. 225: the French Communist party recruits from workers who see no chance of normal social advancement. The North American Negro has been faithful to democratic parties and processes, but his behavior is surprising and generally recognized as requiring explanation. See Wilson Record, *The Negro and the Communist Party* (Chapel Hill: University of North Carolina Press, 1951), chap. viii, on the failure of the party to recruit Negroes. "What intrudes itself upon the observer is the fact that the Party has worked so hard to glean so little" (p. 299). "The degree of loyalty which the Negro has given to the conservative society which discriminates against him is *impressive;* and though this loyalty is often undeserved, it has been *peculiarly* consistent . . ." (p. 302; emphasis added).

Chapter 9

1. "Freedom" has been ambiguous, referring to the conditions necessary for self-realization and to the state of self-realization. I shall use it consistently in the first sense.

2. See David M. Potter, *People of Plenty* (Chicago: University of Chicago Press, 1954), p. 91, on these interpretations of "equality."

3. A constant worry about the democratic state is that the "rise of the average man to political power" will inadvertently result in the vulgarization of all culture. The argument is that the mass market drives all taste to a juvenile level; the popular preoccupation with material goods and personal comfort destroys the "higher" values; and the ordinary man's desire to be like his neighbors and have them resemble him stifles variant behavior and thus creativity. But the facts do not square with this argument. The cultural level of the masses is higher in the modern democratic state than anywhere else at any time, and there are fewer restrictions than ever before upon the "cultured elite." Disapproval of democracy's cultural standards is no doubt based upon the large output of inferior motion pictures, fiction of sex and violence, and drab and senti-

mental products of the graphic arts. In itself, this material is deplorable; but it cannot be condemned without also condemning the methods of production and distribution which make the greatest works of art available to all and which have practically destroyed cultural parochialism, and without implicitly approving a culture of aristocracy or one of folk art, with the political, social, and economic conditions which necessarily accompany them. One final fact is worth noting: the development of one of the great branches of theoretical knowledge—the social sciences—has occurred within the democratic state. This last point is made by William G. Carleton, "Is Democracy to Blame?" *Virginia Quarterly Review*, XXXIII (1957), 225.

4. T. H. Green, *Lectures on the Principles of Political Obligation* (London: Longmans, Green & Co., 1917), pars. 20, 122.

5. Some philosophers have identified the "good man" with the "good citizen." If this means a participation in political life comparable to that of the leisure class of the polis, then no man can be good in the "Great Society." I would prefer to stress the unique *opportunity* for political participation provided by contemporary representative government.

6. See Frank J. Sorauf, "The Public Interest Reconsidered," *Journal of Politics*, XIX (1957), 616–39, for a typical statement. Cf. C. W. Cassinelli, "Some Comments on Sorauf's 'The Public Interest Reconsidered,'" *Journal of Politics*, XX (1958), 553–56.

7. John H. Hallowell, *The Moral Foundations of Democracy* (Chicago: University of Chicago Press, 1954), p. 47.

8. See "Pre-Election Politics," *The Economist*, January 24, 1959, pp. 293–94. "Conservative" parties have also been successful recently in Scandinavia, the Low Countries, North America, and Australia and New Zealand.

9. Richard M. Titmuss, *Essays on "The Welfare State"* (London: Allen & Unwin, 1958), chap. ii, has stressed the limited scope of governmental activity regarding welfare in Britain, where "social services" are usually thought to be very comprehensive.

10. See Dwight Waldo, *Perspectives on Administration* (University, Ala.: University of Alabama Press, 1956). The Fifth French Republic can be interpreted as an attempt to strengthen representative government, which came about only when precipitated by a crisis. It must be remembered that sentiment for a "stronger executive" before May, 1958, was not the monopoly of the Gaullists. See *The Economist*, May 5, 1956, p. 483: "more and more members of the center parties are coming round to presidential government as the only way to sound government," and "it is increasingly respectable on the left to admire de Gaulle." See also *The Economist*, November 16, 1957, pp. 597–98; and Peter Campbell, "The Cabinet and the Constitution in France, 1956–58," *Parliamentary Affairs*, XII (1958–59), 35.

11. This general point is stressed by William H. Harbold, "Democracy and the Service State," *Ethics*, LXX (1960), 135–45.

12. The definitions of these terms are in Robert A. Dahl and Charles E. Lindblom, *Politics, Economics, and Welfare* (New York: Harper & Bros., 1953), pp. 227, 277–78, 324.

13. *Ibid.*, chap. xiv.

14. *Ibid.*, p. 300.

15. Arnold J. Zurcher, "Democracy's Declining Capacity to Govern," *Western Political Quarterly*, VIII (1955), p. 536.

16. Walter Lippmann, *The Public Philosophy* (Mentor ed.; New York: New American Library, 1955), chaps. ii and iv, pp. 28, 42.

17. The electoral success of Dwight D. Eisenhower may have strengthened the opinion that democracy breeds complacency. The key to this success, however, was not Eisenhower's tendency to minimize difficulties, but the remarkable confidence which people had in his ability to meet emergencies, crises, and even disasters. For another interpretation, see T. V. Smith, "Is There a Gresham's Law in Politics?" *Western Political Quarterly*, VIII (1955), 418–24. He points out that campaign promises cannot be taken literally, since they state ideals which are not expected to be realized, but which "nourish the citizen's faith" in democracy and serve as a harmless form of political entertainment.

18. This oversight is especially evident in Lippmann, *The Public Philosophy*. On p. 46, he says the ruler's "duty is to the office and not to his electors." Although Lippmann quite properly wants to stress the former duty, he completely ignores the latter. The democratic officeholder has a duty to both.

19. Cf. Carleton, "Is Democracy to Blame?"

20. On these matters, see Merle Fainsod, *How Russia Is Ruled* (Cambridge, Mass.: Harvard University Press, 1953), chap. iv; Barrington Moore, Jr., *Terror and Progress, USSR* (Cambridge, Mass.: Harvard University Press, 1954), chap. i; and Hannah Arendt, *The Origins of Totalitarianism* (New York: Harcourt, Brace & Co., 1951), chap. xii.

21. See Samuel P. Huntington, *The Soldier and the State* (Cambridge, Mass.: Harvard University Press, 1957), chap. iv and *passim*, for a general account of civil-military relations which shows the subordination of the military to elected personnel of representative governments. See also the references in note 24 of chapter 1, above.

22. J. H. Hobson, *Imperialism* (rev. ed.; London: George Allen, 1938), pp. 113–52. Hobson thought it very probable that the British Empire would destroy British democracy. It is no exaggeration to say that the precise reverse occurred.

23. On the breakdown of democratic control, see J.-M. Domenach, "Democratic Paralysis in France," *Foreign Affairs*, XXXI (1958), 31–44; and André Philip, "The Birth of the Fifth Republic," *The New Leader*, July 7–14, 1958, pp. 9–18. On De Gaulle's restoration of control over the Algerian hierarchies, see Claire Sterling, "Algeria: A Showdown Is Postponed," *The Reporter*, January 22, 1959, pp. 21–24; and "Algerian Anniversary," *The Economist*, May 16, 1959, pp. 603–4.

The collapse of democratic authority was greatly encouraged by special weaknesses of French democracy: the antiquated party system and "weak executive," the powerful Communist party, the army hypersensitive regarding its honor after Indochina, the persistent attitude of a *mission civilisatrice*, and the intransigence of the Europeans in Algeria.

24. See Herbert A. Simon, *Administrative Behavior* (New York: Macmillan Co., 1947), chap. iii.

25. See Dahl and Lindblom, *Politics, Economics, and Welfare,* pp. 261–71.

26. See "Decentralization and Democracy," *The Economist,* April 19, 1958, pp. 217–18.

27. There has been some confusion concerning the modern corporation's position in democracy, and much of it seems to come from a failure to state precisely the *political* problem involved in its "concentration of power." That corporation managers make decisions directly affecting thousands or millions of people is obvious, and that corporate interests must be carefully considered by most politicians is only common sense. For the analyst of democracy, the only question is whether the admittedly vital decisions of the corporation can be controlled by representative government, when the latter wishes to exercise such control.

Robert A. Dahl has pointed out that sociologists tend to emphasize the predominant influence of business groups, while political scientists tend to view business as one among many power groups ("Business and Politics: An Appraisal of Political Science," *American Political Science Review,* LIII [1959], 1–34; see pp. 27–28). This difference in stress is probably the result of asking different questions. The sociologist is concerned with all influence, while the political scientist is interested primarily in influence upon decisions by government.

If representative government maintains its ability to control the corporation, the degree of the latter's influence upon it is not relevant to the larger issue of the health of democracy. The issue is not whether parliaments always act "in the interest of business," for even if this were true the special results of representative government—civil liberties and welfare policy—would still obtain.

28. The power of corporation managers is no longer checked by stockholders, boards of directors, competition with producers of the same product, and suppliers of capital (see Dahl, "Business and Politics," p. 8; A. A. Berle, Jr., *Economic Power and the Free Society* [New York: Fund for the Republic, 1957], p. 10; and Berle, *The 20th Century Capitalist Revolution* [New York: Harcourt, Brace & Co., 1954], pp. 25–52), but other checks remain. Even in a tight oligopoly, there is competition for the "leadership position," as Berle calls it (*The 20th Century Capitalist Revolution,* p. 58); there is interproduct competition (Dahl and Lindblom, *Politics, Economics, and Welfare,* pp. 178–79); and there is at least some control coming from large buyers and large labor unions (*ibid.,* p. 184).

As was pointed out in chapter 4, large business is very sensitive to "public opinion"; it tries to avoid appearing oppressive, arrogant, and generally undemocratic, to all with whom it has direct dealings and to the community at large (see Berle, *The 20th Century Capitalist Revolution,* pp. 54–57). The managers themselves "are invariably influenced by certain great philosophical principles" which "are not derived from within business organization" (*ibid.,* p. 186). When the leaders of private associations—like certain labor unions—seem to ignore these principles, they evoke regulatory legislation.

29. Berle, *The 20th Century Capitalist Revolution,* p. 187. There is some doubt about the effectiveness of business' attempts to manipulate attitudes in its own favor (see Dahl, "Business and Politics," pp. 28–29). In the absence of evidence, the best estimate is that these attempts have only a superficial effect because they are countered by so much contrary propaganda, especially from non-business-oriented political parties.

30. For data on this latter tendency in the United States, see Melvin M. Tumin, "Readiness and Resistance to Desegregation: A Social Portrait of the Hard Core," *Social Forces,* XXXVI (1958), 256–63.

31. See Morton Deutsch and Mary Evans Collins, *Interracial Housing* (Minneapolis: University of Minnesota Press, 1951), p. 127.

32. Using W. W. Rostow's concepts, a "traditional society" is one with 75 per cent or more of the working force engaged in agriculture, a hierarchical social structure with little vertical mobility, wealth and power possessed by landlords, and income above minimum consumption levels spent in nonproductive or low-productivity outlays. A "transitional society" emerges from a traditional society when an elite becomes willing and able to manipulate and apply modern science and useful cost-reducing inventions, to save 10 per cent of the national income, and to lend these savings to entrepreneurs ("Rostow on Growth," *The Economist,* August 15, 1959, pp. 409–16). The transitional period is obviously an unsettled one.

33. It is not possible here to develop a complete theory of democratic foreign policy. The Middle-Class political attitude generally prevents any war not seen as absolutely necessary for national survival. (The "business" or "commercial" spirit has long been recognized as basically pacifist.) Representative governments occasionally can pursue a policy of limited aggression, but they as often as not are then immediately subject to paralyzing criticism and opposition at home, as in the Suez action of 1956. Democratic foreign policy is fundamentally defensive.

34. The "mature" society is characterized by the presence of new methods and outlooks in all sections of the economy and by an effective modern government (Rostow, "Rostow on Growth"). According to Rostow, a newly mature state can choose political and military expansion instead of high mass consumption.

35. There is, of course, frequent conflict between these two basic desires. "Social" acceptance is thought by many to come only from power; hence, the emphasis on heavy industry or upon constructing larger political units (e.g., the United Arab Republic) which often works against raising living standards. Cf. Rostow, "Rostow on Growth," and the preceding note.

36. See "Protection Frustrated," *The Economist,* June 27, 1959, pp. 1159–60.

37. See *The Economist,* May 9, 1959, p. 524.

38. In order to exploit this possibility, Lenin abandoned the Marxist analysis of the foundations of revolution and returned to

the traditional appreciation of the natural conflict between rich and poor.

39. Technical matters of adjusting bureaucracies, assemblies, and policies, although they are difficult enough, require only the same kind of skills and patience necessary for such matters within any single democratic state. The crucial issue is the will to combine, the desire to undertake the technical problems in the first place.

40. See Arnold Zurcher, *The Struggle to Unite Europe* (New York: New York University Press, 1958).

41. Ernst B. Haas, *The Uniting of Europe* (London: Stevens, 1958), is the best description of the separate motives of the major parties and pressure groups in the Six.

42. Again, the best account is by Haas. On p. 158, he remarks how self-interest in a larger group prompts self-identification with the group. It is possible that even as strong a "nationalist" as Charles de Gaulle recognizes the need for a larger community. It has been reasonably suggested that he intends to get his "greatness" in a Franco-German union (*The Economist*, March 14, 1959, pp. 983–84).

43. Zurcher, *The Struggle to Unite Europe*, p. 188.

44. Haas, *The Uniting of Europe*, p. 155: "Certainly it is significant that a *homogeneous* movement combatting such steps [toward Europeanism] has failed to materialize."

45. See C. Grove Haines (ed.), *European Integration* (Baltimore: John Hopkins University Press, 1957), p. 165.

46. The need for uniting western European democracies at the present time is a matter of conjecture. Michael T. Florinsky, *Integrated Europe?* (New York: Macmillan Co., 1955), argues not only that integration is unnecessary but that it would be positively harmful.

47. The American phenomenon of "McCarthyism" was an instance of this type of protest. McCarthy symbolized the antipathy toward the powerful—the bureaucrats, executives, and financiers, all deriving from the educated and moneyed Eastern aristocracy—and he linked this traditional grievance against influence with the insecurities generated by the physical and ideological (primarily atheistic) challenge of the USSR. See Daniel Bell (ed.), *The New American Right* (New York: Criterion Books, 1956); and Martin A. Trow, "Small Businessmen, Political Tolerance, and Support for McCarthy," *American Journal of Sociology*, LXIV (1958), 270–81.

48. The best single treatment of the antidemocratic tendencies of the petty bourgeoisie is Seymour M. Lipset, *Political Man: The Social Bases of Politics* (Garden City, N.Y.: Doubleday & Co., 1960), chap. v. My account follows his statistics and general interpretation.

49. *Ibid.* The movement led by Pierre Poujade has been the best example of this petty bourgeois antidemocratic tendency (see Stanley Hoffman, *Le mouvement Poujade* [Paris: Armand Colin, 1956]; and Peter Campbell, "Le mouvement Poujade," *Parliamentary Affairs*, Vol. X [1957]). Poujade possessed enough flamboyance to attract the mildly dissatisfied, but many French petty bourgeoisie were more than mildly unhappy, since this group has

experienced a more direct and obvious threat to its existence than has the petty bourgeoisie of any other democratic state. In addition, the delayed arrival of large-scale economic organization in France found an especially alert and politically well-entrenched small enterpriser (see Herbert Luethy, *France against Herself* [New York: Frederick A. Praeger, 1955], especially Part IV, chap. ii; and John E. Sawyer, "Strains in the Social Structure of Modern France," in E. M. Earle, [ed.], *Modern France* [Princeton: Princeton University Press, 1951]). The development of large economic units in other democracies has been more gradual and has not been complicated by weak governmental institutions and serious proletarian protest.

50. Lipset, *Political Man: The Social Bases of Politics*, chap. v.

51. See David Lockwood, *The Blackcoated Worker* (London: Allen & Unwin, 1958), pp. 56, 80, 95, 99, for material supporting this supposition.

52. See the discussion of this preference in chapter 8, and in Lipset, *Political Man: The Social Bases of Politics*, chap. v.

53. On the latter point, see Clement Greenberg, "Work and Leisure under Industrialism," in Eric Larrabee and Rolf Meyersohn (eds.), *Mass Leisure* (Glencoe, Ill.: Free Press, 1959), pp. 38–43.

54. Marx, *Capital* (New York: Modern Library, n.d.), Part I, chap. i, sec. 4, and Part IV, chap. xiv, secs. 1–5.

55. "Leisure and Work in Post-Industrial Society," in Larrabee and Meyersohn, *Mass Leisure*, p. 371. Riesman points out that earlier, in *The Lonely Crowd* (New Haven: Yale University Press, 1951), he thought that leisure might thus compensate for work.

56. David M. Potter, *People of Plenty*, pp. 103–5.

57. As an antidote, Potter suggests that an increasingly high standard of material welfare may make occupational position less important. "Upward" mobility may cease to be a "social imperative," and a new sense of status may develop, emphasizing not hierarchy but membership, identity, and one's own place in the community (*ibid.*, pp. 109–10). The trend toward the "organization man" may be a move in this direction. See Robert E. Lane, "The Fear of Equality," *American Political Science Review*, LIII (1959), 35–51, for examples of the tendency of Americans to rationalize their own status positions.

58. It does not appear likely that the people of the democratic state will become satiated with material possessions and therefore no longer influenced by the stabilizing effects of the gifts of fortune in moderation, for there seem to be no limits to the material security for which one can strive. The pattern of American acquisition has shown those people just moving into the Middle Class concerned primarily with physical goods like appliances and automobiles; more sophisticated material goods like houses then become most important; finally, health and education take priority. When these desires are satisfied, the next goal may well be the improvement of "community services," like police, sanitation, and parks, which require the pooling of individual resources through taxation. This development simply illustrates the point that satiation seems relatively remote. The British have followed a different course, with

"cradle to grave" security satisfied first and interest in consumer's goods coming afterward.

59. *The Revolt of the Masses* (New York: New American Library, 1950), chap. vi, p. 42. Also notice the following: "the mass-man sees in the State an anonymous power, and feeling himself, like it, anonymous, he believes that the State is something of his own"; "he will tend more and more to set its machinery working on whatsoever pretext, to crush beneath it any creative minority which disturbs it . . ." (chap. xiii, pp. 87–88).

60. *Ibid.*, chap. vii, pp. 44, 47.

61. *The Public Philosophy*, chap. viii. Similar criticisms of contemporary democracy are given by Jacques Maritain, *Man and the State* (Chicago: University of Chicago Press, 1951); and Reinhold Niebuhr, *The Children of Light and the Children of Darkness* (New York: Charles Scribner's Sons, 1944).

62. The strongest and clearest statement concerning the people's belief in democratic ideals is chap. i, "American Ideals and the American Conscience," of Gunnar Myrdal's *An American Dilemma* (New York: Harper & Bros., 1944).

63. See Lane, "The Fear of Equality."

64. Romain Gary's *The Roots of Heaven*, trans. Jonathan Griffin (New York: Simon & Schuster, 1959), certainly one of the best novels published since 1945, is an interesting commentary on the much advertised "loss of faith" by the democratic artist—especially since it was written by a Frenchman.

BIBLIOGRAPHY

Albig, William. *Modern Public Opinion*. New York: McGraw-Hill Book Co., 1956.

Alexander, Robert J. *The Perón Era*. New York: Columbia University Press, 1951.

Almond, Gabriel A. *The American People and Foreign Policy*. New York: Harcourt, Brace & Co., 1950.

——. *The Appeals of Communism*. Princeton: Princeton University Press, 1954.

——. "The Politics of German Business," in Hans Speier and W. Phillips Davidson (eds.), *West German Leadership and Foreign Policy*. Evanston, Ill.: Row, Peterson, 1957.

Amery, L. S. *Thoughts on the Constitution*. 2nd ed. New York: Oxford University Press, 1953.

Appleby, Paul. *Big Democracy*. New York: Alfred A. Knopf, 1945.

Archibald, Katherine. "Social Orientations among Shipyard Workers," in Reinhard Bendix and Seymour M. Lipset (eds.), *Class, Status, and Power*. Glencoe, Ill.: Free Press, 1953.

Arendt, Hannah. *The Origins of Totalitarianism*. New York: Harcourt, Brace & Co., 1951.

——. "What Was Authority?" in Carl J. Friedrich (ed.), *Authority*. Cambridge, Mass.: Harvard University Press.

Aristotle. *Politics*. Translated by Benjamin Jowett. New York: Modern Library, 1943.

Arneson, Ben A. *The Democratic Monarchies of Scandinavia*. New York: D. Van Nostrand, 1949.

Bain, Joe S. *Pricing, Distribution, and Employment*. New York: Henry Holt & Co., 1948.

Barnard, Chester I. *The Functions of the Executive*. Cambridge, Mass.: Harvard University Press, 1938.

Bates, M. Searle. *Religious Liberty: An Inquiry*. New York: Harper & Bros., 1945.

Beer, Samuel H. "Representation of Interests in British Government," *American Political Science Review*, LI (1957), 613–50.

Bell, Daniel (ed.). *The New American Right*. New York: Criterion Books, 1956.

Bendix, Reinhard. "Social Stratification and Political Power," in Reinhard Bendix and Seymour M. Lipset (eds.), *Class, Status, and Power*. Glencoe, Ill.: Free Press, 1953.

Bentley, Arthur F. *The Process of Government*. Chicago: University of Chicago Press, 1908.

Berdahl, Clarence A. "Party Membership in the United States," *American Political Science Review*, XXXVI (1942), 241–62.

Berle, A. A., Jr. *Economic Power and the Free Society*. New York: Fund for the Republic, 1957.

——. *The 20th Century Capitalist Revolution*. New York: Harcourt, Brace & Co., 1954.

Bierstedt, Robert. "The Problem of Authority," in Morroe Berger *et al.* (eds.), *Freedom and Control in Modern Society*. New York: D. Van Nostrand, 1954.

Blackwell, Gordon W. "Community Analysis," in Roland Young (ed.), *Approaches to the Study of Politics*. Evanston, Ill.: Northwestern University Press, 1958.

Blakeston, Oswell. *Portuguese Panorama*. London: Burke Publishing Co., 1955.

Blanksten, George I. *Perón's Argentina*. Chicago: University of Chicago Press, 1953.

Bone, Hugh A. "An Introduction to the Senate Policy Committees," *American Political Science Review*, L (1956), 339–59.

Brady, Alexander. *Democracy in the Dominions*. Toronto: University of Toronto Press, 1947.

Brogan, D. W. *France under the Republic*. New York: Harper & Bros., 1940.

Brown, A. J. *Introduction to the World Economy*. London: Allen & Unwin, 1959.

Burmeister, Werner. "Western Europe," in Werner Burmeister (ed.), *Democratic Institutions in the World Today*. London: Stevens, 1958.

Burns, James M. *Congress on Trial*. New York: Harper & Bros., 1949.

——, and Jack W. Peltason. *Government by the People*. 3rd ed. Englewood Cliffs, N.J.: Prentice Hall, 1957.

Butler, D. E. *The British General Election of 1951*. London: Macmillan Co., 1952.

——. *The British General Election of 1955*. London: Macmillan Co., 1956.

Campbell, Peter. *French Electoral Systems and Elections, 1789–1957*. New York: Frederick A. Praeger, 1958.

——. "Le mouvement Poujade," *Parliamentary Affairs*, Vol. X (1957).

Carleton, William G. "Is Democracy to Blame?" *Virginia Quarterly Review*, XXXIII (1957), 202–28.

Carter, Byrum E. *The Office of Prime Minister*. Princeton: Princeton University Press, 1956.

Carter, Gwendolen M., John H. Herz, and John C. Ranney. *Major Foreign Powers*. 3rd ed. New York: Harcourt, Brace & Co., 1957.

Cassinelli, C. W. "The Law of Oligarchy," *American Political Science Review*, XLVII (1953), 773–84.

——. "Some Reflections on the Concept of the Public Interest," *Ethics*, LXIX (1958), 48–61.

——. "Totalitarianism, Ideology, and Propaganda," *Journal of Politics*, XXII (1960), 68–95.

Chafee, Zechariah, Jr. *Free Speech in the United States.* Cambridge, Mass.: Harvard University Press, 1941.

Chapman, Brian. *The Prefects and Provincial France.* London: Allen & Unwin, 1955.

Christopher, John B. "The Desiccation of the Bourgeois Spirit," in Edward Mead Earle (ed.), *Modern France.* Princeton: Princeton University Press, 1951.

Clokie, H. McD. "The Modern Party State," *Canadian Journal of Economics and Political Science,* XIV (1949), 139–57.

Cole, Taylor. "Italy's Fascist Bureaucracy," *American Political Science Review,* XXXII (1938), 1142–57.

Dahl, Robert A. "Business and Politics: An Appraisal of Political Science," *American Political Science Review,* LIII (1959), 1–34.

———. *A Preface to Democratic Theory.* Chicago: University of Chicago Press, 1956.

———, and Charles E. Lindblom. *Politics, Economics, and Welfare.* New York: Harper & Bros., 1953.

Davidson, W. Phillips. "Trends in West German Public Opinion, 1946–1956," in Hans Speier and W. Phillips Davidson (eds.), *West German Leadership and Foreign Policy.* Evanston, Ill.: Row, Peterson, 1957.

De Grazia, Alfred. *The Elements of Political Science.* New York: Alfred A. Knopf, 1952.

———. *Public and Republic.* New York: Alfred A. Knopf, 1951.

Deutsch, Karl W. *Nationalism and Social Communication.* New York: John Wiley & Sons, 1953.

Deutsch, Morton, and Mary Evans Collins. *Interracial Housing.* Minneapolis: University of Minnesota Press, 1951.

Djilas, Milovan. *The New Class.* New York: Frederick A. Praeger, 1957.

Domenach, J.-M. "Democratic Paralysis in France," *Foreign Affairs,* XXXI (1958), 31–44.

Downs, Anthony. *An Economic Theory of Democracy.* New York: Harper & Bros., 1957.

Duverger, Maurice. *The French Political System.* Chicago: University of Chicago Press, 1958.

———. *Political Parties.* Translated by Barbara and Robert North. New York: John Wiley & Sons, 1954.

Easton, David. "The Perception of Authority and Political Change," in Carl J. Friedrich (ed.), *Authority.* Cambridge, Mass.: Harvard University Press, 1958.

———. *The Political System.* New York: Alfred A. Knopf, 1953.

Ebenstein, William. *Today's Isms.* 2nd ed. Englewood Cliffs, N.J.: Prentice-Hall, 1958.

Ehrmann, Henry W. *Organized Business in France.* Princeton: Princeton University Press, 1957.

Elliott, William Y., and Neil A. McDonald. *Western Political Heritage.* New York: Prentice-Hall, 1949.

Epstein, Leon D. "Cohesion of British Parliamentary Parties," *American Political Science Review,* L (1956), 360–77.

Fainsod, Merle. *How Russia Is Ruled.* Cambridge, Mass.: Harvard University Press, 1953.

Field, Mark G. *Doctor and Patient in Russia*. Cambridge, Mass.: Harvard University Press, 1957.

Figgis, John N. *The Divine Right of Kings*. 2nd ed. Cambridge, Eng.: Cambridge University Press, 1914.

Finer, Herman. *Governments of Greater European Powers*. New York: Henry Holt & Co., 1956.

———. *The Theory and Practice of Modern Government*. Rev. ed. New York: Henry Holt & Co., 1949.

Fitzgibbon, Russell H. "A Statistical Evaluation of Latin-American Democracy," *Western Political Quarterly*, IX (1956), 607–19.

Florinsky, Michael T. *Integrated Europe?* New York: Macmillan Co., 1955.

Friedrich, Carl J. "Authority, Reason, and Discretion," in Carl J. Friedrich (ed.), *Authority*. Cambridge, Mass.: Harvard University Press, 1958.

———. *Constitutional Government and Democracy*. Rev. ed. Boston: Ginn & Co., 1950.

———. "Democracy and Dissent," *Political Quarterly*, X (1939), 571–82.

———. *The New Image of the Common Man*. Boston: Beacon Press, 1950.

———. "Public Policy and the Nature of Administrative Responsibility," in Carl J. Friedrich and Edward S. Mason (eds.), *Public Policy*, Vol. I. Cambridge, Mass.: Harvard University Press, 1940.

Galbraith, John K. *The Affluent Society*. Boston: Houghton, Mifflin, 1958.

Gary, Romain. *The Roots of Heaven*. Translated by Jonathan Griffin. New York: Simon & Schuster, 1959.

Gentile, Panfilo. "Italy's Greatest Problem Is Lack of Hope," *New York Times Magazine*, December 7, 1952.

Germino, Dante L. *The Italian Fascist Party in Power*. Minneapolis: University of Minnesota Press, 1959.

Gerth, Hans. "The Nazi Party: Its Leadership and Composition," *American Journal of Sociology*, XLV (1940), 517–41.

Gliksman, Jerzy. "Recent Trends in Soviet Labor Policy," *Problems of Communism*, V (July–August, 1956), 20–28.

Godfrey, E. Drexel, Jr. "The Communist Presence in France," *American Political Science Review*, L (1956), 321–38.

Goguel, François. *France under the Fourth Republic*. Ithaca, N.Y.: Cornell University Press, 1952.

Goris, Jan-Albert (ed.). *Belgium*. Berkeley: University of California Press, 1946.

Gosnell, Harold F. *Democracy, the Threshold of Freedom*. New York: Ronald Press, 1948.

———. *Why Europe Votes*. Chicago: University of Chicago Press, 1930.

Green, Thomas Hill. *Lectures on the Principles of Political Obligation*. London: Longmans, Green, & Co., 1917.

Greenberg, Clement. "Work and Leisure under Industrialism," in Eric Larrabee and Rolf Meyersohn (eds.), *Mass Leisure*. Glencoe, Ill.: Free Press, 1959.

Griffith, Ernest S., John Planenatz, and J. Roland Pennock. "Cultural Prerequisites to a Successfully Functioning Democracy: A Symposium," *American Political Science Review*, L (1956), 101–37.

Gross, Bertram M. *The Legislative Struggle*. New York: McGraw-Hill Book Co., 1953.

Haas, Ernst B. *The Uniting of Europe*. London: Stevens, 1958.

Haines, C. Grove (ed.). *European Integration*. Baltimore: Johns Hopkins Press, 1957.

Hall, Arnold Bennett. *Popular Government*. New York: Macmillan Co., 1921.

Hallgarten, George W. F. *Why Dictators?* New York: Macmillan Co., 1954.

Hallowell, John H. *The Moral Foundations of Democracy*. Chicago: University of Chicago Press, 1954.

Hamilton, Walton H., and Irene Till. "Property," *Encyclopaedia of the Social Sciences*, XII, 528–38. New York: Macmillan Co., 1935.

Handcock, W. D. "What Is Represented in Representative Government?" *Philosophy*, XXII (1947), 99–111.

Harbold, William H. "Democracy and the Service State," *Ethics*, LXXI (1960), 135–45.

———, and Dell G. Hitchner. "Some Reflections on Method in the Study of Politics," *Western Political Quarterly*, XI (1958), 753–73.

Harris, Joseph P. "Elections," *Encyclopaedia of the Social Sciences*, V, 452. New York: Macmillan Co., 1935.

Hermens, F. A. *Democracy or Anarchy?* Notre Dame, Ind.: University of Notre Dame Press, 1941.

———. *Europe between Democracy and Anarchy*. Notre Dame, Ind.: University of Notre Dame Press, 1951.

Herring, Pendleton. *The Politics of Democracy*. New York: W. W. Norton, 1940.

Herz, John H. "Political Views of the West German Civil Service," in Hans Speier and W. Phillips Davidson (eds.), *West German Leadership and Foreign Policy*. Evanston, Ill.: Row, Peterson, 1957.

Hiscocks, Richard. *Democracy in Western Germany*. London: Oxford University Press, 1957.

Hobson, J. H. *Imperialism*. Rev. ed. London: George Allen, 1938.

Hoffman, Stanley. *Le mouvement Poujade*. Paris: Armand Colin, 1956.

Hofstadter, Richard. *The Age of Reform: From Bryan to F. D. R.* New York: Alfred A. Knopf, 1955.

———. *Social Darwinism in American Thought, 1865–1915*. Philadelphia: University of Pennsylvania Press, 1944.

Hogan, James. *Election and Representation*. Oxford: B. H. Blackwell, 1945.

Höjer, Carl-Henrik. *Le régime parlementaire belge, de 1918 à 1940*. Uppsala: Almqvist & Wiksells, 1946.

Holcombe, Arthur N. *Our More Perfect Union*. Cambridge, Mass.: Harvard University Press, 1950.

Hook, Sidney. *Reason, Social Myths, and Democracy*. New York: John Day Co., 1940.

Hughes, Christopher. *The Federal Constitution of Switzerland.* Oxford: Clarendon Press, 1954.

Hume, David. "Of the Original Contract," in Ernest Barker (ed.), *The Social Contract.* London: Oxford University Press, 1947.

Huntington, Samuel P. "A Revised Theory of American Party Politics," *American Political Science Review,* XLIV (1950), 669–77.

———. *The Soldier and the State.* Cambridge, Mass.: Harvard University Press, 1957.

Ike, Nobutaka. *The Beginnings of Political Democracy in Japan.* Baltimore: Johns Hopkins Press, 1950.

Johnson, John J. *Political Change in Latin America.* Stanford, Calif.: Stanford University Press, 1958.

Johnson, Paul. "Behind Salazar's Façade," *New Statesman,* November 2, 1957.

Kane, Harnett T. *Louisiana Hayride.* New York: William Morrow, 1941.

Kelsen, Hans. *General Theory of Law and State.* Translated by Anders Wedberg. Cambridge, Mass.: Harvard University Press, 1945.

Key, V. O., Jr. *American State Politics.* New York: Alfred A. Knopf, 1956.

———. *Politics, Parties, and Pressure Groups.* 3rd ed. New York: Thomas Y. Crowell, 1953.

———. *Southern Politics.* New York: Alfred A. Knopf, 1950.

Kirchheimer, Otto. "West German Trade-Unions: Their Domestic and Foreign Policies," in Hans Speier and W. Phillips Davidson (eds.), *West German Leadership and Foreign Policy.* Evanston, Ill.: Row, Peterson, 1957.

Kohn, Hans. *American Nationalism.* New York: Macmillan Co., 1957.

Konvitz, Milton R. *Fundamental Liberties of a Free People.* Ithaca, N.Y.: Cornell University Press, 1957.

Kriesberg, Martin. "Dark Areas of Ignorance," in Lester Markel *et al.* (eds.), *Public Opinion and Foreign Policy.* New York: Harper & Bros., 1949.

Landheer, Bartholomew (ed.). *The Netherlands.* Berkeley: University of California Press, 1943.

Lane, Robert E. "The Fear of Equality," *American Political Science Review,* LIII (1959), 35–51.

LaPalombara, Joseph G. "Left-Wing Trade Unionism: The Matrix of Communist Power in Italy," *Western Political Quarterly,* VII (1954), 202–26.

Laski, Harold J. *Authority in the Modern State.* New Haven: Yale University Press, 1919.

———. *The Rise of Liberalism.* London: Allen & Unwin, 1936.

Lasswell, Harold D., and Renzo Sereno. "Governmental and Party Leaders in Fascist Italy," *American Political Science Review,* XXXI (1937), 914–29.

Lasswell, Harold D., and Abraham Kaplan. *Power and Society.* New Haven: Yale University Press, 1950.

Lawrence, E. V. *Egypt and the West.* New York: American Institute of International Information, 1956.

Lehmann, Fritz. "Distribution of Wealth," in Max Ascoli and Fritz Lehmann (eds.), *Political and Economic Democracy*. New York: W. W. Norton, 1937.

Lehrman, Hal. "Egypt: Potemkin Village on the Nile," *The Reporter*, May 3, 1956.

Lewis, Edward G. "Parliamentary Control of Nationalized Industry in France," *American Political Science Review*, LI (1957), 669–83.

Lindeman, E. C. "Community," *Encyclopaedia of the Social Sciences*, IV, 102–5. New York: Macmillan Co., 1935.

Lindsay, A. D. *The Modern Democratic State*. New York: Oxford University Press, 1947.

Lippmann, Walter. *The Public Philosophy*. New York: New American Library, 1955.

Lipset, Seymour M. *Political Man: The Social Bases of Politics*. Garden City, N.Y.: Doubleday & Co., 1960.

———. "Some Social Requisites of Democracy: Economic Development and Political Legitimacy," *American Political Science Review*, LIII (1959), 69–105.

Lipson, Leslie. *The Great Issues of Politics*. New York: Prentice-Hall, 1954.

———. *The Politics of Equality: New Zealand's Adventures in Democracy*. Chicago: University of Chicago Press, 1948.

Livingston, William S. "Emigration as a Theoretical Doctrine during the American Revolution," *Journal of Politics*, XIX (1957), 591–615.

Locke, John. *Of Civil Government*. New York: E. P. Dutton & Co., 1924.

Lockwood, David. *The Blackcoated Worker*. London: Allen & Unwin, 1958.

Lorwin, Val R. *The French Labor Movement*. Cambridge, Mass.: Harvard University Press, 1954.

Lowell, A. L. "The Influence of Party upon Legislation in England and America," *Annual Report of the American Historical Association*, I (1901), 321–51.

———. *Public Opinion and Popular Government*. New York: Longmans, Green & Co., 1914.

Luethy, Herbert. *France against Herself*. New York: Frederick A. Praeger, 1955.

Luthin, Reinhard H. *American Demagogues—20th Century*. Boston: Beacon Press, 1954.

McCamy, James L. *The Administration of American Foreign Affairs*. New York: Alfred A. Knopf, 1950.

McDonald, Neil A. *The Study of Political Parties*. New York: Doubleday & Co., 1955.

MacIver, R. M. *The Modern State*. London: Oxford University Press, 1926.

———. *The Web of Government*. New York: Macmillan Co., 1947.

McKenzie, R. T. *British Political Parties*. New York: St. Martin's Press, 1955.

Maritain, Jacques. *Man and the State*. Chicago: University of Chicago Press, 1951.

Martin, Kingsley. "Fascism in the Name of Jesus," *New Statesman*, March 2, 1957.

Marx, Karl. *Capital*. New York: Modern Library, n.d.

Mayer, Carl. "Democratic Nationalism," in Max Ascoli and Fritz Lehmann (eds.), *Political and Economic Democracy*. New York: W. W. Norton, 1937.

Merriam, Charles E., and Harold F. Gosnell. *The American Party System*. 3rd ed. New York: Macmillan Co., 1940.

Meyer, Karl E. "Who Won What in Cuba?" *The Reporter*, February 5, 1959.

Micaud, Charles A. *The French Right and Nazi Germany*. Durham, N.C.: Duke University Press, 1943.

Michels, Robert. *Political Parties*. Translated by Eden and Cedar Paul. Glencoe, Ill.: Free Press, 1949.

Mill, John Stuart. *Utilitarianism, Liberty, and Representative Government*. London: J. M. Dent & Sons, 1910.

Moore, Barrington, Jr. *Terror and Progress, USSR*. Cambridge, Mass.: Harvard University Press, 1954.

Morison, Samuel E., and Henry S. Commager. *The Growth of the American Republic*. 2 vols. Rev. ed. New York: Oxford University Press, 1937.

Muir, Ramsey. *National Self-Government*. New York: Henry Holt & Co., 1918.

Myrdal, Gunnar. *An American Dilemma*. New York: Harper & Bros., 1944.

Neumann, Sigmund. "Toward a Comparative Study of Political Parties," in Sigmund Neumann (ed.), *Modern Political Parties*. Chicago: University of Chicago Press, 1956.

Nicholas, H. G. *The British General Election of 1950*. London: Macmillan Co., 1951.

Niebuhr, Reinhold. *The Children of Light and the Children of Darkness*. New York: Charles Scribner's Sons, 1944.

Nilson, Sten Sparre. *Histoire et sciences politiques*. Bergen: Chr. Michelsens Institut, 1950.

The 1952 Elections—A Statistical Analysis. Washington: Republican National Committee, 1953.

Norman, E. Herbert. *Japan's Emergence as a Modern State*. New York: Institute of Pacific Relations, 1940.

———. *Soldier and Peasant in Japan*. New York: Institute of Pacific Relations, 1943.

Oppenheim, Felix E. "Belgium: Party Cleavage and Compromise," in Sigmund Neumann (ed.), *Modern Political Parties*. Chicago: University of Chicago Press, 1956.

Ortega y Gasset, José. *The Revolt of the Masses*. New York: New American Library, 1950.

Overacker, Louise. *The Australian Party System*. New Haven: Yale University Press, 1952.

Owen, Frank. *Perón—His Rise and Fall*. London: Cresset Press, 1957.

Paetel, Karl O. "The Reign of the Black Order," in Maurice Baumont *et al.* (eds.), *The Third Reich*. New York: Frederick A. Praeger, 1955.

Percival, H. W. *Democracy Is Self-Government*. New York: World Publishing Co., 1952.

Perryman, J. N. "On the Meaning of 'Democracy,'" *Public Opinion Quarterly*, XVII (1953), 47–60.

Philip, André. "The Birth of the Fifth Republic," *The New Leader*, July 7–14, 1958.

Pickles, Dorothy M. *France between the Republics*. London: Love & Malcomson, 1946.

———. *The French Political Scene*. London: Thomas Nelson, 1938.

Pierson, William W., and Federigo G. Gil. *Governments of Latin America*. New York: McGraw-Hill Book Co., 1957.

Pinson, Koppel S. *Modern Germany*. New York: Macmillan Co., 1954.

Potter, Allen M. "The English Conservative Constituency Association," *Western Political Quarterly*, IX (1956), 363–75.

Potter, David M. *People of Plenty*. Chicago: University of Chicago Press, 1954.

Rappard, William E. *The Government of Switzerland*. New York: D. Van Nostrand, 1936.

Record, Wilson. *The Negro and the Communist Party*. Chapel Hill: University of North Carolina Press, 1951.

Reischauer, Edwin O. *Japan—Past and Present*. New York: Alfred A. Knopf, 1946.

Rice, Stuart A. *Quantitative Methods in Politics*. New York: Alfred A. Knopf, 1928.

Rich, S. Grover, Jr. "Franco Spain: A Reappraisal," *Political Science Quarterly*, LXVII (1952), 378–98.

Riesman, David. "Leisure and Work in Post-Industrial Society," in Eric Larrabee and Rolf Meyersohn (eds.), *Mass Leisure*. Glencoe, Ill.: Free Press, 1959.

———. *The Lonely Crowd*. New Haven: Yale University Press, 1951.

Roberts, Elmer. *Monarchical Socialism in Germany*. New York: Charles Scribner's Sons, 1913.

Roche, John P. "American Liberty: An Examination of the 'Tradition' of Freedom," in Milton R. Konvitz and Clinton Rossiter (eds.), *Aspects of Liberty*. Ithaca, N.Y.: Cornell University Press, 1953.

Rossi, Angelo. *A Communist Party in Action*. Translated by Willmoore Kendall. New Haven: Yale University Press, 1949.

Rostow, W. W. "Rostow on Growth," *The Economist*, August 15, 1959.

Rousseau, Jean Jacques. *The Social Contract*. New York: E. P. Dutton & Co., 1913.

The Royal Institute of International Affairs. *Nationalism*. London: Oxford University Press, 1939.

Ruggiero, Guido de. *The History of European Liberalism*. London: Oxford University Press, 1927.

Rüstow, Dankwart A. *The Politics of Compromise*. Princeton: Princeton University Press, 1955.

Sawyer, John E. "Strains in the Social Structure of Modern

France," in Edward Mead Earle (ed.), *Modern France*. Princeton: Princeton University Press, 1951.

Scalapino, Robert A. *Democracy and the Party Movement in Prewar Japan*. Berkeley: University of California Press, 1953.

Schattschneider, E. E. *Party Government*. New York: Farrar & Rinehart, 1942.

———. "United States: The Functional Approach to Party Government," in Sigmund Neumann (ed.), *Modern Political Parties*. Chicago: University of Chicago Press, 1956.

Schoenbrun, David. *As France Goes*. New York: Harper & Bros., 1957.

Schorske, Carl E. *German Social Democracy, 1905–1917*. Cambridge, Mass.: Harvard University Press, 1955.

Schueller, G. K. *The Politburo*. Stanford, Calif.: Stanford University Press, 1951.

Schumpeter, Joseph A. *Capitalism, Socialism, and Democracy*. 2nd ed. New York: Harper & Bros., 1947.

Schwartz, Harry. *Russia's Soviet Economy*. 2nd ed. New York: Prentice-Hall, 1954.

Seligson, Harry. "An Evaluation of the Economic Council of France," *Western Political Quarterly*, VII (1954), 36–50.

Sereno, Renzo. "Italy," in Taylor Cole (ed.), *European Political Systems*. New York: Alfred A. Knopf, 1953.

Simon, Herbert A. *Administrative Behavior*. New York: Macmillan Co., 1947.

Smith, C. H. "Liberalism and Level of Information," *Journal of Educational Psychology*, XXXIX (1948), 65–82.

Smith, T. V. "Is There a Gresham's Law in Politics?" *Western Political Quarterly*, VIII (1955), 418–24.

Sorauf, Frank J. "The Public Interest Reconsidered," *Journal of Politics*, XIX (1957), 616–39.

Spearman, Diana. *Modern Dictatorship*. London: Jonathan Cape, 1939.

Spitz, David. *Democracy and the Challenge of Power*. New York: Columbia University Press, 1958.

———. *Patterns of Anti-Democratic Thought*. New York: Macmillan Co., 1949.

Sprigge, C. J. S. *The Development of Modern Italy*. London: Duckworth, 1943.

Stamps, Norman L. *Why Democracies Fail*. Notre Dame, Ind.: University of Notre Dame Press, 1957.

Stapleton, Laurence. *The Design of Democracy*. New York: Oxford University Press, 1949.

Sterling, Claire. "Algeria: A Showdown Is Postponed," *The Reporter*, January 22, 1959.

———. "Can Nasser Ransom Himself from the Russians?" *The Reporter*, May 1, 1958.

Stewart, J. D. *British Pressure Groups*. Oxford: Clarendon Press, 1958.

Stouffer, Samuel A. *Communism, Conformity, and Civil Liberties*. New York: Doubleday & Co., 1955.

Stout, Hiram Miller. *British Government*. New York: Oxford University Press, 1953.

Sturzo, Luigi. "The Philosophical Background of Christian Democracy," *Review of Politics*, IX (1947), 3–15.

Swabey, Marie C. "The Leading Myths of Our Time," *Ethics*, XLIX (1939), 168–86.

———. *Theory of the Democratic State*. Cambridge, Mass.: Harvard University Press, 1937.

Thomson, David. *Democracy in France*. London: Oxford University Press, 1946.

Tingsten, Herbert. *The Problem of South Africa*. London: Victor Gollancz, 1955.

Titmuss, Richard M. *Essays on "The Welfare State."* London: Allen & Unwin, 1958.

Trow, Martin A. "Small Businessmen, Political Tolerance, and Support for McCarthy," *American Journal of Sociology*, LXIV (1958), 270–81.

Truman, David B. *The Governmental Process*. New York: Alfred A. Knopf, 1951.

Tucker, William P. *The Mexican Government Today*. Minneapolis: University of Minnesota Press, 1957.

Tumin, Melvin M. "Readiness and Resistance to Desegregation: A Social Portrait of the Hard Core," *Social Forces*, XXXVI (1958), 256–63.

Turner, Julius. *Party and Constituency: Pressures on Congress*. Baltimore: Johns Hopkins Press, 1951.

———. "Responsible Parties: A Dissent from the Floor," *American Political Science Review*, XLV (1951), 143–57.

United Nations, Statistical Office. *Statistical Yearbook, 1955*. New York: United Nations, 1955.

Veblen, Thorstein. *Imperial Germany and the Industrial Revolution*. New York: B. Huebsch, 1918.

———. *The Theory of Business Enterprise*. New York: New American Library, 1958.

Waldo, Dwight. *Perspectives on Administration*. University, Ala.: University of Alabama Press, 1956.

Watkins, Frederick. *The Political Tradition of the West*. Cambridge, Mass.: Harvard University Press, 1948.

Weber, Max. *From Max Weber: Essays in Sociology*. Translated and edited by H. H. Gerth and C. Wright Mills. New York: Oxford University Press, 1946.

Wigmore, John H. *The Australian Ballot System*. Boston: Boston Book Co., 1889.

Williams, Philip. *Politics in Post-War France*. London: Longmans, Green & Co., 1954.

Wittfogel, Karl A. *Oriental Despotism*. New Haven: Yale University Press, 1957.

Woytinsky, W. S. and E. S. *World Population and Production*. New York: Twentieth Century Fund, 1953.

Wright, Gordon. *The Reshaping of French Democracy*. New York: Reynal & Hitchcock, 1948.

Yanaga, Chitoshi. *Japan since Perry*. New York: McGraw-Hill Book Co., 1949.

Young, Roland. *Congressional Politics in the Second World War*. New York: Columbia University Press, 1956.

Zeldin, Theodore. *The Political System of Napoleon III.* London: Macmillan Co., 1958.

Zink, Harold. *Modern Governments.* New York: D. Van Nostrand, 1958.

Zurcher, Arnold J. "Democracy's Declining Capacity to Govern," *Western Political Quarterly,* VIII (1955), 529–44.

————. "The Political System of Switzerland," in James T. Shotwell (ed.), *Governments of Continental Europe.* Rev. ed. New York: Macmillan Co., 1952.

————. *The Struggle to Unite Europe.* New York: New York University Press, 1958.

INDEX

Administration: and pressure groups, 129; and Middle Class, 129–30; innovations in, 139; democratic control of, 145–46, 160. *See also* Hierarchy

Algeria, 144

Amery, L. S.: on British democratic myths, 177

Aristotle: on Middle Class, 48, 119, 122, 182, 183; on social deference, 187; mentioned, 17, 144

Autocracy: and rules of succession, 18; and welfare policy, 35; and social deference, 36; and civil liberties, 56, 64, 66; and governmental responsibility, 75; and consent, 100; and democratic myths, 109–12; and rich and poor, 123, 128; and functionalism, 129; political processes in, 140; and popular pressure, 142. *See also* Totalitarianism

Bates, M. Searle: on religious liberty, 52

Batista, Fulgencio, 128

Beer, Samuel H.: on interest reflection, 165–66

Bendix, Reinhard: on class theory, 181

Berle, A. A.: on democratic control, 146; on business corporations, 184, 191

Bierstedt, Robert: on authority, 176

Bills of rights, 18

Bismarck, Otto von: and welfare policy, 128

Bourgeoisie, 125–28 *passim*; antidemocratic tendencies of, 152; mentioned, 119, 148. *See also* Classes, social

Britain: House of Lords, 16; role of opposition party, 32; civil liberties in, 53; responsibility of aristocrats in, 75; national community of, 117; scope of governmental action in, 139; parties in, 161–62; power of MP in, 162; political myths in, 177–78; economic policy in, 183. *See also* Parties, political

Brown, A. J.: on comparing living standards, 182

Bureaucracy. *See* Administration

Burns, James M.: on British parties, 161

Campaigning: and nominating, 22; and civil liberties, 57–58; and popular understanding, 79; and promises, 190. *See also* Parties, political

Castro, Fidel, 128, 129n

Chafee, Zechariah, Jr.: on civil liberties, 53, 56

Christian Democracy: and democratic myths, 107

Christopher, James: on French antidemocratic sentiment, 178

Civil liberties, 50–67 *passim*; and periodicity of elections, 8; and uncoerced elections, 9; and franchise, 14; and indirect elections, 16; of minorities, 74; and democratic myths, 111–12; and Middle Class, 132–33; and freedom, 135; and interest reflection, 170; and welfare policy, 172

Civil rights legislation, 131, 147